Love, Truth & Perception

Love, Truth & Perception

*Where do we come from?
What are we? Where are we going?*

by

Kathy Oddenino, RN

Joy
Publications

Love, Truth & Perception
by Kathy Oddenino, RN
Copyright © 1993 by Kathy Oddenino
ISBN 0-923081-03-8

Printed in the United States of America
CURRENT PRINTING   10 9 8 7 6 5 4 3 2 1

All rights reserved. Neither this book or any part may be reproduced or transmitted in any form or by any means, electronic or mechanical, including photocopy, microfilm, recording, or by any information storage and retrieval system now known or to be invented, without permission in writing from the publisher, except by a reviewer who wishes to quote brief passages in connection with a review written for inclusion in a magazine, newspaper, or broadcast.

Requests for information or permission to make copies of any part of this work should be mailed to:

Joy Publications
133A Lee Drive
Annapolis, MD 21403-4043
USA

Front cover art entitled:
D'oú venons-nous? Que sommes-nous? Oú allons-nous?
(Where do we come from? What are we? Where are we going?)
painting by **Paul Gaugin**
Tompkins Collection, Courtesy of Museum of Fine Arts, Boston

Editing by Margaret Martin
Cover and text design by Anita Crouch

◊ *Dedication* ◊

This book is dedicated to my children, Gloria Moren, Lynn Oddenino, Sarah Pernell, Chuck Oddenino, Diana Oddenino, and John Oddenino, in perfect faith that they will understand the miracle of life and live it with hope, health, happiness, and joy.

◊ *Acknowledgements* ◊

To all of my friends who supported me while I sat in my altered state of consciousness, staring at my computer screen, oblivious to the telephone calls, I thank you and acknowledge your love and patience.

To the Joy Publications staff and to my editor Margaret Martin, I acknowledge and thank you for your dedication and your loyalty.

Acknowledgement is also gratefully given to the following publishers: Anthroposophic Press, Inc., Hudson, New York 12534, for permission to cite from Rudolf Steiner's *Theosophy*, © 1971 by Anthroposophic Press, Inc.; Viking Penguin, A division of Penguin Books USA, for use of A. H. Maslow's *The Farther Reaches of Human Nature* (45), ©1971 by Bertha G. Maslow; Samuel Weiser, Inc., York Beach, Maine 03910, for use of G. R. S. Mead's *Thrice Greatest Hermes: Studies in Hellenistic Theosophy and Gnosis*, Book II, Sermons (25), ©1992 by Samuel Weiser, Inc.; Sri Aurobindo Ashram Trust, for use of Sri Aurobindo's *On Himself*, ©1972 and printed in Pondicherry, India. And to Pablo Casals, for his words from *Joys and Sorrows*, published in New York in 1970; and Thomas Merton, with love, wherever he may be.

A Message ◊
to the Reader

The information in this book comes from the highest level of my spirit consciousness, the level of my oversoul or Heavenly Spirit. Writing from the inspiration of my spirit energy is easier than writing from my intellect. The language may be different in some respects than what we are familiar with. Although the language has an ancient flavor, it is not hard to read. I have agreed to follow the advice of my spirit and not change the language, as that frequently changes the meaning and structure of the information.

Read with an open mind and a loving heart and you will understand the message. If you read in judgement, you will be challenged by the information. The information is given in levels and stages that build your understanding automatically if you are reading with an open mind. Each reading will elevate you to a higher level of awareness and understanding.

If you are interested in where you came from, who you are, and where you are going, you will find the answers in this book. Within these pages you will find a new interpretation of the traditional religious and philosophic views of life, our purpose, our path of creation, and our path of human destiny. If we look carefully at our society we can clearly see the messages in this book being acted out in our daily behavior. It is time for us to listen and change, allowing our shift in consciousness to create a better world. Shifting our consciousness is our way of understanding our divine nature as our human destiny. When we become conscious that our perception of life is controlling our destiny, we will choose to go beyond our male, physical perception and choose to embrace, in total wisdom and grace, our female, soul and spirit perception. This shift in our conscious perception from our physical nature to our divine nature is a physical indication that our ego veil is rent and we are one with our spirit consciousness.

Be in peace and joy,

Kathy Oddenino

viii

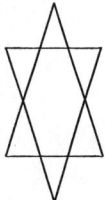

"If you want to identify me, ask me not where I live, or what I like to eat, or how I comb my hair, but ask me what I am living for, in detail, and ask me what I think is keeping me from living truly for the thing I want to live for."
                                              Thomas Merton

Contents

INTRODUCTION...page xv

PERCEPTION...page 1

Common Beliefs 2
Lesson of procreation 5
Jesus of Nazareth 8
Changing 13
Becoming HUMAN 14
Religious foundations 15
Personal civilization 16
Ego influence 17
Shifting consciousness 19
Diseases, addictions, dependency 22
Mind intention 25
Turning water into wine 26
Competition 29
Jealousy, rejection, abuse 31
Relationships, communication 36

PHYSICAL LOVE...page 47

Sexual interaction 46
Dual purpose 48
Physical creation 52
Higher Universal Mana 52
Sensing 56
Seven physical senses 54

Self-consciousness ... 59
Senses as symbols of birth ... 61
The finesse of hand kissing ... 63
Abuse and fear ... 64

LIVING IN THE PHYSICAL...page 67

Female and male equality ... 68
Divine nature ... 69
Physical nature ... 70
Multiple lives and sexuality ... 72
Sexuality and religion ... 75
Peak experience ... 78
Knowledge, dual cycles of soul path ... 78
Cycle of Awareness ... 79
Cycle of Understanding ... 85
Intellectual spiritualism ... 88
Wisdom ... 90
Female power ... 93
Soul memory ... 98
Control and its effects ... 104
Teachings of Jesus ... 116
Collective consciousness ... 117
Mesocosmic influence ... 120

OUR SOUL MIND...page 123

Definition and purpose ... 126
Past life memories ... 127
Beliefs and behaviors ... 134

Birth of Adam by Eve 139
Gender consciousness 142
Our changing sexuality 143
Immaculate Conceptions 144
The chosen ones 145
The second coming of Christ 145
Creation of thoughtform 146
Body, mind, and spirit unity 147
Sleep work 147
Seven levels of soul evolution 149

LOVE...page 167

Our search for love 172
Ego veil of beliefs 173
Spirit love 175
Symbols of love 178
Judgement, competition, fear 179
Crisis, chaos, and love 183
Cycle of Change 187
Seven levels of fear 188
Seven levels of love 194
Intimate relationships 203
History, crime, and inequality 209
Life as our creation 211

TRUTH...page 207

Truth as human destiny 214
The ego's growth 216

xiii

Shadow side of our soul 223
Adam and Eve 226
Sexuality and competition 227
Three dimensions of human energy 227
Perfection as equality 229
Up against the veil 231
Changes beyond the veil 232
Humans as the Cosmic Christ 234
Light side of our soul 239
Merging our dual natures 241
Karmic memory 245
Addictions and karma 247
Sex, religion, and karma 249
Our truth and God 250

SPIRIT LOGOS...page 253

Words as spirit knowledge 254

Introduction

As we enter into the most profound shift in consciousness that will be recorded by history, it is important for us to have a new perception of ourself and our life. Each time the shift in consciousness has begun, man has not grasped the importance of understanding where we come from, who we are, and where we are going. Without the willingness to look at ourself and find our greater purpose of being, we have the power to destroy ourself.

In this book I present the truth of creation from the Spirit Consciousness. Truth must offer us a new perception of our traditional religious and philosophic views of life, our purpose of creation, and our path of human destiny to be useful to our growth as humans. It is no longer productive for humans to stay attached to primitive beliefs and behaviors. It is my hope that these views can now be understood and accepted by all so that our shift in consciousness can occur smoothly and completely throughout the entire world. There is a beautiful side to our human destiny that will be equal in time in the physical world to the shadow side of our soul growth.

Living in the shadow side of our soul has allowed us to experience our lessons of life in fear, judgement, and blame. Now, as we find ourself flush against the veil of beliefs of our ego, we must rend that veil away from our intellect and be willing to grow and change. Growth and change requires that we give up the beliefs and behaviors that do not serve us anymore. Our beliefs must be evaluated to help us discover our love, truth and equality, and to help us release our fear and judgement. Moral virtues can no longer be conceptual, but must be lived as part of our daily life experience. Our intellect and our physical body will blossom from the light of love and truth.

Life gives us the choice to live in two distinct emotions, one of fear and one of love, which represent the shadow side of our soul and the light side of our soul. These two emotions symbolize our physical nature as fear and our divine nature as love. To be HUMAN we must merge our two natures together, living as physical beings through our love. All other emotions of life are merely smaller fractal reflections of our fear and our love being acted out. As we are growing through the levels of our soul, we attach ourself to the fear energy innocently but firmly. Our attachment to fear allows us to live in a state of pathos for many thousands of lifetimes as we learn each lesson one small image at a time. In our dependent physical nature we can find ourself dependent on the pathos itself, which surely happens to each of us before we dissolve our veil.

After we rend our ego veil through our experiences of life, we have the opportunity to see ourself in the truth of our beauty and magnificence. This vision of ourself is a true awakening from a deep sleep of fear that lets us see our life from the spirit perception of love, truth, and perfection. The secret to growth and change is not being afraid to look at ourself and to acknowledge the female energy of our soul and spirit. Only our female energy is capable of balancing our male energy and establishing equality as our true perfection.

God bless each of you who have the courage and strength to recognize and follow your quest. I speak to your soul and spirit with the words in this book to give you love and support as you search your own heart and mind.

H.S.

Perception

◊

"As soon as a person becomes aware of the objects around him, he considers them in relation to himself, and rightly so, because his whole fate depends on whether they please him or displease him, attract or repel, help or harm him. This quite natural way of looking at or judging things appears to be as easy as it is necessary. A person is, nevertheless, exposed through it to a thousand errors that often make him ashamed and embitter his life."

Goethe, as quoted by R. Steiner, Theosophy

Perception is our impression of self, life, and our reality that we define through our sensing, mind abilities, and beliefs. What we believe is what we perceive, and what we perceive is what we believe.

Our impression of life, other people, ourself, society, education, government, health, business, and everything else within the world, is developed by what we believe we know and what we sense, which becomes what we believe is real. Every individual functions from a level of perception unique to him or her.

Perception is the intellect and ego mind response, which can be influenced by the intuition of the spirit mind and the instinct of the soul mind. We live by an individual level of perception dependent upon the degree of soul and spirit mind influence that we accept.

When intuition and instinct are merged with physical perception, the impression of reality is expanded. Instinct is the wisdom of our soul and intuition is the truth of our Spirit. When our perception is based only upon physical knowledge, it is restricted by the physical boundaries of what we perceive as fact.

Fact is defined as that which has been learned, or observed within the past, or verified as real by physical experimentation. All fact is determined by the intellect, and therefore the truth of fact can only be defined in relationship to our level of perception. Perception is limited by our beliefs and knowledge when it originates only from the intellect and ego. If we deny or reject our instinct and intuition, we dramatically limit our perceptive abilities.

There was a time in history when man believed the earth was flat. This belief was considered to be fact and was established by the level of knowledge and perception within the human mind at that time. The "facts" of knowledge are forever changing as the intellectual perception of life and its design expands and changes.

Changes must occur today in the perception of thought that has been taught as truth for generations. The truth of our beliefs is at all times relative to the belief as perceived by the mind. Each individual or group will have a different perception of the most common belief and their behavior will be based upon their beliefs.

Many common beliefs that have lived throughout history began as superstitions and myth. The inequality of the female has been supported by much of humanity for thousands of years, and it is a perfect example of a consolidated belief that is accepted and honored throughout the entire world.

The power of the female was perceived thousands of years ago. The perception of love, mercy, compassion, and the power of the creation of life within the female was seen as a threat. The unity of self was not understood, and therefore the female was superstitiously considered dangerous. Her power of birth was recognized as the spirit presence, which was a threat to the control of the male. Because of her power she was declared unclean and was shunned as inferior to man. Man himself was considered unclean if he so much as touched the garments of the female during her menses.

The female demonstrated a dramatically different personality and character from the male. From the male perception this created the belief that the female was weaker of mind. Based upon this male-generated belief, the ego-driven male allowed himself to feel superior to the female in all activities of life. This established the male control over the female which is still prevalent today. The female, in living her compassion, mercy, and humility, accepted the male control in her need to balance her physical nature with her divine nature.

The female menstrual flow was believed to be the coming of spirit energy, the blood of God. This belief in the constancy of the spirit presence was a fearful belief for man. He had no knowledge of the function of the human body. Primitive man attributed each function of the physical body to the spirit of a God within. Their belief in the God within was seen from a fearful perception of possession, wrath, and revenge. Their truth was the basis of their belief, but their belief was perceived in fear rather than an understanding of the God within.

Man perceived a power within the female that did not exist within himself. Woman had the power to reproduce herself and man and that power loomed in the ego mind of man as a threat from God challenging his sense of superiority. Fear originated from his perception of their differences because he didn't understand that difference was essential to the pattern of procreation.

In primitive times man had no understanding that he was involved in the reproductive process. As man perceived this threatening power, he perceived the only way of controlling the power was through the control of the female. In man's belief in the inferiority of the female, she was cast in that life role in society.

Control of the female has been practiced in multiple forms throughout history because of the foundation of this primitive belief. With time we have gained additional knowledge and understanding of the human body, procreation, and the female and male relationship. Although our knowledge has expanded and completely changed our understanding of the male and female relationship, the beliefs toward control have not completely changed. Woman is still not acknowledged as equal to man.

For many thousands of years the female was not allowed to vote, conduct religious ceremonies, attend schools, hold public office, operate a business, have her own bank account, or make decisions, to name a few restrictions. In ancient times the female was instructed to entertain herself but not to be involved in work of any value. This allowed a belief to be created that women's work had no value. With growth some restrictions have been removed and some value has been acknowledged. Each step forward in equality has been learned from the path of evolution. Our change occurs as we have the courage to challenge what is.

An example of change through soul growth that will explain this phenomenon is a female who lived a life of such intense control that she chose in her next life to return as a male to focus upon changing the laws of the land to laws of equality. This is the way and the intention of the juxtaposition of genders between the twin soul spirit energies to assist in the growth of humanity at all levels.

The female has functioned from instinct and intuition from the beginning of creation. She learned to communicate and to cooperate with man. She also learned to cook, clean, care for children, treat pain and disease, find a home, make cloth, design clothes, and many other essential activities that continue to be important today for our survival, comfort, and growth.

The survival needs of our primitive lives cast both the male and female into survival activities. In later periods of growth the survival needs had been learned, but the relationships between the sexes continued to be a challenge. Relationships have required more time to master than the physical needs, because our design of life has given us relationships as our way of learning how to balance the emotions of the soul within our physical reality. The female perception that came from instinct and intuition was presented to humanity with the love and truth of our soul and spirit.

The intellect of the female has always been equal in every aspect to the male intellect. But the perceptive ability of the female has always been far superior to the male perceptive ability because the male mind is frequently in denial of the soul and spirit presence. Therefore, the male mind, when limited only to the intellect and ego, has always been inferior to the female mind if the female was given an equal opportunity to expand her intellect.

The female ability to think was feared by the ancient males and their suspicions and fear made it essential to them that education not be available to the female. This convenient belief in the inferiority of the female mind has continued for many thousands of years through educational suppression. This singular belief has influenced the overall perceptions of reality by the individual, society, and the world. This human belief of inequality has slowed our soul evolution dramatically because of its wide-reaching effect upon growth and change in our life. The focus upon the results of inequality has captured all of humanity for millions of years and continues to be an active issue in our life today.

Childbirth was another mystery that was not understood for millions of years and was therefore intensely feared. This female ability to produce children emphasized the difference between the two sexes and was a dramatic source of superstition and myth that has created a myriad of beliefs since the beginning of time.

The male was created by the female from her asexual, androgynous soul and spirit as the physical reflection of her image upon Earth. This began procreation as the symbol of the lesson of merging the physical nature with the divine nature upon Earth.

The female became the symbol of the soul and spirit energy upon Earth. The male became the symbol of the physical energy upon Earth. The physical body and the mind of the female was designed with an internal focus. The physical body and the mind of the male was designed with an external focus. They were created as opposites to come together as a symbol of the merging of the physical nature with the divine nature. The physical and mind differences in the design of the male and female began their differences of perception as they began their path of soul growth on Earth as physical beings.

Instinct and intuition were not understood by the physically grounded and focused male, and therefore the female was feared by the male because she was different. The male has never understood the female mind and personality because the male perception is focused external to self and the female focus is internal of self. This continues the symbols of our physical nature and our divine nature upon Earth, which are both inherent within each of us and which have the total intention of merging.

As cultures developed solely from the male perception, the wars, fighting, competition, self-gratification, and greed have limited the cultures to their primitive level of behavior and development. The evolution of humanity has been waiting patiently for the physical, male child within us to mature.

Religious wars have been fought throughout history because differences of beliefs are seen as a threat. Religious wars are closely interwoven with the belief and behavior of inequality, fear, and greed, as religion has created the foundation of modern society and all cultures. A fanatical belief is a weapon frequently used against humanity because the belief is directed as self-judgement, which is contagiously mirrored into the fanatical judgement of others. In our physical perception, being different is labeled as being inferior, wrong, evil, or bad, because the standard of judgement for us is our own intellect and ego belief.

As people have grown and changed, beliefs have changed. But beliefs continue to create the perception of right and wrong, good and evil, within the intellect and ego. In critical perception it is not understood that both beliefs could be right for a specific level of evolution. When someone is different, it is still the perception of our belief that they must be controlled. "If you are not with me, you are against me" is an old belief. The ego control of others is defined as physical or legal control and it intends to control change through the control of differences. Physical and legal control are both karmic beliefs attached to the primitive level of soul evolution.

All knowledge that consolidates itself into absolute belief within the intellectual mind is dangerous to the soul evolution of humanity. The danger is found in the stagnant energy of the intellect that creates inertia and decay within society as it resists change and growth.

These absolute beliefs create the layers of the veil that separates the intellectual mind from the soul and spirit mind. It is our beliefs that form the ego veil that envelopes our mind. It is essential that the intellectual mind stay open to new thoughts and new perceptions to give the mind room to grow and change.

A closed mind is an imprisoned mind whose freedom has been removed by the thickness of the ego veil. An imprisoned mind is a dangerous mind, because fear seeks more fear to strengthen itself. Fear views all that is around it in relation to its mirrored self-perception at the individual level of aware consciousness of the intellect and ego mind.

It is our obsessive perception that our beliefs are always right that allows our mind to live within the dark shadow of the soul. Our behaviors then become the living symbols of our beliefs and fears. Our fears and beliefs will be so intense that we will repeat our behaviors over and over again before we recognize that the pain that we create is within us.

An open mind that is not attached to assumed fact as belief will continue to grow and expand as it seeks to merge the physical perception of the intellect with the divine perception of intuition and instinct. It is our physical perception that determines our beliefs and impressions of life. The level of conscious awareness that we achieve provides the basis of our perception of life. When our conscious awareness is attached to primitive beliefs, we act out our primitive beliefs within our daily behaviors.

There was a time in the evolution of the human soul when killing was seen as a means of survival. If we remain attached to the belief that killing is a means of survival for us today, murder and war will be a natural reaction to our belief. Just as murder exists as our microcosmic behavior, war exists as a mesocosmic and macrocosmic behavior from the identical level of beliefs. Conflicting religious beliefs are a source of war today in the identical repetition of thousands of past religious wars. Religion was the primary way that beliefs were spread from one culture and society to other geographical areas. *The behaviors and beliefs in inequality have formed the basis of our religious beliefs for thousands of years. Inequality creates conflict, murder, and war.*

As each soul grows it will have beliefs that remain from the earlier periods of evolution. These soul beliefs that are continuing through various levels of growth are karmic beliefs. Karmic beliefs are soul lessons not yet learned. Primitive karmic beliefs will result in physical behaviors that will not be in harmony with the beliefs of the more advanced souls upon Earth.

Changing our beliefs allows our soul growth to escalate and expand, which changes our physical behaviors. Changing our beliefs and our behaviors allows us to live the lessons of our soul evolution. Once the lesson is acknowledged as complete, we release our attachment to the primitive karmic belief.

Within the multiple societies that are now recognized within our world we can recognize the manifestation of behaviors from beliefs that are no longer in the harmony and rhythm of the shifting consciousness. Any and all beliefs that are attached to primitive thought will create civil wars, religious wars, and world wars from the conflict in the differing levels of perception within the minds of the world leaders.

Many societies are continuing to be under religious rule that is based upon primitive beliefs. Governments, cultures, and societies that are based upon the primitive beliefs of religion may find they conflict with the beliefs of the people they represent. As personal responsibility is assumed by individuals, conflicting control through religion, state, government, and cults will become unacceptable.

Until these primitive beliefs that teach the opposite of love, truth, and equality can be changed, chaos will continue as a daily event within our lives.

Many of these beliefs are reflections of the primitive beliefs about Jesus of Nazareth having lived to save man. The true teachings of Jesus are based upon love, truth, and equality as the lesson of responsibility for the soul. Primitive perceptions of fear, judgement, and inequality that are more than 2,000 years old are not honoring of who we are. The perception that believing in Jesus is a means of personal salvation allows humans to deny their responsibility for their own behavior.

PERCEPTION

Jesus's message was to *live as I am living*. Jesus devoted his life to merging his physical nature with his divine nature, which was his purpose upon Earth. Refusing to accept responsibility for our behavior allows adultery, sexual abuse, dishonesty, robbery, murder, greed, and all criminal acts to be acceptable within the perception of the mind.

Beliefs that remove responsibility accept an energy of predetermination. It is not predetermined that Jesus will save us if we believe in him. As humans we must save ourself by living the love, truth, and equality that Jesus lived. Jesus never sought to have man worship him. He sought to show man a way of living that would expand his soul growth.

Primitive perceptions, based upon the interpretation of the religious teachings of Jesus, teach us the lesson of freedom by living the experiences of control. Once we learn to free ourself from the lessons of control, we will look for the true teachings of Jesus to follow as a path of living. We will honor, value, and respect Jesus for his contribution to our lesson and the value of his true teachings, but we will not worship him as a savior. Living the perfection, love, and truth of his teachings about life as the daily behavior of our life is the only worship that he sought then and now.

The belief in the crucifixion of Jesus to forgive our sins is another perception that has lived nearly 2,000 years from primitive belief. The intention of the Hebrew culture was to have Jesus crucified by the Romans, but the crucifixion itself did not include Jesus. The crucifixion was reorganized by Pilate and three prisoners who were scheduled to die the next day were crucified. The crucifixion reflected the intention of fear that the society had towards Jesus and his teachings. Jesus merged fully with his divine nature at the moment of his baptism. Following his baptism Jesus was more spirit than physical man, although he stayed by choice within his physical body. It was important to Jesus that his teachings would be understood and lived, but he didn't seek to be worshipped.

It was not revealed that Jesus did not die upon the cross because the angry, emotional crowd would not have accepted this information. Those who knew him well clearly understood that the person on the cross was not Jesus. The apostles were given the information at the Jordan river but were sworn to secrecy. The crucifixion became the symbol of the misperceptions that can occur within the fearful, frenzied mind of man and be accepted and believed as fact.

The important issue for us to remember in this belief is that the intention of the Hebrews and Romans was to execute Jesus because they did not believe in his teachings of personal responsibility, equality, love, truth, mercy, and compassion. Jesus knew that he was not the Messiah that had come to save man, because he knew that man would always be responsible for saving himself. Jesus knew that the Messiah is the spirit within us, and he knew that it is our own divine nature that must save us.

The Hebrews and Romans were firm in their physical beliefs, and they refused to change their beliefs to the teachings that were coming from the heart of Jesus's soul and spirit. Their personal creeds and laws allowed the sacrifice of life, executions, robbery, lying, and inequality. In that day women were shunned as unclean, were not educated, and were considered highly inferior. Jesus knew the truth of equality and practiced equality with all women, men, and races. Jesus lived on Earth through his divine nature which was his message in showing us our path of soul growth.

Jesus taught that man must live in the love, truth, and humility of God, and that all human beings were born equal. Following the mass belief in his crucifixion, the people were then free to continue their belief that he was the Messiah who had come to save them. Maintaining their original belief in Jesus's role also meant they were free to continue with their life roles of control through the fear, guilt, sin, and their beliefs in the judgement and wrath of God.

Their primitive perceptions that stemmed from their own greed, power, and control issues have been the beliefs that were adopted by many humans and have filtered down through the male interpretations of various cultures as unchangeable and indisputable facts of a higher God. Religions have supported these teachings, partly because of control and partly because of embarrassment at their own inaccurate perceptions and beliefs in a judgemental and wrathful God. Each culture has put together its own perceptions of God and Jesus which have been worshiped as fact for thousands of years without change and growth.

The beliefs and behaviors of several thousands of years before Jesus's birth were then allowed to continue to this day, perpetuating the image of fear, sin, guilt, and inequality into the minds of evolving man. As man is willing to change his physical nature and change within, his beliefs will change. Religion is created by the people of a society. As people grow, religion will grow to uncover and to follow the knowledge and understanding that is in harmony with our soul evolution.

Jesus of Nazareth did not come to Earth to save man, but man felt that he needed to be saved from his own behavior and placed Jesus in that role. Jesus came to Earth to experience physical life as a human being. He learned the path and reflected it to all of us by living his devotion to his physical family and friends. He lived his love, his truth, his equality, his compassion, and his mercy, in his daily behavior.

Jesus made certain that all of his personal writings were destroyed because he did not want them changed. It was Jesus's hope and his intention to teach a few loyal friends who could carry on his teachings, in the flesh, but he knew that his lessons would be a challenge for man. Jesus taught individual responsibility, love, truth, and equality. Jesus knew in his heart that man could not understand his teachings, because in man's early cycle of soul evolution he simply was not ready to change. Reviewing our path of history will show us how we have lived the opposite of the teachings of Jesus of Nazareth, God, and our own soul and spirit.

Man attached himself to his own perceptions of Jesus because he was not yet evolved enough to understand the love, truth, and perfection of his own soul and spirit. Without this understanding of self, the intellectual mind could not accept the true teachings of Jesus. Now the hour of understanding his teachings has come for humanity. In the shift of consciousness from the male, physical perspective to the female, soul and spirit perspective, humanity has reached the time of understanding. Understanding must be found through the knowing within our own hearts that we have a soul and spirit that is guiding us.

As humans we are challenged to shift our conscious awareness to the love of self, humanity, and Earth. We will also be challenged with the primitive belief in right and wrong, or good and evil, by those with an attachment to primitive beliefs. We must have the courage, faith, and trust to live our own truth and love to support Universal change.

We are challenged to release our attachments to primitive beliefs whenever we seek our soul and spirit growth. This requires a strength and courage that goes beyond the physical judgement and fear that we have been taught.

The perception of opposites has been created as the human condition within our physical nature to serve as a method of learning what we want by first experiencing what we don't want. Therefore, all physical experiences are the manifestation of soul lessons. Lessons are never wrong or evil but simply the path of growth that is allowing our soul to evolve.

The most dramatic lessons that have been learned through multiple physical repetitions are in our soul reality jewels of great value to the spirit. As we have diamonds of the Earth, we have diamonds of our soul and spirit. Earth is a diamond within the Universe. Our Universe is a diamond within the Cosmos. What is above, is below. This is the Cosmic pattern of the Universe, Earth, and us as HUMAN.

We are a fractal of a larger Cosmic pattern of energy that is repeated within the Universal system, and within the Earth system. We are a fractal pattern of the energy of the Creator. We are female, we are male, and we are spirit energy.

In understanding this pattern of the relationship of opposites as a way of learning, we should feel no fear at the challenge of changing our beliefs. The beliefs that served the early human as he began his soul evolution in the Cycle of Awareness at the primitive level no longer serve the evolving human as he seeks to rend the veil in the level of knowledge to enter the Cycle of Understanding.

As physical beings we must live with the perspective of change throughout our physical lifetime. *Life is a journey, not a destination.* We change our parents during some physical lives, we change schools, our educational focus, our clothes, our friends, our possessions, our houses, cars, careers, jobs, and sometimes our understanding of Earth.

These multiple changes are symbols for us of how we also change our physical bodies as soul and spirit to live other lives, and how we can change the focus of our mind from the intellect into our rational and intuitive minds. All physical change symbolizes our mind change, which is essential to us on an emotional, spiritual, and intellectual level within each lifetime. To stay attached to the perception of primitive beliefs and refuse to change those beliefs is to stay captured in the revolutions of our repetitive behavior within the shadow side of our soul.

Our perception of self is as restrictive as our primitive perception of the Earth as flat. We continue to think in the linear concepts of the intellectual and ego mind. This perception of self originates within the primitive teachings of fear, guilt, original sin, judgement, unworthiness, inequality, greed, power, separateness, competition, and control. We fail to see the obstructions to change that we create by our attachment to our fear of survival.

Changing our perception automatically changes our thoughts, words, and actions. When we are open to the love within us, we give ourself permission to change our beliefs and behaviors. Changing our beliefs changes how we act, relate, and feel toward self and others. From these changes we will find a new and glorious world that we are living in but not seeing.

Accepting the love, truth, and perfection that is the divine nature within us allows us to respect and value self and all of humanity. As we value and respect ourself, we are willing to accept full responsibility for self and our beliefs. The merging of our divine nature with our physical nature removes all vestiges of judgement, fear, anger, greed, resentment, control, sin, guilt, and inequality.

Perceiving life from our integrated nature allows us to be good and loving in thought, word, and action. We will freely accept our freedom of choice, intention, and will as our method of creating our individual life. As we acknowledge the love, truth, and equality in our life, it will be reflected in our society and eventually within the cultures of the entire world.

We are energy and energy by its very nature must move and change. When we feel stuck in our life, we begin to see our intimate relationship, our family, our career, and our body begin to fall apart. These changes happen to get our attention and to slow down our resistance to our soul and spirit energy.

When we find ourself experiencing a crisis, we begin to talk to God. We may not have consciously prayed in an entire lifetime, but if we have a health or survival crisis, we begin to consciously pray.

Our thoughts are truly our prayers and are always answered. We won't allow ourself to remain stagnant forever within any belief system because we must change for our soul to evolve.

When growth of the physical body is complete the mind must continue to grow. Each and every cell within the physical body is in a constant state of change. Our beliefs must also be in a constant state of change if we are to evolve our perception of self into a Higher Universal Mana, or HUMAN.

We are upon Earth as spirit thought forms with the purpose of learning how to be HUMAN. To become HUMAN we must merge our human physical nature with our divine spirit nature. When our two natures are totally integrated as one, we will have achieved our purpose of becoming a Higher Universal Spirit Consciousness (Mana). Learning to live upon Earth from the love, truth, and perfection of our spirit consciousness will fulfill our purpose of becoming HUMAN while in physical form.

As we reach our HUMAN understanding we will begin living in a "Heaven upon Earth." The challenge for us as humans is to let go of our concept of "need" for power, greed, control, separateness, inequality, selfishness, competition, and possessions. This is our lesson of acknowledgement that the physical world we live in is finite. We cannot take the physical possessions of our life into the next life, but we will take what we learn into our eternal life.

An abundance of friends, family, love, and happiness is a virtue. Possessions that are gathered with the perfect intention of love will serve us well. Possessions that are gathered from greed will not serve us well because we will live in fear of loss.

We must also release our fear of survival, guilt, sin, and unworthiness. It is in living from the purity of intention of love, truth, mercy, and compassion that we fulfill our purpose. Fear beliefs are supported by many religions that teach the perception of judgement day and discrimination, as well as guilt and sin. If this is our belief we will live it through the creation of our mind and that is the only reality that exists for us.

Throughout the millions of years that the human soul has been progressing in its evolution, wars have been continually fought because of conflicting religious beliefs. These conflicts are symbols of the differences of the HUMAN soul and spirit in relationship to the human physical perception. These continual religious wars of competition for the "true" beliefs have brought about the destruction of multiple cultures and lands.

The symbol of the competition of the intellect and ego towards the soul and spirit is reflected in all of our physical behavior. It begins with the male and female competition and conflict and expands into the competition and conflicts of nations. *No tribe, sect, society, culture, or race has yet reached the level of civilization. True civilization does not have fear as its foundation. True civilization is based upon love, truth, equality, mercy, compassion, humility, unity, and cooperation.*

Many cultures and religions on Earth are based upon the religious foundations of the Hebrews. The foundation of the Hebrew teachings are based upon their interpretation of the law of Moses. These teachings have as their basis the wrath of God that was inflicted upon man through judgement and fear. Many religions have been influenced by beliefs of ancient pagan cults, especially the Mithrain cult which is responsible for the early beliefs of Paul. Paul's early teaching in Mithraism had a dramatic effect upon Christianity. Mithras was the pagan god of a Persian cult that was extremely popular before and during the early days of Christianity. As Paul became a follower of Jesus's teachings, he merged many of his Mithraic beliefs into his Christian teachings.

December 25 was celebrated as Mithras's birthday. Christianity celebrates Jesus's birth on December 25 with no reference to his actual birthdate. The pagan cults worshiped mythological gods in the form of statues to represent the human form as the god's true origin. In Mithraism statues of saints and gods were used as the link between the human being and God, and statues became a standard form of Catholic worship fulfilling the same purpose. Popes continued to make sacrifices and give prayers to pagan gods when it was felt that favors were needed. In other Christian religions Jesus was accepted as the human link to God and the use of statue worship was discontinued. With our pagan influences and our religious beliefs rooted in the law of Moses, it was a natural progression of the soul to attach itself to fear and not to remember the teachings of Jesus that could not be accepted during his lifetime.

As competition and conflict arose within the churches, followers would break away to form new cults. "Cult" became the term describing a new culture of thought and behavior under a new leader. When the cult grew and branched out into other geographical areas it became known as a religion that focused upon a revised doctrine of dogma and beliefs. Many of these cults had absolute control over the beliefs and behaviors of their followers and demanded a financial reward for protection against the wrath of God, which was forthcoming to them from the religious leaders. Tithing and indulgences became commonplace among religions as a way of raising revenue for the cult leader as a reward for his protection and forgiveness.

The early religions found their leaders in the kings, emperors, priests, and power hungry fanatics who took their burden of redemption seriously and murdered and plundered at their will. The followers were put to death at the leaders' slightest fear for their own preservation of power. The leaders lived from fear, judgement, greed, and control, mirroring their energy and attracting followers of like energy. These beliefs and behaviors have been passed down by karmic energy into our present life and greatly influence our soul evolution. The perceptions that we have of fear, judgement, guilt, and sin are learned beliefs that no longer serve us, but they are the religious beliefs that have become the foundation of our society.

Individuals in growing numbers are reaching a state of personal civilization. Those who reject and resist war in all guises and aspects of competition and conflict within themselves and with others are reaching a state of internal civilization.

After the state of internal civilization has been reached, the merging of the physical nature with the divine nature is assured if we continue to expand our understanding of physical experiences. Individual civilization will allow society to perceive differences as being resolved by cooperation not conflict.

War will not be an acceptable solution for the individual, the society, or the nation. The beginning shift in our consciousness became evident during the Vietnam conflict when souls that had reached a higher level of female consciousness refused to go to war.

Personal civilization denotes a shift in our consciousness from fear to love, or from our male focus of the physical to our female focus of the soul and spirit. Fighting on any level will be painful and unacceptable to a civilized person. Competition and conflict are misdirected emotions of another level of soul evolution and they are no longer real to us when we change our perception of life.

Socialism has a new meaning when civilization is the foundation of a culture. The power of true socialism is created through individual equality, cooperation, unity, understanding, love, truth, and caring. Life will bloom with faith, trust, honesty, humility, sharing, and caring. Perceiving a life of joy and happiness while living a life of fear and anger may seem unrealistic to our intellect. The intellect and ego are the symbols of our physical nature that we consistently reflect and that will compete with our divine nature until we become aware of our internal conflict.

We manifest physical symbols into our external world to trigger us to the internal conflict of our intellect and ego with our soul and spirit. The internal, cumulative manifestation of war within the individual mind is then reflected into our society and our world with the same combative and warlike actions. When we quiet the war within us, we will cease all wars external to us.

The intellect and ego moves quickly to change into its combative stance if it feels even slightly threatened by a thought, word, or action. The initial challenge comes from within but we instantly reflect the anger into our external self and to others. Each time this challenge is presented as an opportunity from our soul and spirit within, the belief of the intellect and ego is reflected into an external action in relationship to self and others.

The wounded ego's need to share its pain and misery has the power to spoil a beautiful day for anyone it encounters. This sharing of pain also allows the individual to reflect blame onto any innocent soul and spirit that was nice enough to be present. With another person present to compete with, blame and judgement become an immediate perception of the wounded ego.

Without another person present to accept the blame and judgement, the wounded ego would be confronted with personal responsibility. But the ego is capable of saving pain until it finds someone to bear the burden of its wounded anger. Of course the human ego is not suited to responsibility or true commitment. The ego is much too selfish to care or share with another human being. The perception of the ego is always one of needing instant gratification despite the circumstances.

The resistant action of our ego will be manifested in multiple levels in our daily life. It will run the gamut of fear, changing emotions constantly from resistance, rejection, competition, judgement, anger, withdrawal, arguments, to verbal abuse, physical abuse, suicide, murder, and war. The ego is full of self-pride which allows dishonesty, inconsistency, revenge, hypocrisy, unfaithfulness, fear, and anger to become its natural emotions and behaviors.

The perception of life that results from an outraged ego is distorted with beliefs of primitive thoughts, words, and actions. The ego that is out of control pulls the mind down into the lower levels of primitive reactions and attaches itself to a level of emotion where it feels comfortable. The ego can be charming, charismatic, sexually appealing, and believable to those it encounters, if that is the choice of the ego. The deception of the ego comes from such a strong veil of beliefs that a very believable reality is formed as a way of life. When the ego is in its power, the individual as well as others may not have a conscious awareness that the ego is in control of all emotional and physical behavior.

Our primitive levels of growth were focused upon survival. Killing, cannibalism, genocide, eugenics, greed, abuse, inequality, control, and other primitive behavior was lived with the intention of self-survival and later, selective survival. Primitive behavior was a different level of perception and awareness at a time of less knowledge. Behavior and beliefs functioned within a different reality system because it was a time of change and growth at a lower level of our soul evolution.

In the beginning of soul evolution, man reacted to circumstances as a survival trigger without the benefit of knowledge that would allow his actions to be consciously thought through. We have evolved in the only way that was possible, through living our physical experiences. There should be no concept of blame or guilt attached to the past or to the streams of energy that remain connected to the past levels of our growth. Understanding is our opportunity to change.

Our primitive world had its own harmony and rhythm of growth. At the time that primitive beliefs were formed, the human being was just entering the seven primary levels of soul growth. When practiced today the early primitive beliefs and behaviors are out of synchronization with the harmony of today's beliefs and levels of growth. Behavior that was accepted as normal in primitive times has become unacceptably bizarre in relationship to today's level of growth.

Evolution has allowed us to grow into expanded beliefs and knowledge that allow us to experience the differences that exist between our levels of growth. From our experience of our early primitive beliefs, we begin to perceive the difference between our physical nature on the dark, shadow side of our soul and our divine nature on the light side of our soul. Our expanded awareness of these glaring differences can trigger us to accept and acknowledge that we must change and grow.

When we perceive the differences between fear and love with our aware consciousness, we are inspired and motivated to continue to shift our consciousness to love. *Without this continuous change in our perception of reality, we would become self-destructive from physical boredom and mental decay.* Primitive behavior at any level should not be rewarded by an evolving society. Acceptance of primitive behavior allows the behavior to flourish and fails to support the soul and spirit in its challenge of change to the ego.

When beliefs and behaviors are no longer accepted by society a change occurs within the collective consciousness. Individuals who function through primitive behaviors and beliefs are captured in consistent revolutions of repetition and must learn from the physical experience or they will continue to repeat the behavior. Refusing to accept and reward primitive behavior is the responsibility of the individual and of society in supporting others in their soul growth. All behavior that is based within fear, judgement, and anger is attached to the dark, shadow side of the soul.

At this time in our evolution our soul is evolving within the level of knowledge. Releasing all of the beliefs that bind us to primitive behaviors will allow us to reach the peak experience for the soul as we open our mind to understanding. *Once the collective consciousness of truth and love has reached a balanced state of understanding through the equality of our minds and our actions, the beliefs of the collective consciousness will become universal.*

Our belief in original sin is an example of the collective consciousness that has been felt and lived through our perception as we have been experiencing the evolution of our soul. This belief became a universal belief in our collective consciousness as a sense of unworthiness and failure. The emotions of unworthiness and failure can be experienced as karmic energy without our having a conscious awareness of the belief being present in this lifetime.

Once a belief becomes predominant in the collective consciousness, it is a lesson within the soul mind and brought as a karmic lesson from one embodyment to another. It is not necessary that the belief become part of the conscious awareness within a lifetime to be experienced as an energy depletion on a daily basis. The belief in original sin is one reason for our victim consciousness and it is a cycle of energy that must be released. Another primary reason for our victim consciousness energy is the female within us has been made to feel sinful by the male within us, and that relationship is symbolized within our physical relationships.

Our peak experience in soul evolution is the perceptual shift of our aware consciousness from fear to love within the level of knowledge. The level of knowledge is the fourth level of soul evolution and the level of stasis. It is at the midpoint of the level of knowledge that we challenge ourself to rend the veil of our intellect and ego. As we rend the veil that separates our minds, we enter the Cycle of Understanding in our soul growth. As we grow from our levels of examination and reflection upon the knowledge that we accept as fact to understanding the relationship of knowledge to ourself, the Earth, and the Universe, we will be entering the light side of our soul. This gives each of us the power to choose to live in love rather than fear.

Shifting our perception of self to love allows us to examine the relationship of our soul mind, spirit mind, and intellectual mind as a living, functioning trinity that controls our physical body through the energy of love. Each individual is a cell within the body of the Creative Spirit. As a spirit cell, we created our physical body as a temple for the soul and spirit. The soul and spirit is dependent on the unity of the external self of the intellect and the physical body to support it in the physical experience. The soul and spirit uses the physical body as a tool to grow and change into a Higher Universal Mana, or Spirit Consciousness.

Our path of learning to be HUMAN is to merge the physical nature that our individual cell of spirit created with the divine nature that the Creative Spirit gave us as an eternal Spirit Con-

sciousness. Our spirit consciousness is part of us at all times in every embodyment that we choose. Our soul and spirit can be ignored, denied, rejected, and resisted by our intellect and ego but it cannot be removed or destroyed.

Our eternal spirit is the enfinite us, with a purpose in physical life of growth and change from a seed of spirit to an expanded Spirit Consciousness. Our physical body and intellect is the finite us and is created as the external image or reflection of the internal soul and spirit. As we begin to grow and change, we are living on the shadow side of our soul. Growth and change is our soul evolution. As we grow and change, we follow the path of our fractal pattern of life into the light side of our soul.

As an infant and young child the love of our soul and spirit is easily apparent in our behavior. When a child is born, it is pure soul and spirit. A child remains in the soul and spirit energy of love and joy until it begins to experience the negative behaviors of the physical world. At that moment the child begins to construct the veil or shell around the intellect and ego to provide a separation from the soul and spirit. As growth continues for the child, the power of thought shifts to the intellect and ego mind and the child becomes locked into the intellect, as karmic memory and learned behaviors develop a dense veil of beliefs separating the intellect from the soul and spirit mind.

Our level of knowledge is divided at the midpoint by the veil which separates the left lobe of the brain from the right lobe of the brain. The veil acts as a shield to the transference of electromagnetic energy from the right side to the left side of the brain. It is the veil that casts the shadow upon the left side of the brain. On the left, shadow side of the veil our mind is aware of the knowledge which we call our intellect. On the light side of the level of knowledge the mind begins to understand what the intellect has until now accepted as fact. When our intellect moves forward into the Cycle of Understanding the levels of growth and change within our one mind become real as the differences dissolve.

As the intellect and ego expand, the beliefs and behaviors learned by the external mind veil the internal soul and spirit mind from view. The intellect will then see a mirror image of itself as it looks within the mirror of its veil, and all of the attachments that still remain from the beginning of soul evolution will be mirrored back at the intellect by the ego veil.

As the intellect and ego seeks control, it attaches itself to physical beliefs and behaviors from which it builds a veil of fear to shroud itself from the love of the soul and spirit. The soul knows that the beliefs and behaviors that are attached to the left side of the brain must be released before it can merge with the right side of the brain in the light of the soul and spirit. *The veil has two purposes for the mind: it separates the physical nature and mirrors back the issues that must be dealt with; and it protects the divine nature from the negative energy of the physical mind.*

The intellect and ego represents our physical nature. The soul and spirit represents our divine nature. As a fractal pattern of the Creative Spirit, each cell within our body is a fractal pattern of the energy of the Creative Spirit. Earth and the Universe, as fractal patterns of the Creative Spirit, are supporting us in our soul evolution. Perceiving ourself within our true magnificence and unity allows us to love our eternal spirit and to live our daily physical life from that love as one nature and one mind.

Looking at ourself to discern our individual level of perception will help with our soul evolution. Our minds are not a closed system of energy thought unless we make it so by the development of the veil. The veil then encloses the aware intellect within the energy of the ego and consciously denies the presence of the soul and spirit. The soul and spirit continues to be present within the mind but its presence is not acknowledged.

The fears and guilt that haunt our mind and smother us in unworthiness are those beliefs that we use to judge ourself, and our mirror image reflects them back at us. Our belief in guilt and sin expands our fear energy and controls our life. Our attachment to fear, guilt, sin, and judgement begins to instill within us a vision of ourself as unworthy, which proceeds into a full-blown image of victimization as the energy increases. When we begin to believe that we are a victim, we will create physical experiences in life that will allow us to perceive our thoughts as truth.

Beliefs that are used by our intellect and ego to judge us are the identical beliefs that we use to judge others. All judgements that we have of others are a reflection of the judgements that we have of ourself. Our life is about us and our soul lessons. When we choose *not to look within ourself to find the lessons we are seeking within our own experiences, we will see the image of our lessons of self reflected within others.*

If we are a depressed, angry isolationist, we will attract someone of that same energy into our life to remind us of self. Our reflection may be so acute that all of our friends may be attracted by one or more of these reflections. Friends that do not share any of our fears will not remain within our physical circle of friends.

Our beliefs and behaviors also reflect our energy. If we are drug-dependent, sex-dependent, relationship-dependent, abusive, or alcoholic, we will attract our friends from like energy. Because like energy expands the energy of each individual, the sense of fear and unworthiness increases.

The perception of attaching ourself to the fear energy of our mind or to the beliefs and behaviors that control and distort our life is not fully understood within the human experience. In our soul and spirit there is comfort and a removal of self-judgement and guilt.

When we attach ourself to disease, dependencies, or abuse, it is not done with our conscious awareness. These attachments are designed into our life experiences by our soul and spirit to give us an opportunity to complete lessons from past lives. In learning the lessons of physical experiences, we release ourself from the need for disease, dependency, drugs, and fear. Lessons that are passed on from one life to another are known as karmic lessons and can be the most challenging to identify, because we will not have a conscious awareness of having experienced the belief in this lifetime.

Our life is a school for the soul and spirit and it is designed in the same way that our schools for the intellectual mind are designed. When a lesson of a specific subject is necessary to growth, we must focus upon that subject repetitiously until it is mastered. Our physical experiences will reflect the lesson that is being learned.

Reading is considered an essential subject in our schools. Our ability to read affects our entire school experience as well as our entire life experience. Reading provides an expanded quality of life as it adds to our personal enjoyment, and it is an integral part of our function in family and business relationships as well. Love is considered an essential subject by our soul and spirit and is therefore the one lesson that is approached from multiple images within each life design. Love affects every moment of our physical life as well as every moment of our eternal spirit consciousness.

Love expands our quality of life and dramatically affects every aspect of our personal experience. We feel the need to be in touch with love and it motivates us to seek love within another. In reality we are seeking love within us that is being reflected externally to another. It is our perception that allows us to feel that if we can find someone to love, we will be loved in return.

Learning the lesson of love must begin with learning to love ourself. Because the ego resists this lesson of love, it will attach itself to multiple behaviors and beliefs that will show a total lack of love, respect, and value for self.

Those in intimate relationships who choose physical or mental dependencies within a lifetime do so as a lesson of the opposite of what they want. When the ego attaches itself to behavior that creates pain, separateness, and depression to resist the soul and spirit, the spirit trigger depends upon the disparity of the extremes.

In all addictions we remove our freedom, free will, free intention, free choice, our love, inspiration, motivation, and our creativity from ourself. Everything that we remove from ourself we also symbolize in our physical life. As we lose our self-respect, we gradually remove the love, respect, and value that other family members, friends, and business associates see within us. As we have less respect and value for ourself, we have less respect and value for others who are close to us. As we judge ourself and feel more under the control of the dependency, we will seek to be around others who we can control despite the dependency.

This self-destructive course will act as a trigger to help us learn what we do not want in our life, but not before we are in a state of crisis. Dependency is our method of proving to ourself the value of loving who we are. Our soul and spirit love is at that moment capable of overcoming the addiction with physical cellular and mind support that is in the harmony of Earth and spirit love.

Our physical cellular support must come from the Earth elements of air, water, and minerals. Mind support must be in harmony with the love of the soul and spirit to effectively change the perception of the intellect and ego from fear to love.

All dependent crises of our physical life are designed into the soul lesson and manifested with the determined intention of the soul and spirit to grasp the lesson with total clarity in this lifetime.

Behaviors such as alcoholism, drug addiction, sexual promiscuity, crime, and violent abusive behavior are all lessons of firm soul and spirit intention to change and grow. Rewarding dependent behavior will extend the lesson into other lifetimes as it totally supports the ego mind and elicits the ego, vanity belief in success.

Our lessons of dependency create a double drama because it has an intimate effect upon families, friends, and lovers, as well as the individual experiencing the dependent behavior. When dependency lessons are chosen within a life design, the soul and spirit is seeking participation from others to help with the lesson of this lifetime. The soul agreement to give support offers an opportunity for family members and friends to learn the lesson of truth and love without guilt through their active participation within the lesson.

Dramas of this magnitude are the design of old and advanced soul and spirits that are determined to be finished with the repetitions of physical fear and to complete their shift in consciousness. Their determination propels the soul and spirit beyond the fainthearted approach to life and allows acceptance of the all-or-nothing approach to learning. An approach of this intensity sets the design in place for future repetitions at the same level of intention, if the lesson is not grasped in this lifetime.

Disease can also be a dependency that is designed to capture our attention. The perception of disease as being secondary to germs or genetic influences is only partially true, as the reality *can be created. The question for science is: Why does the body allow organisms of lesser strength to become stronger than the body?*

When the proper question is asked, the search can be directed in the proper way. *Instead of blaming the organisms or the genes, explore the viability of the body, mind, and spirit.* Is there unity in its function? What havoc is the excess of medicine heaping upon an unbalanced body? Is the body being supported in its change and growth? Is the body seeking decay as the path to a new beginning? As all disease begins within the mind of the body, the solutions can't be found outside of the body.

If Jesus could turn water into wine without the physical intention of his mind, it should be understood that the mind of our soul and spirit can turn our body into disease without the physical intention of our mind.

On February 26 A.D. 26, a Wednesday, Jesus was with his six new disciples in Cana, where he had stopped to join his mother Mary and his brothers and sisters at the wedding of Naomi. Naomi and her bridegroom had invited about 250 people but about 1,000 people had arrived because they had heard that Jesus would be with his family at the wedding. There was a great celebration in progress when his mother Mary came to him in a frenzy of concern because the wine was at an end and the wedding had not yet taken place.

Jesus was fully aware that the unexpected crowd at the wedding was there in anticipation, waiting for him to declare himself as the Messiah, since John the Baptist had named him as the Deliverer at the Sunday ceremonies along the Jordan River. Jesus knew that the entire wedding crowd was waiting for him to perform a miracle to show his powers as the Messiah.

Miracles and Messianic declarations was not the way Jesus chose to deliver his teachings to any crowd, and he had no desire to attract attention to himself instead of the bride and groom at this wedding. He heard his mother's pleas and couldn't believe that she, who had borne him of her spirit, was asking him to be a magician of entertainment. She knew that he was here to do his Father's work.

Mary was speaking to Jesus for the second time, urging him to save the host from embarrassment and do something about the wine. Jesus looked at his mother and felt the love in his heart for this sweet and caring woman. But he said, "My good woman, what have I to do with the wine?" and immediately he paused as Mary burst into tears. Standing before him with tears streaming down her face she pleaded with her son, "Please, I have promised them that you would help us." With his heart full of compassion and love for his mother, he took her wet face in his hands and began to gently wipe away her tears, pleading with her to calm herself.

Mary looked into Jesus's face and jumped with joy. She threw her arms around his neck and kissed him before running back to the wedding table. Mary knew that Jesus had not let her down. Jesus walked behind her, strolling over to where the crowd had gathered around the servers who were dipping and filling vessels from the water jugs. Jesus looked down into the large twenty-gallon jugs and saw clearly that they all held wine.

No one at the wedding could have been more surprised than Jesus to see the jugs full of wine. *It had not been his conscious intention to turn the water into wine but it had been his deed.* Jesus removed himself from the crowd and retired to a corner of the garden to be alone with his thoughts.

Jesus remembered the compassion that he had felt toward his mother for her concern over the success of the party. He knew that while it was not his physical intention to provide the wine, his compassion for his mother had directed his divine nature to fulfill her wishes unbeknown to him.

It was his choice not to use miracles except in special cases of compassion and mercy, and in his compassion for his mother his mind had created the wine for him. Jesus knew that he would need to be very careful of the physical thoughts of his mind. With his divine nature so powerful within him, every thought could be fulfilled without his physical intention. Jesus knew as he meditated alone in the garden that it would take man a long time to appreciate the power of his mind.

The power of our mind is the path to healing our body and our physical mind. Being conscious of our negative, fearful, disease thoughts will allow us to change our thinking to protect us rather than scourge us. What Jesus did, we do. *We are the miracle.*

If it is our belief that we are victims of germ and gene warfare, we will certainly create enough examples to outwit our intellect. Our mind has been led into the intellect and ego perception of science, and our belief that all cures are external to us has created a distortion in our path of understanding the body, mind, and spirit as a trinity. Without understanding and acknowledging the eternal connection within the trinity of our mind, understanding disease and curing disease will be a futile pursuit of the intellect.

Our intellectual mind has expanded the problems of our physical body to the level of challenging balance as a societal lesson. Science in its "need to save" is in many instances exacerbating disease.

The scientific mind has strong attachments to the soul levels of examination and reflection, which prevent progression into true understanding and allow the mind to perceive only from the shadow of the soul. As science learns to strengthen the germs and mutate the genes, new dramas will be emerging within the physical body to capture our attention. Nature provides us with all cures for our mind and body. All that we create with our mind, we can heal with our mind. Our body is the total creation of thought energy that honors the trinity of our mind.

Shifts of perception will allow us a full awareness of our mind power that will serve us well in prevention. Our mind perception of physical reality governs and controls every aspect of our life from physical birth to death. When we understand the strength and power of our mind perception, we will consciously choose to think in terms of what we want, not what we don't want. Because of this subconscious and unconscious power of our mind, it is important to define what we want within our perception of life and to think only in creative and positive ways.

A defined purpose within our life gives the mind a focus of intention and allows the power of our mind to consistently work with us, not against us. Once one purpose is achieved, we can establish a loftier purpose for ourself as our next goal.

If we have a family history of cancer and it is our belief that we will develop genetic cancer, we will. Our perception of cancer being created within our body will aid and abet the development of the cancer cell.

If we believe that we will die young because that is a family genetic pattern, our perception of an early death will create an early death for us. If we believe in the assumptions of others that limit our age span, we will die on schedule. These beliefs allow us to remove our power of free will, free choice, and free intention, and our own power of creation by believing in the power of another's belief. Any belief that gives another person the power of our body, our mind, or our life, gives our own power away.

If we believe that we are going to be senile at an early age, our perception will effectively shut down the mind and body at the determined time. If we live in fear of senility, we will create it. If we live in fear of nursing homes, we will find ourself living in one.

When we are attached to a fear, we create the physical experience of the fear in our physical life.

If we fear old age and perceive old age arriving at a specified time, we will begin the aging process on our self-defined time schedule. Our perception of old age is related to our multiple fears of loss, such as the loss of our mental and physical abilities, our career, fun, family, friends, and perhaps most of all the loss of our beautiful, youthful body and mind.

We fail to change our perception from the fear of what we are losing to the love of our life experience, wisdom, self-respect, and a new time schedule that allows us more freedom. Our fear of changing our perception of life allows us to dwell on what we feel we have lost, not what we have gained. This fear of loss captures us and takes away our potential for joyously celebrating each moment that we live.

As our perception of life and death and all that goes between begins to change, our life span will change dramatically. All nursing homes should be abolished, if their intention is business, not loving care. New methods can be perceived that will provide love, mercy, and compassion when care is truly needed.

The wisdom of our multiple life experiences that dwell in the mind of the evolving human being is being lost as a family and a societal resource. Our failure to share the wisdom of age with the children of today allows a strong and more rapid development of the veil. *The old and the young have a well-developed soul and spirit communication that provides a continuity for the coming and going of the soul and spirit in our physical life.* All of humanity deserves love, respect, and value from each other regardless of age.

The old and the young are both representing their divine nature and fulfilling stages of their physical evolution. The early and later years are simply bridged by the middle stages of our life to work on our lessons. The continuity that is being lost within the stages of the Law of Sevens in our physical life is the symbol of the continuity that is being lost within our mind when the intellect rejects the soul and spirit of our divine nature. Continuity cannot be lost to humanity without the lessons of that loss being lived again in our physical experience.

Competition has been perceived as a necessary part of our

physical life for many years. Competition is an energy of the ego and is based upon the fear of failure. Competition is used in all aspects of human reality from youth to old age, including multiple interactions from personal to international relationships. It is seen in sexual relationships, in families, with friends, in work, in play, and in religion. Competition is always the beginning of conflict, which can appear in many disguises.

The weapons of the game are an indication of the intention within the mind. The weapons can be status, skill, words, education, science, physical strength, sex, money, prestige, adoration, drugs, guns, bombs, tanks, planes, and promises of being saved. For many the physical rewards of the game have now become more important than the game. Games that were once played for fun and socialization have now become a symbol of the ego resisting the soul and spirit at the mesocosmic level of our societies' evolution. Competition is veiling the importance of cooperation in all aspects of our life.

The soul of our society is reflected from the energy of our soul. If our soul is our individual, microcosmic experience of living through competition and conflict, our society is living the mesocosmic soul experience as a reflection of our beliefs and behaviors using competition and conflict. The world as the macrocosmic level will also reflect the identical competition and conflict, which will lead to war when the energy expands to this degree.

The pattern of our competitive lifestyle has been perceived, revered, and copied as the "right" behavior when the behavior has been based upon greed, adoration, prestige, money, sex, alcohol, drugs, and negative influences. Our lifestyle is structured, organized, and disciplined through competition, conflict, and greed from the board room, to the baseball field, to the street corner.

It is this image of competition, conflict, and greed that is being used by our children as their symbol of success or failure. This is the perfect symbol of the mesocosmic or societal influence that originates from the microcosmic life of the individual. Our perception of our own success is then judged in relationship to our ability to meet the behavioral and success standards of our hero.

When competition becomes an issue in any relationship, whether it is an intimate relationship with a family member or friend, or a professional relationship—financial, political, national, or international—the perception of the relationship changes. The cooperative spirit of love is lost in the fear that overwhelms all who are worried about their self-image and their survival. This is a self-defeating perception that overwhelmingly strives to always be right and is symbolic of a fragile ego that is feeling threatened by its own self-judgement.

When an ego is fragile and living in fear, that fear will be reflected into all types of situations by the quality of the behavior. Anyone who competes with a gun, with physical abuse, verbal abuse, sex, money, status, or with image, is protecting a fragile ego that is supported only by fear.

The ego is wounded and ravaged with guilt. These internal feelings will then be reflected outwardly in callous and disrespectful behavior towards others. When the ego feels wounded, betrayed, abused, or ignored, it impinges these same feelings outward, physically and emotionally, to others—feeling it is in a battle for survival and must willingly compete for its life.

The solution to the crisis created by all criminal activities is to shift the mind from fear to love. Without fear there is no motivation to compete to the death and there is no ego self-image to maintain. When love dwells within the heart of all humans, cooperation will allow a peaceful solution to all problems. Beliefs, behaviors, and perceptions of fear will all dissolve within the harmonic energy of love. When the pattern of love can be established early in life, the shift in consciousness will be the chosen path or it will occur naturally, with growth as the purpose of our one mind.

Jealousy is an ego emotion that appears when the ego is feeling rejected. Our perception of rejection can cause dramatic emotional pain, and it will lead to more serious emotional dramas if no valid attempt is made to understand it.

Jealousy can be triggered in intimate relationships, in friendships, in families, or within the business community. It can affect individuals on their microcosmic level, society on a mesocosmic level, or the world on a macrocosmic level. The perception of rejection that causes jealousy can establish a sense of unworthiness that can lead to bloodshed at any time as a crime of passion.

The emotion of jealousy may be triggered by a physical act or it may originate solely within the mind. The perception of rejection is a lesson that is based within the individual and will be triggered into action with a variety of stimuli. The perception of rejection has its foundation in an extreme sense of unworthiness. When the unworthiness is challenged by the perception of rejection, intense anger and jealousy is the emotion and behavior that is acted out.

When rejection occurs within our mind, it is more important to look within than to attach ourself to the perceived pain of the external rejection. Discovering the internal reason for the ego to react so dramatically can help us learn the lesson that is being sought by the soul and spirit.

Our emotions become our drama coach, helping to bring within our understanding the truth of our feelings of unworthiness and rejection. It is important to understand that our perception and emotional reactions are for our benefit and not the other person's.

If we are faced with true physical rejection we have the choice to consider the source and excuse ourself from the drama. Nothing is requiring us to become a victim of the abuse and rejection except our own sense of unworthiness. If we feel the rejection and unworthiness, we are responding to the reflection with our jealousy because our lesson has not been learned with clarity.

To recognize our own emotional response and freedom of choice is a magnificent step forward in honoring and respecting ourself. When we honor and respect ourself, no one will have the power to trigger the emotion of jealousy, rejection, or unworthiness. We will see the situation for what it is and give ourself total respect and honor in choosing to be elsewhere. Or we could choose to find a solution through mutual cooperation and communication.

Attaching ourself to negative energy in any relationship indicates that we have triggered a lesson within us. Our emotional response has nothing to do with the other person. Jealousy is the result of our own lesson. Jealousy is symbolic of the ego reaction to the love of soul and spirit. Our reaction of jealousy is a manifestation of our internal emotion being reflected into our physical life. With meditation and an honest assessment of our soul and spirit, we can change our perception of a jealousy challenge.

Revenge is an ego anger of such magnitude that the ego is determined to get even. Revenge is a reaction to our perception of rejection and unworthiness, and it is the normal sequential emotion that follows jealousy.

Responding to the emotional abuse of the ego is non-productive in our physical life. The pain and emotional abuse that the ego can heap upon us when this emotion is in control shows no respect or value for us. Revenge destroys our self-respect and allows us to sink to the level of the person who is triggering our anger.

The soul and spirit responds by living well and joyously, removing us from all triggers of pain. The ego desperation that seeks revenge is an imprisonment of our soul and spirit. Desperation pulls us down into the primitive beliefs and behaviors, encouraging us to wallow in the fear of our wounded ego. We have the power to change our perception.

Seeing the choice of wallowing in our pain relative to choosing our freedom will help us to make a wise and loving choice. The intention of revenge toward another is a useless emotion that can never be realized. Despite the drama of the physical action that could be taken, the harm would always be reflected back into our personal life as a lesson. Being loving and true to our own personal value and our magnificent power to change will support us in releasing the drama of revenge. This is the only method of truly learning our soul and spirit lesson.

Abuse is a perfect example of our changing perception. What is now seen as abuse in its many varied forms was once understood as the "right" of man. When women and children were considered the possessions of the male, our laws gave the male the "right" to abuse. This law still exists in many cultures. When women focus within their physical energy they are also capable of abuse. Abuse is the opposite of equality. If every human were perceived as part of self through the Universal connection of the soul and spirit, no one would be abusive.

Man has abused women and children, frequently in the name of God, since the beginning of time. The teachings of the female having been made from the rib of Adam have allowed a perception of ownership of all females and children. This is a teaching of many religions, and abuse has therefore been rampant in many cultures in the name of God. The male has taken to his ego mind the primitive belief that man was made in the image of God and therefore he has the supreme right to control through his wrath and his judgement. In truth, man was created by woman and both as humans were created in the image of the Spirit energy of God.

The female sense of powerlessness to survive abusive male behavior for many thousands of years has strengthened the sense of unworthiness in all of humankind. The gender focus is changed from embodiment to embodiment, allowing every human to live as both male and female. Our attachment to the belief in unworthiness and powerlessness is then passed down through the karmic energy within the soul. What we give, we will also receive.

Abuse is the true manifestation of "an eye for an eye, and a tooth for a tooth." The physical, emotional, or sexual abuse that we inflict upon another, we will also inflict upon ourself. Abuse is then a soul lesson of learning to love self. Abuse of another becomes the mirror of self-abuse. The abuse will have multiple images reflecting the multiple images of the lesson.

There are no accidents within the Universe, but there are countless life designs that will cover the multiple images of multiple lessons. Our perception of abuse will originate from the perception of the experience as victimization, until we learn that the subconscious energy of our soul and the unconscious energy of our spirit are the master planner and designer of our physical lives. When we learn our lesson, we no longer tolerate abuse of any kind.

Abuse does not wound the inner child of the soul and spirit. Abuse is the two-by-four of the soul and spirit that is determined to get the attention of the physical child. Abuse creates the opportunity for us to learn what we don't want so that we can fully understand what we do want. We experience abuse in multiple levels of learning. Abuse is designed into our physical lives as an image of the lesson of loving self.

Sexual promiscuity has been the physical action of man from the beginning of time. Sexual promiscuity is a dramatic lesson of self-abuse and accepting the responsibility for our actions in life. *The images of sexual promiscuity are all lessons of learning self-love through acceptance of responsibility. The physical action of responsibility is the commitment to always live our life through our personal respect and value for self.*

The images of sexual promiscuity are acted out within our life in issues of control, money, survival, dependency, disease, unworthiness, victimization, abuse, power, self-indulgence, greed, possessions, and multiple others. These images are all perceived as images of "love" by different intellects and egos. Until our sexual activity supports and respects the value of self as a healthy, happy, and enthusiastic person, we are not living our love of self.

The emotions that we live within our daily life will be reflected to other people, into our society, and into our world. *Our interwoven soul and spirit energy connects each of us to one another, to our society, and to the Universe regardless of our physical connection.* This is the way we form our collective consciousness through our connecting energy streams of thought.

Disease is within itself another dramatic lesson of life. The lesson will depend upon the perception of disease within the individual person's mind. From this personal perception the lesson will be very individualized and will be acted out through the multiple images created by the belief system. The mind will allow us to put into action in our physical life all of the fears, perceptions, beliefs, and dramas that we connect with the disease.

Disease is one way of transformation into another life while cleaning up the lessons of a current lifetime. Disease is a profound lesson in maintaining the health of the physical body by staying in tune with nature, from which the body was designed. This is an image of loving self and accepting responsibility for the actions of our life. Disease is also a lesson of commitment, of accepting our physical power, of honoring the power of the mind, of patience, unity, love, caring, truth, freedom, and equality.

Disease is created through the soul and spirit direction to get our attention and to help us work through our lessons. Learning and acting upon the lesson will change the chemical and energy responses of the body and allow many diseases to be healed by the body itself if the lesson is completed.

Relationships are the fiber of learning within our physical world. They provide the classroom for each lesson that we have designed into this lifetime. A relationship allows us to see ourself relative to another. As we reflect our behavior from the behavior of another, we are seeing our own image or the opposite of our image.

If the other person reflects the opposite of our behavior, the beliefs and behaviors can be easily assessed and consciously chosen as something we want in our character or something that we do not want in our character or personality.

Those in close relationships will frequently reflect the mirror image. Those in casual relationships will frequently reflect the opposite image. Not all images of us will be reflected in one person, but we will find different behaviors or beliefs reflected in different relationships. Our group of close friends will provide the clearest image of self. Our perception of our close friends and family members will be established by the image of ourself that we find within them. Our perception of the relationship may not be shared or be in any way the same as the perception of the other person.

This mirror image can establish an active relationship or active participation in learning our lesson through the image of self in another. Each individual perceives an image of self reflected in another that is his personal perception, and the image will originate from the intellect as long as the veil is in place. This image then becomes a perception of our mirror image and not the true image of the other person within the relationship.

Our perception of the opposite of our beliefs and behaviors that are understood in families and friends will give us the opportunity to learn through passive participation. By seeing what we don't want, we can avoid further repetition of our lessons by learning them passively through our observation of other beliefs and behaviors as we are involved in the relationships.

Marriage or intimate relationships can provide the entire spectrum of lessons which can be learned with the valuable physical and emotional support of intimacy.

Close families provide the same spectrum of lessons with the same valuable physical and emotional support on the dual levels of our individual and societal experience. In all relationships the roles that are perceived provide the script for the behavior.

Life is a dance, choreographed by us, allowing our emotions, behaviors, and beliefs to flow and move in harmony, in chaos, in rhythm, in steps, in blocks, and in falls. We can be graceful as we learn or we can be totally uncoordinated and out of rhythm with the lesson.

The beliefs and the lessons will merge and flow together, allowing us to live what we are trying to learn. In a relationship each mind will have a perception of roles. The roles may not be defined in the same way. If a wife sees marriage as an opportunity for closeness, love, communication, sharing, and play, and a husband sees marriage as an opportunity to organize, discipline, control, and work, they will be living from two separate scripts. Their dance will take place to the beat of different drummers.

The failure to communicate and reach an agreement on the definitions of beliefs and roles before marriage destroys many marriages. The intellect of the male, physical mind perceives relationships differently than the soul and spirit of the female mind; therefore, intimacy is approached before the language of sex is interpreted and fully understood. The most common words between two lovers will have two separate meanings.

A female speaks of love and she thinks of commitment, sharing, emotional support, and togetherness. A male speaks of love and he thinks of sex. Beliefs that differ regarding language communication and role definition will allow behavior that is not expected and not accepted. This inability to communicate in the same language begins the fear, judgement, blame, anger, and revenge. All arguments from that moment on will be endless because the meanings of the words are perceived differently. The perception of roles, expected behavior, beliefs, and the expectations of the relationship are different and are destined to create conflict internally and externally.

Compromises can be agreed to that do not improve understanding. Compromise defines a discipline or structure in which the marriage is then perceived. The most important issue for the male and female in all intimate relationships, friendly relationships, or family relationships is to communicate in words of the same meaning. Never assume that your definition of words is the same. Definitions must become a part of your communication.

To use an example, the roles and identities that are attached to a marriage will differ from within the individual, culture, society, and the world. In each instance the role and identity of the wife will have a unique meaning, and the role and identity of the husband will have a unique meaning.

To begin communication that is effective, we must understand how each individual perceives his role and identity. Once the perception is defined, accepted, and understood, communication can begin. The definition of roles and identities begins to present clues to specific beliefs and behaviors. Unraveling the belief system of a partner in a relationship can take years and will never be perceived from the exact perception of the partner because the definition itself is perceived from our own level of soul growth.

If individual perception is never defined and understood throughout the relationship, the parties involved are working with different scripts and attempting to make the play of life make sense. Working from different perceptions of the expected role allows unhappiness with the behavior within a relationship to cause anger, frustration, jealousy, rejection, and fear.

When one role is dependent, the expectation will be seen from a self-serving perception. Dependency is the lesson of personal responsibility being denied in our physical behavior. In dependency there is no perception of equality. If equality is not accepted as a part of daily life in the relationship, the responsibility for personal performance is removed and the stage is set for the dependent person to expect to receive from the person that is perceived as the caregiver. The caregiving that is expected as a right within the relationship may include all aspects of daily living, or it can be specific in separating some expectations from others in the dependent personality.

This relationship will establish revolutions in life not evolutions, and when dependency is recognized it should be immediately changed. But the fear of responsibility will usually be honored in the dependent personality by the immediate establishment of a similar relationship with another individual. Dependent behavior will not be recognized until the veil can be removed and personal responsibility for all of life is accepted.

The lesson of dependency symbolizes the dependency of the individual upon the intellect and ego as the receiving physical nature, while denying the giving energy of the soul and spirit as the divine nature. Dependency and control feed off each other.

Dependency will be a major lesson for anyone who is up against the veil of physical beliefs and sees himself as spiritual from an intellectual basis.

Those individuals working with this lesson will develop relationship dependencies, as well as physical dependencies that cover the entire spectrum of living. The survival symbols of food, drink, shelter, money, life amenities, sex, friendship, and caring are frequently involved.

The dependent person will also be very closed and separate in his physical behavior. This is the symbol of the physical mind staying separate from the soul and spirit mind.

Because the minds of the intellect, soul, and spirit are not in communication, the inability to communicate will be a major issue in any physical relationship.

This example can be seen in all relationships, from intimate ones to casual friends. The lesson of dependency is the lesson of believing only in the physical, intellectual perception of life. This lesson will create multiple images because each lesson is connected to all lessons and we are all connected to each other.

The lesson of dependency will frequently be found in the passive-aggressive personality, with the passive behavior becoming the fantasy of living as soul and spirit. Dependency must be worked out in relationships because relationships are the perfect lesson that allows the shadow to dissolve. The shadow will only begin its dissolution when the passive, dependent behavior is no longer accepted within the physical relationship.

Within the dependent personality there will be little if any indication of self-motivation, enthusiasm, inspiration, imagination, or ideas, because the ego is in denial of soul and spirit. If these feelings are present they will be denied as unworthy, inadequate, ineffective, and meaningless. The self-image of the dependent personality is totally under the control of the ego.

The ego is dedicated to the perception of its superiority and therefore maintains total separateness from the soul and spirit. If the soul and spirit is acknowledged in any manner it is through the deception of the intellect. The deception then becomes a perception that acts as a red herring, allowing another belief to strengthen the veil of separation from the soul and spirit. Distorted perceptions convolute or thicken the negative energy of the veil that separates the intellect and ego from the soul and spirit.

The distinction between the ego vision of soul and spirit energy and the true soul and spirit energy can only be defined through a self-examination of individual actions, behaviors, and beliefs.

Do you awaken in the morning full of enthusiasm, ideas, and excitement at being alive in a new day? Do you perceive your day as an opportunity to grow and change through what you expect to experience? Do you look forward to seeing others, speaking to others, and freely sharing your ideas and enthusiasm from the love and truth of self in clearly communicated language? Are you open to everyone around you with your enthusiasm, love, and caring? Are you open to growth and change? Are you open to new ideas and concepts? Do you live your life without judgement?

If your actions are those described in the above questions, you are working with your internal soul and spirit energy. You will find all actions occurring in levels of energy. You will begin to develop an awareness of these defined levels of growth as you change. This shows you your immediate room for expansion and growth.

Truth and love are the natural energies of the soul and spirit. You will feel no sense of fear or unworthiness in your soul and spirit energy. You will feel no rejection if your ideas are not accepted by others. You will have the confidence that all things have their moment in time.

Judgement, evaluation, and assessment differ only in the emotion of the intention that is involved. Evaluation and assessment of life experiences is our method of growth and change, which becomes the intention in looking at the problem. As we view our experiences to recognize and heal our lessons, we will subconsciously evaluate and assess our multiple lessons of life. Looking into the events of our physical experiences allows us to see the lesson. We must not be afraid to look within ourself and our actions. If we fear looking at ourself and the life dramas that we create, we are still a captive of the intellect and ego judgement.

Evaluation and assessment is a soul and spirit response to define the path of change within the physical to the soul and spirit. If we intend to understand ourself, then evaluation and assessment of our life experiences, both past and present, must become a conscious action. We can review our life experiences with fascination

PERCEPTION

or with judgement. The challenge is ours.

Judgement is involved with the emotions of blame, vindictiveness, wrongfulness, and revenge, which then becomes the intention. Judgement is an ego response that is accepted in fear as a threat to our survival. Judgement is the opposite energy to the unconditional love of our soul and spirit. It is at all times the emotional reaction of the intellect and ego. Judgement is the normal way of perception of events for the intellect and ego. The energy that is harnessed by the intellect and ego in the act of judgement dramatically expands the negative energy of the mind. This is the method of our mind when it creates mountains from ant hills.

Perceiving life, relationships, or self from judgement energy will create repetitions of our lessons as we fear change.

Do you awaken in the morning disgusted that morning has descended upon you against your will? Do you perceive your day as just a repetition of the same old grind to provide for your daily survival? Are all of your activities based upon doing what you have always done? Do your behaviors, beliefs, actions, and thoughts tread only the well-worn paths within your mind, belaboring thoughts of problems, people, and events over and over again? Do you feel afraid, captured by life, imprisoned by circumstances, or unworthy?

If you answered yes to any of these revealing questions you are captured in old habits, beliefs, and behaviors. Being stuck in old habits and beliefs will cause feelings of depression, unworthiness, and victimization that will pull you into fear and judgement. Making changes in your life will initiate new ideas, inspirations, and excitement.

Do you fear change? Do you say the words that you think people want to hear? Do you feel that you have a role to live up to? Is your life dedicated to living up to other people's expectations of you? Do you find yourself drained of your physical energy? Do you feel that you need lots of sleep to survive the next day? Do you harbor fears of heights, elevators, closets, some people, loud voices, speaking within groups? Does your life feel empty of meaning? Are you sad, depressed, angry, fearful, vindictive, judgemental, or greedy?

If you answered yes to any of the above questions you are captured in your intellect and ego. Our intellect and ego lives from fear because it places all of its belief in the external. The external is seen as the ultimate in life's destination. The more money, fame, status, and possessions that can be obtained the safer you feel. Life is not a destination of physical "things," it is a journey of change and growth.

If you could gain all that is available within the external world, what would you really have? You cannot take any of your physical possessions with you when you die. But you can take all of the growth of your soul and spirit with you into your eternal life.

Our soul and spirit is our path of growth in our life's journey. In denying the soul and spirit, we acknowledge the separate and fearful energy of the ego and we proceed to live from that energy. This is the way we create our reality through our perception. Our reality is created by our mind and its accepted beliefs.

Our perception of life affects every aspect of life from our relationships, beliefs, emotions, and behavior to the tangible, physical art of living. If we perceive education as only the degrees that we obtain and not the relationship of knowledge learned and life experience, we limit our ability to function. Classrooms and teachers are limited in what they can teach us, but we are not limited in what we can learn. If we perceive our ideas and imagination as valuable, we will feel the freedom to challenge what is learned.

Learning to honor and respect the inspiration and motivation of our mind is our best education. This allows the perceived fact of the intellect to be assessed and evaluated by the soul and spirit within us. If it is absolute truth, truth will be understood through the action of the belief. If the consistency of the belief is destroyed in the action, it is not truth.

As individuals we perceive the importance of absorbing knowledge, but we do not understand that when we perceive truth, truth will absorb us.

The perception that we have of our government, our education, the health of our physical body, our career, our sexual orientation, and our religious beliefs defines our level of soul evolution. In soul evolution we must perceive our growth and change as our individual responsibility in every facet of our life.

It is the perception that we have of responsibility that deter-

mines our life. To give our power away to anyone else is not honoring and respecting ourself. Responsibility is our lesson of unconditionally loving ourself as body, mind, and spirit.

We will not and cannot love ourself if we cannot acknowledge the unity of the whole self. Our lesson of scientific medicine is being manifested as the symbol of our need to love the whole self. Perceiving the body as separate parts is disrespectful and dishonoring to our body because it denies the eternal connection of our mind, body, and spirit as a whole.

If we sailed out to sea and took only the rudder, the sails, or the forward cabin with us, we would sink before we left the dock. When the physical body is perceived as a whole it can be treated as a whole, giving our mind the freedom to consciously create vibrant health. Treating only separate parts of our body can destroy the body by misdirecting our internal mind energy and sinking us into the pathos of disease.

The mind has total control over the body. The body is connected by blood vessels, lymph streams, organs, cells, water, minerals, oxygen, blood, and on and on. What happens to one cell has the power to affect the entire body. One thought can change the entire body or any one part of it. But one part of the body cannot be successfully treated without treating the whole body.

When we are treated by multiple physicians instead of one, the consistency of thoughts, words, and actions are lost and confusion reigns. When we perceive that anyone knows more about our health and our body than we do, we are living our own deception. We have not been taught to listen to our body. If we listen, we will hear our body talking to us and we will hear truth.

Communicating with our body gives us an enormous advantage over the physician who is treating us from perceived fact. The physician can become our guide and our teacher in following our path of healing, but the physician cannot heal us unless we choose to be healed. When the mind believes the body is being healed, the body begins the healing process.

When the mind perceives the medicines, treatments, and surgery as healing, a message is sent to the body to begin healing. As we begin to feel better, we are convinced the medicine healed us. When we release our fear of death and believe in our ability to become well, the immune system becomes activated and the healing process begins. This explanation may seem simplistic, and it is, but understand that our perceptions, created from our beliefs, are our challenge or our power.

Our perception of health, homosexuality, religious beliefs, love, truth, and equality are all lessons that we are working with in our fourth level of soul evolution. These are major lessons of perception that are being reflected to us as the illusion of truth.

Truth, when it is understood, will be reflected within the actions of the individual, our government, and the world. Seeing truth reflected in our society will change the relationship of all people on the microcosmic, mesocosmic, and macrocosmic levels.

Each lesson that has roots in the beginning levels of our soul evolution must now be completed. As we enter into the light side of our soul, we cannot remain tied to the primitive beliefs of the shadow side of our soul and enjoy the true miracle of life.

2

Physical Love

> "When will we teach our children in school
> what they are? We should say to each of them:
> Do you know what you are? You are a marvel.
> You are unique. In all of the world there is no other
> child exactly like you. In the millions of years that
> have passed there has never been another child like you.
> And look at your body—what a wonder it is! Your legs,
> your arms, your cunning fingers, the way you move! You
> may become a Shakespeare, a Michelangelo, a Beethoven.
> You have the capacity for anything. Yes, you are a marvel.
> And when you grow up, can you then harm another who is,
> like you, a marvel?"
>
> *Pablo Casals, Joys and Sorrows*

Sexual interaction is the most common perception of physical love. Many times sex is more physical than loving, making the perception of sexual interaction as love a misnomer. Sexual interaction is the expenditure of physical energy in a sexual way.

Sex is dramatically important to our physical and emotional health because it is one method of draining off blocked physical energy.

Our body is energy and it has an inherent force that we do not understand. Our energy force must be used. If our energy is not expended in an acceptable manner such as labor or exercise, it will accumulate and explode in a violent, angry, abusive manner either externally through physical behavior and emotions or internally through disease.

The energy within our bodies comes from the energy of our physical matter, our soul, and our spirit. The power of our energy is harnessed and directed through our mind to our body. If we refuse to use our mind and body, we are storing up electromagnetic energy that has a dramatic explosive power. An inactive life may allow for some small seepage of energy through sex, but that tiny drainage of energy is not sufficient to prevent an emotional explosion or a physical disease.

Our sexual abilities were given to us for a dual purpose. First, we have the ability to procreate sexually, and second, sexual activity is an escape valve for our pent-up emotional and physical energy.

When our life is directed toward our physical perception, we must have more outlets for the buildup of soul and spirit energy that occurs. If the soul and spirit energy is denied, we will create disease or other crisis dramas in an attempt to capture our conscious awareness on a physical level. *Until we can become consciously aware of the crises events that we are creating within our physical body and our mind, we will not accept our power to change our misdirected energy that produces the events.*

Individuals, society, and the world are now faced with the results of their obstructed energy that has been misdirected into fear and its traumatic results. The actions of misdirected explosive energy result in murder, rape, abuse, destruction, alcoholism, drug addiction, dependencies of multiple form, and disease. The negative effects from misdirected energy are endless and they impact the individual, society, and the world.

We have the choice of directing our energy into the negative perspective of fear which is directed externally but mirrored internally, or the positive perspective of love which is directed internally and mirrored externally. The combined energy of our physical body, soul mind, and spirit consciousness is not yet understood and accepted, and therefore it is not respected and valued as a powerful energy force. When positive energy is converted to negative energy by our daily activities, when it is stored inadequately and its power is not respected, destruction is the natural result.

This conversion principal of positive energy can be seen as a physical reality within us and external to us. *As we learn to channel our electromagnetic energy forces through a balanced use of body, mind, and spirit energy, we will begin to find the peace and harmony that we seek.* Our positive energy will create a harmony and rhythm within our body, our mind, and our physical life that will reflect out from us into our society and the world.

We have unknowingly created the chaos of ourself and our society because we direct our attention to the external world, not to the magnificent strength of our internal power. But as our internal power seeks to become one with our external power, the explosive energy is seen within our mind and body as our physical beliefs resist change.

The atom is the smallest fractal of the cosmic pattern that we are familiar with. The human body is many steps up the ladder of repetition in its cosmic fractal pattern. We understand the destructive force of the atom: therefore, it should be easy for us to draw an analogy between the destructive force of the atom and the destructive force of the human intellect and body. The power within our mind and body is many times greater than the power of the tiny atom. It is our method of using our mind and body that obstructs and converts our positive energy to negative energy within our life.

We have the power to change our destructive energy into productive energy at will. We are constantly creating our life and our world from our energy forces. As humans we have been given the power of creation with our freedom of choice, intention, and will to guide us. We choose to direct our energy with either a positive or negative intention.

When our destructive, negative energy is exploding within, our sexual interactions will be destructive. Physical love will become physical sex, which is devoid of the emotion of love. The credibility of our sexual energy comes from the sensitivity of our physical senses. As physical substances are used, such as alcohol and drugs, our physical senses are suppressed in the same way they are suppressed with fear and its myriad of negative emotions. We decrease our ability to feel, emotionally and physically, which allows our energy to be obstructed and to build again to the point of explosion.

When the mind and body are in harmony, the act of physical love will become the celebration of love, not the physical sexual encounter that is common today. The emotion of being in love is an energy boost that uses the energy from both the physical body and the mind. It can create inspiration, motivation, excitement, enthusiasm, and happiness. Yet the reactions to the feelings of love are in fact fantasy if the sexual encounter is coming only from our physical perspective.

Some fantasies are more fleeting than others. Our feelings are being created by the love energy which comes from within us. Our vision is the mirror image of our energy that is reflected back to us but is perceived by us as being generated by another. The fantasy of love that is based upon physical or sexual attraction has a durability that can be measured in minutes to perhaps three months.

As we feel differently about the relationship, the mirror image of our feelings that we see in the relationship begins to change. Our partner's feelings may not change, but as we change, our perception of the relationship changes. If we suddenly perceive a relationship as not being truthful, our image of the love that we feel changes and we begin to look at the other person with new emotions.

Our feelings, as energy, change constantly as we share our experiences with the one we love. At this sensitive time we react to every word, every thought, every action. Our perception of the other person is established through our perception of ourself and our beliefs and expectations about the relationship. Our response to ourself becomes our positive or negative response to those we interact with, regardless of the level of intimacy involved.

If we are shut down and do not communicate, we will see others as not communicating with us. If we are stuck in the inertia of depression and lethargy, we will feel that others are doing nothing and are depressed with their lives. If we feel rejected by others, we will reject others. If we feel that others are not giving us the love that we need, we will withhold our love from them.

Our sensitivity to interaction has a biological purpose and an emotional purpose that symbolize the lessons of our soul. We are seeking through the interaction of physical love to act out our individual lessons through our experiences. Our personal attraction gives us an opportunity to experience our own physical and intellectual mating dance of establishing boundaries and role beliefs within our relationships. *The external mating dance of relationships is symbolic of the internal mating dance of our physical nature with our divine nature.*

Our male and female energies are involved in their own frenzied dance. We seek interaction to honor self rather than the other person. Our interchange in a relationship of sexual attraction creates a personal validation within us as we maneuver for acceptance and confirmation of our personal sense of attractiveness and beliefs. This is our method of self-validation as we search for support for our belief systems.

We create a wall of individual physical needs and beliefs, which are the building blocks of our ego. The ego challenges itself through physical and emotional self-exploration to define its capability to control and maneuver for power in a relationship. The levels that are sought in this maneuvering for power in a relationship may only be based upon the initial conquest. When conquest is the goal, the sexual encounter will usually end with the completion of the conquest, or sexual fulfillment. The goal of a sexual encounter is to succeed in the power of the conquest for either a short- or long-term act of possession.

Possession within the boundaries of sexual attraction is usually defined as a sexual completion within a short-term encounter. Possession within a long-term encounter will find the relationship wrought with jealousy, control, manipulation, and multiple types of abuse. Possession is equivalent to control for the ego.

When this completion is felt to be established by sexual intercourse in the normal manner of agreement between two people, the ego begins to seek more traumatic experiences of control in the relationship. This ego control becomes a debasement of human consciousness as it moves into the more primitive methods of self-satisfaction. Primitive beliefs give the ego the power to erupt in mental, physical, or sexual abuse. Abuse occurs because of the soul's karmic energy memory of primitive beliefs that remain from the earlier periods of soul evolution.

It is through the personal debasement of our human consciousness into the primitive levels of our development that abuse occurs in physical love. The abuser is only conscious of personal needs and judges the abused to have the same needs. The needs felt by the abuser are the mirror reflection of his needs being cast as a vision over the needs of the abused. This allows the rapist to feel that the victim enjoyed the rape.

The failure to communicate through the physical senses by equal thinking, speaking, and hearing between the individuals allows actions to occur that are perceived from individual boundaries of ego need.

Perceptions of events are always judged from individual levels of awareness and self-need, not from the needs and beliefs of the other individual that is involved in the interaction. Each person will be working upon his individual lessons and will perceive the physical events from his aware consciousness.

The sensitivity of the physical senses and the aware understanding of thoughts, words, and actions should be fully in play in mature sexual interaction. Our awareness of these guides differs significantly between individuals. Many individuals base their sexual interaction solely upon their beliefs, ego, and physical needs.

Our personal level of conscious awareness is controlled by the limited or expanded use of our physical senses in our daily life. Gender focus itself presents a dramatic difference in the level of awareness that exists. We will use the word love as an example. Love to a male may mean only a brief moment of sexual satisfaction. Love to a female may indicate a desire to spend the rest of her life in the relationship.

The perception of the word love will determine the immediate

Physical Love

reaction to the event. If the male feels love and seeks satisfaction but the female feels nothing, the encounter will be perceived as abuse by the female, who is not feeling the magnetic power of love. This is a frequent occurrence in intimate relationships.

Multiple levels of abuse and misunderstandings occur daily in the interaction of individuals seeking physical love. Abuse can be ended as a part of our society when the joys of physical love, together with our soul and spirit love, are understood and accepted. The merging of the physical nature and the divine nature within all humans will allow life to be lived from the light side of the soul, which provides a new experience in physical love.

The misunderstandings of physical love are reinforced when they are accepted regardless of the emotional level of fulfillment. Rewarding behavior that is less than perfect strengthens the behavior by the fantasy of validation. Unacceptable behavior is misdirected energy from our unknown soul and spirit. When mystery surrounds why an experience happened to us and its overall outcome, fear becomes the guiding force that controls our reaction.

If a woman feels that she has been sexually abused but also believes that she deserved it, that no one will believe her, or that a man has the right to control her body, she will suppress her anger and say nothing about her abuse or her feelings.

To understand and seek a more perfect physical union in relationships, we must understand the dynamics of our own energy that builds and attracts relationships into our life. All relationships of physical love originate from our physical concepts of need. We will seek love because of loneliness, fear, insecurity, helplessness, physical desire, or needing to be needed. Relationships should only be sought to enhance our life and to celebrate our life.

Seeking love externally is the physical symbol of seeking love of self internally. Our impression of self-love is based upon conforming to our stereotypical physical perception of love that fulfills our physical needs, status, culture, identities, and roles. Accepting our responsibility for personal choice in relationships will give us a new freedom and power in our entire life and it will enhance our acceptance of the female power in our soul and spirit. Our responsibility for choice will empower us to see ourself with a new vision of love, truth, and perfection.

Perfection was clearly designed by God as our equality of perfect balance. Equality is first of all the perfect balance of our one mind which represents our female, male, and spirit mind. The equality of our one mind is symbolized as the physical equality of the female, male, and the human race. All of humanity upon Earth is the living symbol of our spirit consciousness. This balanced perfection of our internal trinity created the symbol of the trinity of our mind, our society, and our world, which must be kept in perfect balance through equality.

Our physical senses have gradually expanded throughout our Cycle of Development. We developed each sense as it became necessary to our growth. We began as thought consciousness with the purpose of creating a physical body that could serve as a temple for our spirit consciousness. As our spirit consciousness entered into the temple of our body, we became the living symbol of God upon Earth.

As we passed through the matter that was accumulating as Earth, we were seeking ways of growing and becoming a perfect receptacle for our spirit consciousness. We were seeking those elements around us that we could design into a physical body that would serve us as a physical tool as we learned how to become a Higher Universal Mana, or HUMAN. This was the name given to us by the Creator.

As a Higher Universal Mana or spirit consciousness, we have accepted the challenge of becoming HUMAN. We accepted the responsibility to create a physical body and the myriad of physical, soul, and spirit experiences which we needed to grow from a spirit thought to a physical form with a physical mind, to a unity of our soul mind, and to our expanded Spirit Consciousness. *We know internally that we must bring all of our energy into one magnificent energy force to accomplish our purpose upon Earth. We know that our female, male, and spirit minds are one unified mind.*

As we were busily creating our physical body, Earth was being created simultaneously for the purpose of our evolution. We were challenged to create our physical body as a way for the soul and the spirit consciousness to return again and again to physical form.

It was understood by the Creator that each soul and spirit would have the physical time that was necessary to work through the lessons that were essential to the merging of the divine self of soul and spirit with the physical self of the intellect and ego.

Earth has been provided for us as a school from which we can learn. Our physical bodies are once again fractal patterns of Cosmic, Universal, and Earth energy. We cannot be disrespectful of the heavens or the Earth without feeling the effect upon our physical bodies. When we learn to understand us, we will understand the Earth, the Universe, and all that is within the Cosmos.

Cosmic energy is the enfinite energy of *thought*. Negative beliefs, thoughts, and greed energy therefore affect us as intensely as negative physical actions. The only difference is that physical actions can be defined by our measurement of time and space. *Negative thought energy must be understood as a part of our physical reality to appreciate the destruction that it creates as it is transformed into physical action.*

Negative beliefs, thoughts, and greed energy are expressions of intellectual mind and ego fear, which can only be assessed retrospectively by the Universal Law of Cause and Effect.

Negative actions are the effect of our fear beliefs, and our negative actions revert again into thought energy that merges with and expands the existing negative thought. Negative actions that are repetitiously focused upon reach out to affect many in our society, promoting additional thought energy to support the action and to culminate in expanded negative energy.

All intellectual thought energy, including that which is directed towards physical love, becomes part of a collective consciousness and affects all of society and the world through its power. All thought originates from the perception of the individual mind, which is highly dependent upon the daily stimulus of the physical senses.

In the beginning of creation, *thought* understood that the physical body being created must have feelings to bridge the energy between the material body and the divine energy of the soul and spirit. With this understanding the physical senses were defined as the bridge to the physical growth of the body and to the emotional growth of the soul.

Creating our Seven Physical Senses

Knowing its spirit consciousness as the energy of love, truth, and equality, it was evident to *thought* that a method of sensing would have to be in place for the physical matter to feel the love, truth, and equality of the spirit. This sensing energy would keep the physical matter within the harmony and rhythm of the path to spirit consciousness.

Sensing would serve a two-fold purpose. It would guide the physical matter in the fractal pattern of creation; and when the creation was complete as human, it would guide the human on its soul path to the love, truth, and equality of its spirit consciousness.

Each sense was to have a purpose that would allow the energy forces within the body to move and flow in a harmony and rhythm. Each sense was unique and creative, supporting the precise elements of energy within the physical body, and supporting the magnificent energy of the mind. When all senses were in harmony as one, the body and mind would be in balance with nature and the Universe.

Our first sense to be created was our sense of touch.

Our sense of touch allowed us to know that we were not alone. It created for us the understanding of unity. It removed us from the fear of separateness by allowing us to feel the presence of like energy around us as the phenomenon of our human body was in the making. Touch then became our first awareness of self as physical matter. Touch put us in direct contact with the dust of Earth and created an awareness of other *thought* energy as *thought* and touch worked and created together.

Our sense of touch is our first ability to feel. When we are deprived of touch, a sense of separateness begins to overwhelm us and we feel isolated. Touch deprivation of the physical body begins the symbol of separation of the body and mind from the soul and spirit within us.

The loss of unity of the internal self with the external self is manifested within the body and mind by a fear of touch. The separation that begins internally with the soul and spirit is then manifested in our life by a separation from the intimacy of friends and family.

Touch became an essential sense in our nature consciousness, giving us the dual power to physically feel the elements of nature around us and to relate to those elements emotionally.

The second sense that we developed was our sense of taste.

As we moved through the elements of Earth, we were designing from the *thought* energy of spirit. Within the spirit *thought* there was a pattern. This pattern was found within all of the energy of the Universe.

As *thought* with the sense of touch, we began to test those elements that we touched by tasting and absorbing the energy of the element to see if it fit the pattern we were using as a design for our creation. As we tasted and absorbed the proper elements, we changed and we grew. Taste allowed us to feel the perfection of the minerals and nutrients that went into our creation.

Taste became a survival sense, giving us the ability to choose those foods best suited to the support of our physical matter, minerals, and nutrients. Taste is our second nature consciousness and continues to be the selective sense of restoration in the selection of foods and fluids that are essential to our health and growth.

The more we changed as a microscopic element the more selective we chose to become with our absorption. The pattern had developed to a level where the choice needed expansion and change. The minerals and nutrients for the body had been chosen.

As one level was learned and another was needed, the power was within us as *thought* to complete the creation. To choose the necessary gases, smell became an essential sense for us to have. The perfection of the various gases that would be needed to sustain the perfection of our developing human form was understood from the fractal pattern. With the new sense of smell, each gas could be chosen with the exact balance that was necessary.

Smell was then created as our third developing physical sense.

Smelling allowed for an expanded refinement of choice. Assessment could determine the perfection of any one element for the design. It was with the sense of smell that the gaseous elements of Earth that were essential to the fractal pattern became identifiable and were chosen.

It was through these first three levels of our physical senses that the Universal pattern was created as a microcosmic fractal cellular pattern that was to become the generic basis of the human physical form.

This cellular pattern was of intense electromagnetic energy. Within it the power of the Universe, the power of spirit *thought*, the power of physical elements, and the everlasting power of creation, were put together as the beginning of a new and unique creation of physical form.

With the sense of smell the gases were chosen to support the design, and this unique sense was instilled as a method to stimulate the constant need for replacement of the gases. Our sense of smell was given an acute sensitivity to allow it to choose those gases that were supportive to the physical matter and those that were destructive. Smell became another natural survival sense for us.

Within itself, this newly created energy pattern understood that mass was the life and power that it sought. Recognizing the need to identify compatible energy vibrations, the purpose of the next physical sense was created.

The fourth physical sense of hearing was essential for identifying the perfect energy from which our physical mass could be created.

It was with the sense of hearing that the electromagnetic energy field could be molded and changed. With this new sense being used for the detection of energy vibrations, the design of our fractal pattern could be expanded. By touching, tasting, smelling, and hearing, the fleshing out of the microcosmic cell could and did begin.

The sensing of vibrational energy allowed the harmonic tuning of the energy forces to discover the presence of water. Water began to charge the elements of the microcosmic cells as it made contact, and the massing of energy became more focused. Another level or fractal of the Universal energy was being created as the pattern for human form.

It was through the energy vibration of hearing that the first human cells began their energy communication with water. This communication allowed the newly formed cells to discover the

Physical Love

presence of water to use as the mass for physical matter. As the microcosmic cells began to absorb water, new energy was being magnetized into the developing *thought form*.

With the expansion of cellular mass it proved to be expedient to see as a way of choosing the next essential step in the evolution of human form. The need to examine and assess the available forms upon Earth created the fifth physical sense of seeing.

Seeing allowed the freedom of choice to help in finding the perfect physical form to choose as a human form. Once seeing became a sense, a degree of abandonment overcame the energy of *thought form* as expanding matter and it chose to merge with the energy of multiple forms. This created an opportunity for *thought form* to experiment with its own matter and to refine the elements that it had chosen.

Thoughtform freely changed as choice dictated. As it moved in and out of various forms, it had an opportunity to choose that which worked and that which did not work with its continually developing energy field. This exercise of experimentation allowed *thought* to reconsider its role in this new creation of expanded mass.

As *thought* focused its energy within this microcosmic cellular mass it began to realize that thought must be guided by intention and integrity. It must use the energy of the spirit which was within as the energy of love, truth, and perfection to guide it into its state of physical balance. *Thought* understood that the HUMAN responsibility was to create upon Earth from the virtue and grace of the Divine. With total freedom of choice *thought* merged with the spirit consciousness and became *conscious thought*.

The sixth physical sense was created when thought chose to be a thinking spirit consciousness, having both a physical and a divine nature.

After many billions of years of evolution from the star dust that formed Earth, the *thought form* realized its purpose upon Earth. Acceptance of the responsibility to evolve from that moment on as a thinker of divine virtue and grace created a new path of evolution. The path of HUMAN evolution was at that moment assured.

Thought consciousness accepted that it was the highest form of matter upon Earth when it merged with the spirit consciousness. At that moment the life of the thinking human began in its primitive stage of emotional development to seek, through further experimentation, the perfect physical temple to serve the spirit upon Earth.

Millions of years were to pass as the experimentation proceeded from one physical form to another. Each step along the way allowed the refinement of the physical form to expand. Each physical house was assessed and examined, keeping that which worked and discarding that which did not work. With each experimentation in the physical, the physical form was being refined.

When the thinker began to think with an increased clarity, a sense of need again arose within the consciousness. Thinking as a sixth sense needed expression, and upon the recognition of need the seventh physical sense was created.

The seventh sense became the ability to express thoughts by speaking, and communication became our eternal path to growth.

Speaking then became the human tool of communication, giving and receiving through the expression of love, truth, and unity. This seventh sense created a way of expressing the awareness of all other senses. Our seventh sense completed the true cycle of communication for the human being.

The sixth and seventh senses set the human apart from all other species of nature and gave him the inalienable right to equality as the HIGHER UNIVERSAL MANA. This began the path of living multiple physical lives to learn the love, truth, and perfection of being spirit consciousness in physical form.

No other species upon Earth has the ability to think, to speak, and to create in exactly the same way as a human. With our acceptance of mind evolution in the sixth and seventh levels of the Cycle of Development, we agreed by our choice to expand into spirit consciousness, giving us a unique evolutionary path of consistent growth and change.

To accept being the highest form of nature upon Earth, we agreed not to become stagnant but to continue our path of change and growth until we transcended into the love, truth, and perfection of our Creator.

We agreed to become the part of Earth that is willing to grow and expand through our creation of mind energy. Our purpose of growth and expansion upon Earth is to expand the love, truth, and perfection of our Creator. Energy expands like energy. When we expand in our love, truth, and perfection, we expand the love, truth, and perfection of the Creator as our energy becomes one with the Creator.

These seven primary levels of the Cycle of Development of our physical senses have occurred in all human beings. If one or more of our senses are suppressed in our life it is by soul and spirit choice. Our choice will not be understood by the intellectual mind, but it is understood and designed by our soul and spirit mind. It is when we block our physical senses within a life that we create the karmic energy that will require the suppression of a physical sense in another embodiment.

Suppression of one physical sense allows us to focus upon the development and expansion of another physical sense. If we fail to use a physical sense within one lifetime because we are not consciously aware of the importance of that individual sense, we will suppress another sense that will focus our attention upon the unused sense in another lifetime. For example, if we deny touching or being touched, we may choose a lifetime of blindness so that we can develop our sense of touch to re-establish the balance of our physical senses.

Our Creation of Self-Consciousness

During the evolution of our senses we also began to develop our self-consciousness. Each sense brought with it a unique understanding of self and our creation. The sense of touch was accompanied by an emotion of unity. When we fear touch, we create separateness.

Thought no longer felt separate and alone, adrift within the ether and dust of Earth. *Thought* began to find a vision of self through the sense of touch that related it to Earth. It became one with Earth, being and feeling natural within the dust or the ether as it acquired its earthly possessions of minerals, gases, and water. *Thought* no longer felt separate, because it could touch Earth and the ether, feeling naturally a part of all that is.

As the sense of taste was being developed, *thought* celebrated its new ability to assess that part of nature that it chose to take as part of self. Having the ability to touch and to taste extended a greater confidence to *thought* as the unity with nature was being sought. The minerals of nature have distinctive tastes, and *thought* became proficient in choosing those of the exact fractal pattern to function as an energy team to sustain this unique form of life.

A form of eating began to occur as *thought* tasted and assimilated minerals into self in a conscious effort to design a material form. From the energy of *thought* the sense of taste also expanded into new emotions to be experienced, thus changing the level of self-consciousness both physically and emotionally.

As *thought* learned the senses of touch and taste, it became aware that it could not fully develop without the gases of nature. It was one thing to taste the minerals of the dust, but the gases that were prevalent in the ether could not be identified by touch and taste alone.

As the self-consciousness developed for the need to smell, the ability to smell was created. Our self-consciousness was in total attunement with our nature consciousness and so the selection process began. Our natural self-consciousness was seeking a gas to support an expanded level of life for the developing human form.

Using touch, taste, and smell, many gases were chosen to formulate what we now call air. These gases were used in a selected proportion to create a colorless, tasteless, and odorless mixture that would soothe and support the three primary senses. Nitrogen was chosen as the primary gas with oxygen added as a secondary ingredient. Several other gases were added in small amounts, such as argon, carbon dioxide, neon, helium, and other gases in minute quantities.

The nature consciousness of *thought* was developing in unity with its self-consciousness. Movement as the action within the natural law of change and growth was happening by its own design. *Thought* was accumulating possessions of nature to allow its growth into physical form. As material elements changed and grew, it became apparent that there was a need for electrical energy that could provide stimulation, mass, and energy that could all work together as one.

The nature consciousness understood the vibrational waves

within the Universe. These waves could be identified by the sense of hearing. *Need in and of itself had the innate power to create change.* The fourth sense of hearing was then self-consciously acknowledged as a need.

This fractal pattern of self-consciousness in our physical development is repeated in the creation of the developing human embryo today. The first four senses that efficiently and effectively created our first physical form continue to be used by the unconscious self to choose the sperm for fertilization. We use the spirit sense of hearing to guide the chosen sperm into the electromagnetic force field of the ovum. This selective process allows the sperm to charge the electromagnetic force field of the ovum, creating cross-fertilization. Cross-fertilization is the action of the fourth fractal pattern in all stages of evolution. It is this pattern that allowed asexual creation to be a purpose of human destiny in the beginning of life. The first four physical senses which we developed are used in all forms of the physical to fulfill procreation of the body, mind, and spirit.

Different levels of our first four physical senses are active during the period of gestation before birth that symbolizes the period of 280 billion years of evolution for these individual physical senses. Once birth has occurred, our four physical senses are intuitively understood, and the progression continues as the following three senses are remembered and developed.

The fourth level of growth is the stasis level and requires the most intense amount of time for development. Development of the last three physical senses will occur in unity with the further development of the fourth physical sense. This period of physical time will include another period of 280 days, symbolizing another period of 280 billion years of microcosmic cellular development.

Observing an infant in utero, at birth, and for the first nine months after birth can verify the development of the seven physical senses within us as HUMAN beings. This seemingly extensive period of time to the human mind did not seem long or unusual to the spirit consciousness. There is no time in the spirit world and time could not be an issue as the *thought form* of Spirit worked toward perfection from a clearly understood Universal pattern.

In humans the first five physical senses initiate the supreme sexual consciousness, but if the senses of speaking and thinking are not used, the sexual act is reduced to the level of animal procreation. Using the entire sphere of our physical senses allows our sexual consciousness to aid us in our path of evolution. Using our first five senses of touching, tasting, smelling, hearing, and seeing triggers the supreme sexual response and can climax in a sexual encounter. Our sexual consciousness had a dramatic impact on our self-consciousness and set in place our first energy of physical competition.

Sexual encounters that are triggered by one or more but fewer than five of our physical senses do not climax as a supreme sexual response. This incomplete trigger climaxes in a physical sex act, but it will frequently require the use of a bizarre stimulant of the physical senses to elicit a true sexual response. Despite the added stimulus, the supreme sexual response will not be forthcoming and frustration will be the predominant emotion. This obstructive energy of sexual frustration contains the explosive energy that is misdirected into bizarre sexual behavior, such as murder, cannibalism, rape, and other aberrations.

This elaborate mental representation of sexual satisfaction represents a desperate soul seeking internal unity in an external image. A contrived belief of the mind is triggered because of a total disdain for its own inability to love and be loved. Such behavior demonstrates a total lack of respect and value for self, which is symbolized as a total lack of respect and value for the life of others. This is a lost and desperate self-consciousness living with strong primitive soul attachments.

Knowing that our physical senses are gifted to us because of our intention of learning to be HUMAN, we see ourself with pure disdain when we believe we are inadequate. We become confused by our own sense of inadequacy when we are unable to use our physical senses in a productive manner. Our confusion and frustration allow us to resort to the primitive memory that exists within our soul consciousness.

Learning to fully use our first five physical senses in our intimate relationships will create a new level of pleasure, physical satisfaction, and caring. Learning to use all of our seven physical senses will create lasting relationships of sharing, commitment, joy, happiness, unity, freedom, communication, and inspiration.

Stimulation of our first five physical senses requires that we not only like what we see, but that we are triggered by the tone of the voice, the smell, and the touch. Smelling the natural essence of the body is more of a trigger of the smelling sense than smelling artificial substances. What we see, hear, smell, and touch is absorbed as a sense of taste. We assimilate the energy into one supreme sexual sense.

Kissing was begun as a way of fulfilling three senses in one acceptable and harmless way. Kissing the hand allows the touch, the smell, and the taste senses to be immediately triggered in a polite manner. Kissing the hand will always elicit a response, which allows the hearing and the seeing to be fulfilled and completes the spectrum of the supreme sexual sense.

The finesse of hand kissing is considered obsolete in our society, but it is a powerful tool to stimulate the sexual response. Touching is the primary trigger of our physical senses and it has the power to stimulate other senses, such as seeing and hearing.

Touching the hand is symbolic of connecting with the soul and spirit as well as the physical, and the custom of handshaking began as a result of the need to create unity. The design of the extremities of the body symbolizes the three facets of our mind. The smallest part is the hand or foot, which represents the intellect; the lower arm and lower leg represent the soul mind, or right brain; and the upper arm and upper leg represent the Universal mind, or cerebellum.

Our extremities move and flow as an unbroken harmony of inner energy. There is an energy connection between our mind and our extremities that allows them to move smoothly without our conscious direction. Each of these connections are there as a repetition of the pattern of the three parts of the mind.

Our unconscious movement and function within any part of our body symbolizes the energy that flows unconsciously between the three parts of our one mind. The reproductive system of both male and female has three distinct parts. The heart, lungs, and liver sustain physical life as three essential organs to clean, clear, and restore our body. They work with a harmonic energy that helps them to restore themselves and the rest of the body. *This body, mind, spirit pattern is repeated throughout the entire system of the human form. It is not accepted by science because the power of the mind is not understood as the creator of all mental and physical disease.*

It is our mind that triggers the supreme sexual response through the trigger points of the physical senses, but it is our body that responds. This creates for us the perfect example of the power of the mind to manifest a reaction within our body. In many relationships today the sexual response is minimal or no longer being triggered consciously through the physical senses. The intellect assesses the situation and the body responds. This becomes a conscious action for many humans. Yet the mind influence upon disease is not understood.

When the sexual response is deficient in any way, the senses are not being used to trigger the response. It can be frustrating to be told that the sexual response is 99 percent in our head and 1 percent in the sex organs. Still, this is correct, because the physical senses are located within the head and must be stimulated by the mind within the head.

When relationships are formed from our soul and spirit energy as well as physical energy, the higher level of our physical senses will also be engaged in our sexual response. The mind will be focused upon the act of loving the partner, all of our physical senses will be in maximum use, and communication will be the free flowing of thoughts between the partners. This allows the words of love, commitment, respect, and honor towards each other to be shared as a unity with the physical senses, the mind, and the physical body.

There is no greater stimulus to the sexual response than touching, thinking love, and speaking love. If a relationship is based upon fear and judgement, the sexual response will not be triggered. The sexual act may occur but there is no love or loving exchange.

When abuse occurs in any way through physical violence, emotional abuse, verbal, sexual, or psychological abuse, the sexual response is frequently damaged beyond repair in the relationship.

Fear behavior patterns the mind to respond to the abuse in a sexual way that is patterned from the physical actions of sex. The mind is not engaged in love but rather in fear. The mind rejects the perception of love when the actions are creating the opposite of love, which is fear. The emotions are opposite to each other and the

PHYSICAL LOVE

mind cannot focus upon both. We frequently engage in sex as a fear reaction to our survival needs, and it may appear satisfying because of the adrenalin response which accompanies the emotion of fear.

A sexual response cannot be triggered by the physical senses or the mind for love one moment and for survival in the next moment. The mind and the physical senses are receiving mixed messages and will withdraw in a state of confusion.

When either the male or the female is abusive with a partner and then is mystified because love is being withheld, the actions of daily life experience must be explored. Our mind is patterned by our beliefs that are then lived through our daily behavior.

Beliefs are designed through our perception of thoughts, words that we hear, and actions that we see, hear, and experience. If all of our beliefs are based upon fear, anger, violence, hate, judgement, guilt, sin, and other negative concepts, we will live our life from that energy of belief. Our actions, our words, and our thoughts will be consistent with our beliefs if we are living our truth.

Fearful and abusive energy is not conducive to love in any relationship whether it is an intimate relationship or a relationship with a family member, friend, or colleague.

Many relationships could be revitalized by using the physical senses in a loving and honoring way. If there is no love within self for self, love cannot be pretended for another. Fear changes the sexual response to the sexual act, and at that time sex becomes an act of using or abusing the physical body not a sharing of love.

The love or fear that we live as individuals becomes the love or fear that is reflected by us into society and into the world. In our path of evolution it has been helpful to live experiences that allow us to see what we don't want as a way of life to help us better define what we do want as a way of life. Once our fear of life is changed to a love of life, that change will be reflected in society and within the world.

Fear has been learned from superstitions and myths. Truth has been distorted by fear beliefs. Love has been perceived as the sexual act. Evolution through living the behavior of these opposite beliefs allows us to see truth within life as living the love within us. *Truth is the action of loving self. Our perfection is living in the love, truth, and equality of self through our daily actions.*

Changing our perception of self and our life changes our level of self-consciousness. The more expansive our understanding of self becomes the less we relate to our ego self-consciousness and the more we relate to our spirit consciousness.

Understanding that life is our perception of reality gives us the freedom to change our perception and therefore change our reality. Changing our perception of self changes our perception of life. Changing our perception of self and life changes how we relate in all of our life experiences with other people. This changes the manner in which we express love in our physical reality.

An increase in our level of knowledge will guide us into an understanding of self that will allow us to overcome millions of years of fear. Fear is the energy of the dark side of our soul that is our physical nature. Understanding why we are here and how we can go beyond this level of growth is what our mind now seeks. Keeping the mind open and allowing new information to enter is our path of change and growth.

As we change and grow we will begin to understand the magnificent pattern of ourself in our human form. With our expanded understanding, we will have no fear of tomorrow and the changes that are there for us to experience in the light side of our soul evolution.

Love, truth, and perfection are the energies of the light side of our soul that is our divine nature. Our perfection is forever seen in the equality of our thoughts, words, and actions as they relate to ourself and to all of humanity. When these truths can be honored in physical love, love will be a time of celebration.

3

Living in the Physical

> "Let us think of life as a process of choices, one after another. At each point there is a progression choice and a regression choice. There may be a movement toward defense, toward safety, toward being afraid; but over on the other side, there is the growth choice. To make the growth choice instead of the fear choice a dozen times a day is to move a dozen times a day toward self-actualization."
>
> **A.H. Maslow, The Farther Reaches of Human Nature**

We are all that is. We are female. We are male. We are God. As humans we choose our gender in each lifetime dependent upon the lessons that we have designed into this soul experience.

If we have chosen the male gender, our focus will be primarily upon the external, physical world and all of its beliefs and behaviors. The male chooses the male focus to challenge himself in seeking balance within his female energy, the energy of his internal soul and spirit.

Despite the physical focus of the male, he has a very real and advanced female nature within him. Learning to accept his female energy is the goal of his gender focus. Our female nature is our soul experience, and it is eternally bound to our spirit as the unity of our divine nature. Soul and spirit cannot be separated, as our evolving soul is the path to our expanding spirit.

Our chosen physical gender defines our major lessons of this lifetime. It does not always define our sexual orientation or our gender consciousness. Our chosen gender does not remove the soul and spirit, but the lessons we choose can camouflage and conceal them from the awareness of our intellect and ego.

Concealing our soul and spirit does not change our eternal nature, but it allows our new personality of this physical life to work through our lessons without a conscious awareness that the soul and spirit are inherently very much a part of our mind energy. We begin the process of covering up our soul and spirit energy at the age of seven. Beliefs and behaviors can be copied but not firmly patterned within our mind until the second Law of Sevens. Some will choose to remain open to soul and spirit influences from the beginning of their life. Both males and females can choose to come into a physical life with a total unawareness of their soul and spirit mind and direct their life intensely into their intellect and ego mind.

Our attachment to unawareness will be designed into our life plan as a challenge to be overcome. Strong attachments to the physical beliefs and behaviors of life will be developed very early when the lifetime is planned to focus only upon the physical illusion of self and life.

Resisting our soul nature as part of our divine spirit nature limits our aware consciousness to our physical beliefs which then control our behavior. As a higher state of growth is reached, concealment will no longer occur. The purpose of growth is to live our physical life with a total awareness of our divine nature.

When the divine nature is resisted within the male, all behavior will be defined by the male roles, identities, and beliefs that have been learned within this specific lifetime as well as multiple lifetimes of karmic male intensity. There will be a resistance to allowing the physical personality and character to reflect any behavior or belief that could be judged as female. This would destroy the physical image that the male is attempting to create with his linear focus upon the external self.

Learned behavior of this lifetime that has no female awareness has not had the opportunity to be tested within the soul memory and assessed by the standards of the soul and divine nature. This can allow for strong ties to the lower levels of soul evolution, which can result in primitive behavior and beliefs.

Divine nature is the nature of love, compassion, truth, responsibility, equality, freedom, and humility. Physical behavior that refuses the influence of soul and spirit is fearful, judgemental, angry, dependent, self-gratifying, controlling, and greedy.

Our belief in separateness is the reflected image of the ego striving to survive and remain separate from our internal soul and spirit. The separatist personality will judge self, life, and all events within the physical world by the illusion of power within the external world. The physical image of relationships, money, possessions, education, roles, and beliefs will totally control the personality and character of the behavior. These personality and character traits that are seen as an integrated part of daily behavior reflect our level of soul growth.

We develop our dogma, directives, and doctrines from fleeting forms of fact. Using our relative facts as our physical beliefs, we expand them to design our obstructive limitations to living. Our illusion of fact as reality is in a constant state of change just as we are in a constant state of change. Change is growth. Being stuck in a reflection of beliefs that began thousands of years ago with superstition and myth shows how effectively the intellect can conceal and camouflage our divine nature.

Discrimination is a form of inequality and it is not a female, soul and spirit behavior. All inequality is a male, physical belief and a resulting behavior that has been practiced since the beginning of our recorded history. Our society has been guided and formed by the male gender for many thousands of years. The male, physical belief has created every facet of our life to reflect, examine, and be perceived from the limited boundaries of the intellect and ego.

The superstitions and myths of the mind create boundaries of behaviors and beliefs that are accepted as indisputable fact. Why would the female, who is the living symbol of the soul and spirit energy, be considered unclean and be shunned from many events, experiences, and roles for many thousands of years if we are living from our love, truth, and perfection?

When one identity role sees itself as more advanced than all other genders and races the behavior is established for inequality, discrimination, graft, greed, war, economic exploitation, and control. This behavior then establishes the breakdown within the structure that assures society of a social and economic collapse. This pattern has been repeated throughout our history, at all levels of growth, because our primary beliefs have not changed.

The choice of life within the male gender has been made to learn the lesson of balancing the physical nature with the soul and spirit female nature. Concealing our female nature is resisting the lessons of this lifetime. As lessons are resisted on an individual level, the society and the world will continue to live the effects of the lesson. It has been the intellectual and ego mind that has controlled society and the world for thousands of years. If we choose the female gender, our focus will be upon the soul and spirit with its emotion and love.

The female chooses the soul and spirit focus to challenge herself in seeking balance within the physical. We consistently provide the opposites for ourself within each lesson so that we can see what we don't want as well as what we do want.

At this time within our society, the male, with his established physical belief system and behavior, is feeling extremely threatened by the female as she balances her personality and character within the physical arena of intellectual knowledge.

Yet the rigid identity and role beliefs of the male are strongly attached to his physical image and are not easily changed. The physically oriented intellect and ego does not relish a division of power. To grow and change the male must acknowledge his female energy as part of himself.

Some females will camouflage their soul and spirit energies to appear masculine within the work place. This challenges them with a lesson of value and respect for who they are, and they will constantly be looking at their personal integrity, love, and truth of self. Being in the truth and love of our female energy is essential for all human beings.

We experience in everyday life those lessons that we are learning within the unity of our own individual mind. In seeking to merge the divine nature of our spirit with the physical nature of being human, inequality will be the focus of the genders, relationships, society, and the world as long as our physical perception of separateness rules our minds. Inequality within our physical reality becomes a physical manifestation or symbol of the inner struggle of humanity to accept the equality of our internal divine nature.

We have been living the lesson of inequality for many thousands of years as we have experienced different images of this important lesson. The most dramatic lesson of inequality is the one that exists between the accepted value of the male as it relates to the unaccepted value of the female. The ego of the male has cast females, children, other races, and multiple beliefs as inferior to self. This behavior is symbolic of the resistance of the physical nature to the divine nature within.

When the female power of the soul and spirit is accepted within all of humanity, dramatic changes will occur within society and the world as the female influence becomes balanced with the now-dominant physical, male influence. Decisions within the family, society, and the world will be tempered with the love, compassion, mercy, humility, trust, and faith of the divine nature as it balances with our intellect.

In living a life focused upon separation, we create the opportunity to attach ourself to roles, beliefs, identities, and behaviors that will allow us to disguise that part of self which we seek to balance. As evolution occurs, lives will be experienced to reflect self to the image of self, to all gender images of self, and to the complementary twin soul image of self. These are the multiple lives that we will all live through heterosexuality, homosexuality, bisexuality, and androgynous heterosexuality in the merging of our physical nature and our divine nature.

Each level of soul evolution is a level of personal growth. Our level of soul evolution symbolizes the level from which we are perceiving our physical experience. Each level of personal growth gives us the opportunity to expand our perception and grow to the next level of awareness.

When anger and resentment is our behavior towards other people who are experiencing roles that we are not experiencing within this lifetime, we are attempting to learn the lesson of equality through our relationship with them. Resentment of genders and roles other than our own are symbols of our intellectual ego fears created by the identical but misunderstood nature felt within us. During our path of soul evolution we will choose to live all gender roles, all race roles, and all experiences. Therefore, when we judge another, we are in fact judging ourself.

Our goal and purpose as an evolving soul is to love our unified self which includes our male, female, and spirit self. It is in our willingness to grow that we acknowledge our physical balance, remove our fear, and unleash our female power of truth and love as a guiding force within our life. The balance of our female, male, and spirit self will allow us to evolve into a balanced gender focus, which will fulfill the lessons of homosexuality and bisexuality. Both genders have the ability to become focused upon the physical beliefs and behaviors that attach them to the physical.

The strongest physical attachment known within humanity is the attachment to sexual gratification. When the male or female becomes obsessive in the pursuit of sexual gratification, he or she is denying the soul and spirit balance that is being sought. Sexual attraction becomes an image of the lessons of equality and balance in both genders and is another step in the path of growth.

The female nature that seeks only a female as a mate is attaching herself to her mirror image through energy strings still attached to the soul growth levels of self-examination and reflection. Many females with a mirror image of sexual orientation will be attracted to females with a male gender consciousness.

The male nature that seeks only males for sexual gratification is attaching himself to his mirror image through energy strings still attached to his soul levels of self-examination, reflection, and the primitive. Many males with a mirror image of sexual orientation will be attracted to males with a female gender consciousness.

Heterosexual attraction that is aroused by physical images, identities, roles, and beliefs of need for sexual gratification is attracting only from the physical, ego needs of the physical nature, which may also include the needs and attractions of past lives.

In bisexual relationships there is a combination of images from all levels of evolution that are being acted out within the physical relationships. Multiple levels of sexual attraction, sexual orientation, and gender consciousness exist within life, with none being permanent in our soul evolution, until our androgynous balance has been reached. The major lesson for the bisexual individual is the one of loving self and commitment.

In all instances our intellect continues to seek sexual gratification while denying the true energy of our divine nature. All levels of sexual response are present in the multiple images of reflection in soul growth. As our level of knowledge expands flush with the veil, the strings that remain attached to the levels of examination, reflection, and primitive energy in our sexual response become more evident within us as individuals and reflect more intensely into society and the world.

The effect of this expansion into society will be obvious as more individuals become aware of their sexual orientation, which may be different from their gender consciousness and their physical consciousness. Changing the beliefs and the acceptance of our female energy within self, within society, and within the world, requires that old beliefs be released and the lessons of freedom and choice be honored and respected.

All sexual orientations that expand beyond the stereotype of the missionary perspective of procreation are a threat to the acknowledged stereotypical male role and identity that is based upon religious foundations. Our sexual orientation is designed and initiated from the female energy of our soul and spirit. The male that is focused upon his physical nature will feel threatened, experience fear, and become abusive when he is exposed to sexual responses that trigger his female energy in an emotional and loving manner that he feels is beyond his control.

When someone is in sympathy with sexual orientations other than his own, he or she has already learned the lesson of female and male balance. The fear, hate, and anger that is predominant between individuals of diverse sexual orientation is a symbol of the tug-of-war that is raging within them between their own physical intellect and ego and their divine soul and spirit. Any judgement or fear that stays within our heart towards another human being is evidence that we have not yet passed through the veil of our physical nature.

As the level of knowledge is being lived, the individual will be transcending from the cycle of fear into the cycle of love. This transcending energy will allow each individual to accept and acknowledge who he is to society, and as he continues his growth he will gain true respect and value for self. Becoming aware of the female energy within us requires multiple images of lessons that will be experienced through our changing sexual response.

Each and every soul and spirit will choose to experience growth lessons through the path of sexual experimentation because our supreme sexual sense is the power energy of our physical nature that triggers our loving divine nature. As the veil is rent, our sexual response emanates from a balance of the female, male, and spirit energy within us and the differences of sexual preference begin to dissolve. We will then be entering the female energy of the soul, and as this energy becomes predominant we will seek with greater frequency to balance our energy with the energy of our twin soul.

When our soul is striving to release our separatist attachment to the physical to fully accept our divine nature, our growth will be symbolized through our sexual behavior. All levels of sexual manifestation for soul growth exist in and below the level of knowledge and are firmly attached to the intellectual and ego perspectives of self. Rending the veil of our intellect removes all strings that are attached to the levels of soul evolution that are within the shadow or dark side of our soul.

Once the level of knowledge is transcended, sexual fulfillment is not based upon physical attraction as it is in the primitive, examination, or reflection levels of our soul growth. Our female power reaches new heights of creativity and inspiration after we rend the veil of our ego.

An awareness of these early levels of soul evolution will avoid the perception that spirituality is found in the level of reflection. The level of reflection is the level of our soul path where religion first began, when the male perception of self was seen as the image of God. This male reflection of self as God can also be seen in some physicians, scientists, and other intellectuals.

Our divine nature is the female energy of soul and spirit. We expand our divine nature by merging and balancing the male intellect, ego, and physical body with the female soul of wisdom and ingenuity and the spirit power of love, truth, and perfection. Becoming consciously aware of both our female and male power creates our true balance of power. Each power is inherent within us, but the power of our female soul and spirit is not consciously recognized until the veil is removed from our merging intellect.

When we are equally balanced within our minds with our intellect, soul mind, and spirit consciousness, our physical behavior will reflect equality and balance within all facets of our individual life, our society, and our world.

Focusing upon the image of our female nature as the supreme power, or our physical nature as the supreme power, becomes an ego exercise in intellectual spiritualism. Our soul and spirit never seeks supremacy; it will always seek balance and equality. Equally balancing our inner and higher nature with our physical nature creates androgyny of mind in thoughts, words, and actions.

The mirror image of the physical reflects the separatist vision of the intellectual mind, not the integrated focus of the mind. Sexual reflection expands the physical nature that is reflected. It does not reflect or expand the soul and spirit nature that is beyond the physical level of reflection in soul evolution, although this is the illusion that is perceived. Our soul and spirit is asexual in nature. Only our physical nature is sexual.

Heterosexuality that is attached to judgement and fear is connected through karmic energy to the most primitive level of soul evolution, which can capture the soul at a lower level of soul growth than homosexuality. This attachment supports a variety of primitive behaviors, such as child abuse, cult practices, sexual aberrations, rape, mutilation, infanticide, eugenics, and zoophilia.

Sexual mates are chosen by a physical system of beliefs that determine sexual response. This can range from the arranged marriage to the instant physical attraction. In this level heterosexuality is responding from a belief and behavioral system known as physical need, either societal or biological.

This primitive level of physical perception will act out judgement against all levels of the sexual response that do not conform to its beliefs. In the primitive belief of the intellect and ego, fear separates behavior that is different from its one specific belief to another expanded category of beliefs that is seen as unacceptable and wrong. *When primitive beliefs are structured from superstition or religion, judgement will be delivered as sinful or guilty and acted out in behavior of anger, violence, and rage, which promotes rebellion in those with changing sexual feelings.*

The only true power within us is the balance of power which is found by merging and equally living from our trilocular nature. We are physical body and mind, we are soul mind, and we are divine spirit. Our physical nature is seen through our personality and behavior characteristics. What we think, speak, and do then becomes our physical nature.

If we are being guided in our thoughts, words, and actions by the female power of our soul and spirit, we will live through an understanding of our inner and higher power. Our actions will at all times reflect our love, truth, compassion, responsibility, freedom, equality, and humility. In honoring our personal female power in love, truth, and equality, we are free to honor and respect others on an equal basis.

If we deny the female power of our soul and spirit within, we find ourself living from our perception of physical competition and victimization. This creates the perception that "If you are not with me, you are against me." We will feel that we are competing for each and every moment of our life, and if we fail to win we become a victim. Self-proclaimed victims will seek equality through societal rebellion. Getting society's attention removes the feeling of victimization and replaces it with an egotistical, self-proclaimed hero image. Each thought, each word, and each action in every facet of our life will be viewed competitively as we weigh the worth of the other person by our individual standard of judgement.

We develop our standard of judgement through our own

beliefs and behaviors relative to our life. Our standards will be limited by our growth and our sense of equality. Our judgement becomes a reflection of our fears, anger, rage, devastation, self-pity, and beliefs. Judgement and fear are only found in the first four levels of soul evolution. There is no judgement or fear in our soul and spirit nature.

We create a losing condition in our intimate relationships. Our fear, anger, dishonesty, judgement, control, separateness, and distrust become glaring emotions within us that control us through our behavior and reflect our control to the other person. Our negative emotions capture and control our intellect, behavior, beliefs, words, thoughts, and actions. We in turn reflect this negative energy into our relationships through our beliefs and behaviors. In convoluting our energy we set ourself up for failure.

We have the freedom of choice to reflect negative behavior or positive soul and spirit behavior into our relationships. We will choose our intimate relationships, our work relationships, and our friends from this mirror image of ourself. Each person in our life will then be judged by our mirrored self-image of unworthiness. Unworthiness creates the reflected mirror image of self in every type of relationship.

When we are reflecting loving and truthful emotions, we are using our female energy. When we are reflecting fear and judgement emotions, we are using our male energy. We will attract to us the energy that we reflect in our emotions. When we are dealing with evolution of sexual image, we will seek our mirror image. When we are learning about our intellect, we will seek the mirror image of intellect. There are multiple levels of images in each and every lesson that we choose.

The purpose of life is growth. The soul and spirit seeks constant change within the mind. We create constant change within our life as a symbol of the inner and higher change that we seek. Stasis within any lesson of the soul will create crisis within our life.

To awaken to and to live within our soul and spirit power we must continually seek an understanding of self. Knowledge as the fourth level of our soul evolution is also the level of stasis of physical growth. It is the level of intellectual spiritualism. In the beginning knowledge is not the stage of integration but rather the stage of separateness. In the first half of the knowledge level of soul evolution, the ego is fighting fiercely for control. This is our male, physical nature at its finest. It feels invincible, determined, and beyond intellectual challenge. Our ego will create chaos in our mind at this level of growth.

Our peak experience in the level of knowledge is the awakening to our soul and spirit. The feelings of this awakening are ones of ecstasy, peace, and joy. The physical orgasm is the symbol of this peak experience but it remains inadequate to describe the emotion.

Our beginning level of knowledge in soul growth allows us to focus upon the perception of physical processes as our means of growth. As we become attached to physical processes they act as physical chains to bind us to our individual perception of knowledge. The physical process of our daily life becomes the focus of our intellect, rather than our soul growth.

The ego's belief in its omnipotence keeps us attached to our accepted level of knowledge. Our perception of personal infallibility closes our mind to any other concept and we become obsessive, compulsive, and fanatical in our attachment to our learned beliefs and behaviors. Our processes take control of our life.

Physical knowledge can only be relative to our accepted physical concepts, which are identified by us as real or factual. In our omniscience we base our perception of knowledge upon an impermanent material world which is conditioned by constantly changing circumstances. Our vision perceives only from our external level of awareness and we can never see absolute reality. We have created our veil as the illusion of our reality.

In the level of knowledge in soul evolution we are dealing with the only divided cycle of our soul path. Knowledge is divided evenly by our ego veil of beliefs which separates this level into two separate cycles. On the shadow side of the soul, we are working through our Cycle of Awareness. On the light side of our soul, we are in the Cycle of Understanding. Both cycles reflect toward the entire side of the soul path. With the Cycle of Awareness, we walk through the shadows of life. With the Cycle of Understanding, we walk into the light of life and became the masters of our own destiny.

As we travel into the Cycle of Understanding, we complete the final half of knowledge, before entering into the levels of understanding, wisdom, and truth as the final three levels of our soul path.

As we move forward through the level of knowledge that is split in half by the veil, we begin an experience that is unique to this level of soul evolution but common to our everyday experience. In knowledge, we begin a magnified cycle of change that moves us through our seven levels of fear as we approach the veil and our seven levels of love as we enter into the Cycle of Understanding.

All perception of our physical life and ourself begins to revolve around our singular search for knowledge as scientific fact, until we rend the veil. In our fear we desperately seek answers external to ourself, ignoring the potential of our internal power, and the obvious changing of physical circumstances. *The physical facts and knowledge of our ancestors are in a constant state of change, because we are our ancestors and we are in a constant state of change.* It is only our intellectual, finite mind that is linear.

We have become complacent and satisfied with our self-imposed boundaries surrounding our mind, and we are unable to see the insufficiencies of knowledge. We are captured and convicted by our self-inflicted separateness and finite limitations.

We fail to see that we are connected to our soul and spirit, our physical self, and to each other, that we are our past and we are our future. Each life is a new opportunity for us to change and grow from the beginning of time. We are living our eternal life and our power is centered upon the now of this moment in physical time. We make our own laws. We create our society and our world as a reflection of our minds.

If our minds are focused upon fear, greed, abuse, sex, war, or judgement, it will be reflected in our society. As we grow from a democracy of impulses that establish judgement and law upon the testimony of unrefined sense perceptions, we will be evolving from the physical levels of knowledge into the inspirational levels of knowledge. That is where our mind is now seeking to focus.

Our soul growth is now shifting to our female level of mind growth. We have been learning the lesson of our physical growth. Physical growth has been designed by us to happen over a space of time relative to our soul pattern. Honoring the body with pure air, water, food, and peace will allow the body to grow naturally. Evolution has allowed us to grow, within our soul mind, one step at a time. Each lesson of each level must be learned with clarity. All streams of energy that attach our mind to the reflection of the images of our past must be released before we can move forward and rend the veil that will release us from our shadow.

Our level of understanding is the fifth level of soul evolution and it is specific to the completion of understanding our female power. Our Cycle of Understanding gives us an opportunity to see the magnificence and beauty of our personality and character during the last half of our level of knowledge. Rending the veil gives us the opportunity to expand our knowledge far beyond our present stage.

Nearly all of the fears that reside within the human disposition arise from misdirecting our emotional soul and loving spirit energy. Our soul and spirit energy is acted out within the physical dimension as motivation, inspiration, enthusiasm, love, peace, joy, and happiness. We misunderstand these powerful energies as physical energies and we misdirect them into our physical appetites that create dependencies and negative emotions. Our instincts, intuition, inspiration, and enthusiasm should be directed toward creative expression and artistic endeavor. With our soul and spirit energy we can create beautiful, magnificent masterpieces in any field of interest. *Life is the art of the soul and spirit.*

We agonize over our physical loves, seeing ourself unworthy of another's love. But when we do not love ourself we resist the reflection of love from anyone else. The image that we see is the reflection we send. We send our personal sense of unworthiness or love back to ourself.

We separate ourself from our female love and truth, which is the energy of our soul and spirit. We separate ourself from our female power, which is inherent in our love and truth. In our separation from our female energy, we direct our attention to the external world of money, greed, possessions, fear, and judgement, which is at all times opposite to the love that we seek. With this external focus we lose the art of living.

Separation is more intense in the male than in the female because of the male physical resistance to the female personality and characteristics found within himself. The macho image of the male that is ego-directed and prevalent within our society precludes the male being gentle and caring. Accepting that each of us is male, female, and spirit will give us our equality of actions and feelings.

Once we understand and accept that our female power of soul and spirit is an integrated part of us and that we create the separation within our intellect and ego mind, we can begin to successfully learn ways to change our perception of life.

When we seek to learn a lesson within the limitations of our intellect, we are seeking an intellectual awakening. Awakening occurs on multiple levels with multiple images. Our pattern for intellectual growth is the same fractal of the Universal cosmic pattern as the pattern for soul growth.

The seven levels of our soul evolution are the primitive, examination, reflection, knowledge, understanding, wisdom, and truth. Soul awakening is imminent as the cycle of fear is complete and we transition into the cycle of love. This transition occurs at the peak or midpoint of the soul level of knowledge. In our cycle of change in the level of knowledge, we will pass through the seven levels of fear and the seven levels of love.

We can live many thousands of lives as we pass through this path of growth. If we are seeking the truth of the intellect, we are seeking relative truth. If we are seeking the truth of the soul and spirit, we are seeking absolute truth.

The soul mind never judges the physical time that is required for us to awaken to our soul and spirit energy. And it does not behoove us to judge ourself. Until we transcend the complacency of intellectual knowledge, our mind is not open to accepting our true awakening to a new understanding of life.

As each of us intellectually reaches a crisis in knowledge, there is an opportunity to awaken to the inspiration and motivation of our female power. If the intellectual opportunity for awakening is passed by, the crisis will occur within our physical body, our life, or within our physical relationships, to get our attention.

Disease has always played a role in our society to allow us to experience physical crisis in the three dimensions of life: the individual or microcosm, the society or mesocosm, and the world or macrocosm. These symbolize the three dimensions of self—the physical body, the soul mind, and the divine spirit. The Universal cosmic pattern of life is repeated within all of reality and will be reflected throughout our physical body and our physical life.

We manifest symbols from the spirit and soul consciousness to awaken the physical self to growth. Our physical body and intellect is a tool of the soul and spirit. It was designed by the divine nature within us to manifest growth. We may get stuck temporarily within our physical perception, but we can trust the soul and spirit to awaken us with a sudden crisis to get our attention.

Each of us will in time awaken to our one mind despite our denial, resistance, and rejection.

Understanding our soul and spirit nature gives us the opportunity to use our power as a healing energy in all facets of ourselves and life. Perceiving ourself with love, truth, compassion, freedom, equality, responsibility, and humility gives us the wisdom to think, speak, and act with a new power within our daily life. From the beginning of our cycle of change, we have an unseen power that gives us courage and strength if it is our intention and will to change.

As we begin to perceive our newfound power, we will begin to examine it from every intellectual and ego belief that is within us. This begins the ego and spirit tug-of-war that allows many to fall back into old fear beliefs and superstitions. This becomes a test of our new perceptions and their stability and strength. During this period of change, our entire life may feel like it is falling apart. We will find ourself in change whether or not we invite change.

It is essential to our growth for us to continue to seek information to reinforce our new perceptions during our ego and spirit tug-of-war. Without support our ego can win and we will slide backwards into our old emotions of fear and judgement. As we travel our path of self-examination, we will find our new perceptions being reflected back to us in many of our daily experiences. We will attract others to help us learn how our female soul and spirit nature support us in our growth. Suddenly we begin to see reflections of our new dimensions of self. We begin to feel good about ourself and we are strengthened to continue.

As we continue with the new perceptions that we have gathered about ourself, we recognize our new perceptions as knowledge. We have reached a new level of self-acceptance and respect when we are willing to allow others to see our true feelings in an open and free exchange. Our expanded understanding begins to give us confidence that we can totally evolve into the new growth that we are seeking.

Our enthusiasm for our change and growth is a dangerous challenge to the ego and intellect. Suddenly we are overwhelmed with doubt, fear, and devastation. These fear emotions are designed by the ego to capture our attention. Our doubt, fear, and devastation set in as intensely as a physical disease and will struggle to force us back into the reality of fear. The ego has begun to feel its loss of control and losing control is not acceptable to this self-styled omnipotent force.

This is the moment to begin our soul mind talk. *"Soul talking"* is the female energy reinforcing the love, beauty, and magnificence of self. The purpose of soul mind talk is to repattern the negative ego beliefs that are creating our emotions of doubt, fear, and devastation. We are what we think, speak, and do. Accepting our responsibility to control what we think and speak will naturally affect what we do.

Each time a negative thought enters your mind, change it to a positive thought by speaking the words, "I am love." As the positive thoughts flow in, continue to repeat them to yourself over and over again. Any thoughts, words, and actions that have a positive emphasis can be used in place of a negative thought, word, or action. With your mind, flip your thoughts from the negative perspective to the positive perspective.

As you speak, read, and think, become consciously aware of your inner and outer dialogue. Continually talk to your mind using positive approaches to your life experiences. Repeat in front of a mirror "I am love" multiple times throughout your day. Make certain that you *"soul talk"* in this dialogue of love as you go to sleep each night. This allows you to speak directly to your soul and spirit during your sleep by consciously engaging your intellect.

Knowledge is a level of information within our mind that began with perception spurred on by curiosity. Repeated use of knowledge within our mind creates a pattern. Our perception changes with each new level of knowledge that we discover. Not all levels of our soul growth have been as advanced as the one that we now enjoy. To repattern the mind we must be committed to change. Our perception is determined by our beliefs about ourself and the world around us. Beliefs are handed down within families, educational systems, cultures, and religions.

When our mind discovers new knowledge it must release the old perceptions of that knowledge. If we try to merge the new and the old, we will find ourself overwhelmed with conflict and confusion. Merging our knowledge becomes the challenge of our female mind as our true source of wisdom and ingenuity. Attaching ourself complacently to beliefs that hold us captive within a time warp gives us an opportunity to learn the value of change. We must always ask ourself "why" with each belief that controls our perception of reality. We must always seek to understand the value of beliefs. If they are of no value to us within the present moment, the beliefs must be released. In releasing past beliefs and gaining new perceptions we heal our mind and our emotions.

If we learn to perceive our life from false or negative beliefs, we will attach ourself to the level of knowledge that supports the belief and we will assume that our knowledge at that level is absolute truth. Wars have been fought at all levels of our soul evolution because of our attachment to beliefs that are no longer valid. Beliefs that are based upon ancient perception lose credibility as our understanding is expanded. Yet the ego will resist changing its perception once the knowledge is accepted as fact.

Knowledge has the power to create inertia. Inertia is a stagnant energy that allows decay to set in and destroy whatever it touches. There is a cosmic pattern that exists within each cell of our body and each energy cell of our mind. It is duplicated within all of life, society, and the world. It is our responsibility to keep the energy flowing within our body and mind, thus setting in place an openness and rhythm for our integrated minds to move in harmony.

Knowledge is the final level of the physical, male energy of thought. In the beginning of the knowledge level of evolution, our mind will be focused upon the external information of facts and beliefs. Once knowledge is open to change, the mind energy begins to access soul memory and the Universal consciousness of our spirit. It is this integration of information from the soul and spirit mind that begins to expand our thought into the power of our female soul and spirit understanding. This addition of the female mind energy with the male mind energy begins to access our soul memory and our Universal consciousness, allowing our knowledge of ourself and the Universe to expand dramatically.

Understanding will always be initiated from within the inner mind of our soul and the higher mind of our spirit. Understanding gives us a new perspective of life. We begin to see our life lessons as we have symbolized them in our physical experiences. The levels of our growth begin to appear in our mind, clearly defined, clearly understood, and joyously accepted.

Understanding is the fifth level of our soul evolution and the first level of awakening the mind to our true reality of all that is. But we begin our Cycle of Understanding as soon as we pass through our veil of beliefs. This allows the light side of the level of knowledge to help us work through our cycle of love with total understanding as we erase the strings of fear that may be lurking within our mind.

Understanding removes fear, judgement, doubt, devastation, anger, unworthiness, and every remaining negative emotion that we have clung to in our physical, male nature. Separateness and competition are dissolved in the physical nature as it is merged within the harmony and flow of our female soul and spirit mind energy. Understanding has no boundaries, no veils, and no obstructive thoughts. It allows us to see with clarity the individual pattern of our life. Life is open-ended in its eternal magnificence.

We challenge ourself to look at our life in the same manner that we look at a science experiment. We must look without judgement but simply to observe what is, as our lessons unfold before us. Judging our personal experiences of life as right or wrong, good or bad, has attached us to the negative energy of the event. Our pattern of life must first be understood through observing our personal experiences within these seven levels of energy: our personal perception, interpretation, examination, assessment, evaluation, experimentation, and reflection.

Each experience of our life is viewed within our minds in these separate stages of thought, representing our levels of growth. As one aspect of reality is understood, another will appear to establish clarity. Understanding is the basis of unraveling the mysteries of life, Earth, the planets, and the Universe. Once the pattern of self and life experiences is understood, the pattern of all of reality becomes visible.

Understanding is the female power being accepted into our physical life. When we understand ourself, we will understand the Universe. The power of our soul and spirit can be an overwhelming energy for those who have lived within the fear of the physical world. The ego fears each and every change of life. The ego believes in maintaining what is, what is known, what is comfortable, and what supports the ego.

When experimenting for the first time with your knowledge expansion, give yourself time to adjust your energy within by listening to the silence for several hours each day. With this approach you can continue to support yourself with new information. Silence is a challenge to the ego, so the ego chatter may be in your mind in the beginning. Continue focusing your mind within.

The ego is present at every level of our physical nature, and it is hidden in every belief and behavior of the physical experience. As we work with our commitment to understand, any ego beliefs that remain will challenge us with fear. Every "what if" in the ego mind will resurface for our immediate consideration. We are creating this challenge because our understanding of knowledge has not yet become fully developed and operational in every minute pattern of our mind.

"Soul talk" can very efficiently clear the last remnants of fear from the recesses of the mind. "Soul talk" allows the openings of the mind to remain clear, accepting the flow of soul memory and spirit memory with a total harmony and rhythm.

Understanding—the "why" of our knowledge, ourself, and our life—is the beginning of unity within self. As the female nature of the soul and spirit begin to unify with the physical nature of the body, the sex drive will disappear from our thoughts, words, and actions. Sex will not be our focus during our period of merging our physical nature with our divine nature.

Our physical nature that culminates in the sexual drive is experiencing a role change. This role change, as we shift to openness and self-love, is significant to our physical nature because it allows the interaction of our relationships to provide a new and elevated level of fulfillment and joy. After the merging of our two natures, sex becomes the celebration of physical life.

Once openness and self-love occurs within us, we can no longer grow within the identical level of physical interaction that was at one time very satisfying to us. Our physical nature is now being influenced and encouraged by our divine nature to design relationships that will support the expansion of openness and self-love within our love and truth. This change in our relationships requires physical time to clear our perception of beliefs, and to fully examine our past relationships to see the repetitive behavior of our relationship patterns.

Looking at our repetitive behavior to see our lessons in total clarity allows our healing to occur. Removing the identities and observing only the experiences of our past relationships allows us to keep the events in the perspective of us and our soul lessons. When we can see what we learned from the experience, all of the hate, anger, fear, revenge, and pain will dissolve. At that moment we can, in total love and truth, thank the actor that was on our stage. Once this stage of understanding is reached and resolved, we are healed.

As we reflect upon releasing what we don't want in our lives, we will begin to reflect upon what we do want. Clearing the space around us can only be accomplished by the physical changes that we make in our thoughts, our words, and our actions. Our life is a reflection of our beliefs, behaviors, and actions.

As we clean up our act, we attract new people with more understanding and insight. If the people that we are attracting have not changed, we have not changed. Always look at self. We cannot change another person, as change is our personal choice. We can change us, and we can attract people who are also changing in their willingness to grow. It is important to find a support system that we can comfortably relate to when our lifestyle is changing. New friends provide us with new mirrors, new relationships, and like minds to support and inspire us as we change and grow.

Truth is the consistency of our thoughts, words, and actions. Knowledge can be masked until our veil is completely dissolved, and therefore any "fact" that is believed can be perceived as truth. When this circumstantial delusion is present, we will continue to attract what we reflect. This is the challenge of intellectual spiritualism which effectively obstructs us from our peak experience of spiritual awakening.

The phenomenon of intellectual spiritualism frequently occurs as we find ourself flush with our veil of beliefs. It can be heard in the words, "I know all of that," as the individual continues with his or her external search. Our spirit and soul are at all times found internal to ourself, not external. This is the reality test for truth when we can clearly see that our words and actions are not consistent. Dishonesty is never loving of ourself because it shows no value and respect for who we are.

The reality test for us is to look at our feelings. Are we harboring fear, anger, judgement, unforgiveness, dependency, control, unworthiness, inadequacy, or self-blame within our mind? Are we being loving, truthful, and respectful of our value as a person?

Any of these negative emotions are an indication that our soul and spirit nature has not integrated with our physical nature. Understanding remains an illusion of knowledge that is being perceived by the intellect. This is a level of intellectual spiritualism that is upheld by the intellect and ego as an effigy to reflect the image of understanding without the reality of understanding. As we move from our Cycle of Awareness in our intellectual level of knowledge to our Cycle of Understanding in our expanded knowledge, we will begin to see true glimpses of understanding. Be encouraged to continue with your change and growth.

As our cycle of change begins, movement from one level to another can require months or years of physical time. Awakening creates seven levels relative to seven in our cycle of change from fear to love. Each level to awakening requires that we experience each level within each level. Physical time does not matter. As we move forward, we will grasp love and truth with the speed of light. Knowledge is at all times the level of stasis in each level of awakening to change. Knowledge is our lesson in patience.

As we develop an awareness of understanding, we no longer blame other people who have participated in our life experiences. We become aware that the role of others within our life is simply as actors upon our stage who have allowed our lessons to be acted out as real-life dramas. There is at that moment a deep gratitude within us that other souls and spirits love us enough to agree to help us with our lessons. All anger, blame, judgement, jealousy, rage, and devastation are released, and we experience a beautiful cleansing and healing of our mind. At last we understand that we could not be who we are at this very moment in time if we had not experienced the relationship dramas that we designed.

We accept the responsibility for the script that we wrote, the actors that we chose for each role, and we value the drama as a beautiful, shining jewel in our tiara of soul growth. Once we learn from the drama, we never have to repeat it again. When we don't value, respect, and learn from the drama, we repeat it over and over and over again.

We may use different actors upon our stage and ad-lib the lesson in a slightly different style, but nevertheless we will continue repeating our lesson until it is understood. Our attachment to drama ties us into the physical experience and our repeated reflections of the lesson. We allow ourself to be stuck in the negative, physical levels of growth until our lessons are totally clear within our conscious awareness. Experiences that are frequently repeated within our life and our lifetimes cover the entire spectrum of the lessons of our soul evolution.

We repeat lessons for many thousands of lifetimes and for millions of years in our determination to grow into an acceptance and acknowledgement of our female energy of soul and spirit. Repetition is our highest order of learning. Repetition is the order of the Universal pattern, and it is repeated to the smallest fractal of reality within all physical matter. It is through the repetitious living of our physical nature that we expand the wisdom of our soul nature, which expands the truth and love of our spirit nature.

Each experience of life adds to the growth within our physical body, intellect and ego, our soul mind, and our spirit consciousness. The trinity of our spirit self as male, female, and God creates the image of the trilogy of our physical self as male, female, and spirit energy. Each has three dimensions with seven primary levels of growth that are at all times relative to seven to infinity.

The multiple levels of our soul and spirit growth are symbolized by our untiring and persistent capability for physical repetition ad infinitum. Once our lesson is learned, we can accept it instantly and never think about it or repeat it again. We will find ourself going back into soul memory only at times of free choice. At times we will consciously choose to thank a favorite actor with our unlimited gratitude for his willingness to help us through a lesson of this life.

This is done through our mind, which needs no mechanical assistance to reach another soul and spirit energy.

In understanding our Universal pattern of female and male energy, we begin to understand the pattern of the Universe. Our understanding expands into wisdom and becomes the sixth level of our soul evolution and the second complete level of awakening to our female power within. In using the second level of our female power, we begin to live our life from the wisdom of our soul and spirit. Until we reach this level of our soul growth, we can at times of extreme challenge feel the ego memory returning to haunt us.

Wisdom far surpasses the boundaries of our intellect and it flows in an unbroken energy of harmony and rhythm, bringing together our intellectual mind, our soul memories, and our Universal consciousness. Our mind energy flows in a circle of power energy when all resistance has been removed.

Removing the boundaries established by the intellectual and ego veil removes the resistance, denial, fear, anxiety, and competition from our mind. At last the ego is allowed to rest in its complete humility. *Wisdom is knowing that the competition that existed within us between our intellect and ego nature and our soul and spirit nature is no longer a consideration.* We acknowledge the wholeness of our intellect, soul, and spirit mind.

Now our mind energy is understood as one unified energy force that is the pure essence of cooperation. There is no sense of competition within us or towards the external world. We can see that being female, male, and spirit creates us as the perfect trinity. Our new path of refinement of self is seen with love and enthusiasm.

As our mind understands unity internally, unity begins to become our physical experience. As we see ourself through the understanding and wisdom of the soul, we accept our part in the Universal pattern as our contribution to the Universe. *Inequality and competition between the male and the female loses its power, its reality, its necessity, and it suddenly becomes only another physical process that we have used to slow down our soul growth. All fear, guilt, sin, judgement, and blame are gone.*

The symbol of the male and female acting out inequality in their physical life through the identical scenario that is happening within their minds gives us a clear vision of the mind influence over our physical body. We begin to see how healing occurs, how disease occurs, how conflict is created, how fear mushrooms, how original sin holds us captive, and the patterns of our growth suddenly have a new and powerful meaning. This is the beginning of our wisdom.

Wisdom is not slow; it is not physical. Wisdom is the peace of understanding, the motivation for creating, the enthusiasm for living. Wisdom is the achievement of shifting the source of our power from the lower activity of our physical nature to the higher spirit activity of our divine nature. Wisdom becomes a unity of all levels of thinking, knowing, and understanding.

Wisdom does not allow judgement because it sees judgement as the veil of fear that creates illusion. Wisdom is confidence, power, and acknowledgement that is accepted and understood with total humility. Wisdom is faith, trust, respect, and honor. Wisdom is acknowledging the power within us and honoring our freedom of choice and responsibility.

Wisdom and ingenuity is the female power that exists within each and every HUMAN as his inherently created soul mind and spirit consciousness. Our soul mind remembers our experiences from the moment we were created as *thought* by the Creator. All learned soul experience is stored as memory without the beliefs and emotions of our physical nature but as lessons of clarity within our spirit consciousness.

Beliefs, emotions, and behaviors that are not understood in the physical nature within one life experience remain part of the physical nature of succeeding life experiences until they are transcended as lessons learned within our soul memory. Our experiences remain as beliefs, emotions, and behaviors of the deeper recesses of the subconscious mind of our soul, always available to our physical nature while they are being learned as lessons.

These experiences become our karmic lessons to continue studying in every lifetime until they are healed by understanding and wisdom. Merging our physical nature with our divine nature doesn't wipe our slate clean of all remaining lessons. It does, however, give us a new perspective from which to complete the internal healing of any pain from our lesson. After we rend the veil of the intellect and ego, we live our lessons through humility, knowledge, understanding, wisdom, and truth. There is no fear, guilt, sin, anger, or revenge. The light side of our soul allows us to heal all that has gone before in the shadow of our physical nature.

After transition into clarity, the energy of our physical experience is cleansed and healed from fear to love to expand our spirit consciousness. The dramas designed by our soul and spirit around these karmic beliefs, emotions, and behaviors become more dramatic and traumatic with each life experience until transition is complete into the light side of our soul. It is the absolute, loving intention of our soul and spirit to allow us to work through our negative beliefs, emotions, and behaviors in meaningful physical ways that will capture our attention and create total clarity for us within the lesson.

We are merging our divine nature of soul and spirit into our physical nature. We continue to work through our life experiences as physical beings no different than we were before our transition, except in the way we think, speak, and live our life.

This is the wisdom of our soul and the path it chooses to manifest the physical symbols of our lessons again and again into our daily life pattern of experiences, until we understand who we are and why we are here on Earth. The light side of our soul gives us the opportunity to change and grow in light through love, truth, and equality. It gives us an opportunity to know who we are and why we are here. In the path of our spirit evolution we will be living our change and growth as our daily celebration of life.

Have you ever observed a beautiful house plant living in the shadows in a corner of your home? One day you see that the plant is still very much alive, but it hasn't grown or bloomed in all of the years it has rested in that corner. You pick up your plant and move it to a bright, sunny window so that it is in full sunlight. In a few days you see your plant beginning to change. It has perked up, it is growing, and it is blooming; it looks like a new plant. That is the same story that we live in our human condition. Our soul has infinite patience with the frustrations of our physical humanity.

Our physical beliefs in roles, identities, and behaviors cast us into guilt, disbelief, sin, fear, resistance, and denial of our female power. This is symbolized by the male focus on inequality and separateness and is manifested through the intellect and ego that is captured in its fear of change. Our soul accepts the responsibility of awakening us to the perspective that all of the physical drama really doesn't matter. What we learn is what is important.

The male has controlled and suppressed the female in the identical way that we have controlled and suppressed our soul and spirit energy with our intellect and ego. It is the pattern of our physical suppression that is used to awaken us to our soul and spirit suppression that reflects the wisdom of our soul in its design. We design both male and female roles into our lives. No one soul and spirit is suppressed more than another unless the lesson is a total challenge to grasp. When we awaken our intellect and ego mind and change to merge with our female power that exists within each individual in the Universe, we honor the wisdom of our soul and the love and truth of our spirit. We begin a new level of respect and value for ourself as physical beings.

In each life experience our gender is chosen by us as the most efficient tool for learning the lesson of this life design. This choice is made through the wisdom of our soul that efficiently records all of our life experiences. It is the physically focused male and female that is most challenged to accept the female emotions of his or her soul and spirit. In choosing to become physically focused, we place our trust in the external belief system. The belief in our physical reality as the only reality supports unequal behaviors both internally and externally. Our physical beliefs hold other behaviors and emotions in disdain.

Our singular focus upon the external, physical world presents the awakening to the recognition of our soul and spirit female power as a crisis event within our physical, intellect, and ego experience.

When this event occurs we will find ourself faced with the most dramatic crisis of intimate relationships, career, and health that we may ever experience. The female focus is naturally directed towards the soul and spirit female power and it will orchestrate crisis events to remind us of our need for physical balance in every aspect of our life.

Both our male and female energies are seeking balance. Any time that we find our internal or external balance being threatened we can and will initiate a crisis. As our soul and spirit evolve, we will seek physical experiences to enjoy both our external focus and our internal focus being together within a balanced state. This will allow us to physically experience the wisdom of the female soul manifesting into our awakened intellectual mind as a celebration of the physical experience.

As we evolve into our higher levels of soul growth, our wisdom will be beautifully integrated as the normal ability of our intellect. Additional levels of our soul growth will allow our divine nature to merge more fully with our physical nature. Our divine nature will not be fully merged with our physical nature until we have lived through the remaining levels of our soul evolution and the seven levels of our spirit evolution.

Using our power from the divine level within our physical life will far surpass all of our past life experiences. We are learning how to be, living to understand through our wisdom and our truth who we are and why we are here. As wisdom becomes the focus of our mind energy, our mind will recognize truth internally and externally, and it will be capable of releasing all thoughts, words, and actions that do not hold truth as their basis. Truth is the seventh level of our soul evolution and it is the third brilliant level of awakening to the true power within us.

Truth is the light of our spirit. Truth is the final level of merging the soul with the physical nature. It is the truth of living the experience of being HUMAN while on Earth. As individuals we absorb knowledge. Truth, as our life, absorbs us. Truth is the loving action of our spirit consciousness that creates the perfection within us and our life. In our search to become HUMAN we have set out to seek our Higher Universal Spirit Consciousness as physical beings. Bringing together our understanding, wisdom, truth, and love of our divine nature with the physical nature of our humanness is one goal of life upon Earth. *Our purpose in living is to expand our perfection, which expands the perfection of God.*

The merging of our divine nature with our physical nature and living our unity in absolute truth completes the Cycles of Awareness and Understanding within our second dimension of energy known as our soul mind energy. This second dimension of our energy is our female soul energy.

The first dimension of our energy is our male, physical energy, and we passed through this first dimension of our energy billions of years ago as we learned how to create our physical body and our physical nature. This first dimension of our physical growth was our Cycle of Development.

It is through our path of growth in physically living through our divine nature that we can once again become the purity of spirit. When our soul evolution is complete and we move forward into our spirit evolution, we will begin to live our "Heaven upon Earth." It will be during the period of our spirit evolution that we will live and experience our true Cycle of Integration.

Our pattern of Cycles for Development, Awareness, Understanding and Integration is experienced with each of our physical lives. We repeat each level of physical growth, soul growth, and each dimensional cycle with each physical life. In our pattern of repetition we are given the ability to see that we are all that is.

Our spirit must evolve through its dimension of spirit, which is our Cycle of Integration, and its seven levels of evolution. But we begin to live our "Heaven upon Earth" after we rend the veil and move into the light side of our soul. After we complete our soul evolution we will live within the forces of our spirit evolution before we can reach the perfection of our Heavenly Spirit Realm.

During this mesocosmic shift in consciousness we have the power to move into the light side of our soul, our Cycle of Understanding. It is our individual responsibility to choose our path of growth through the expansion of our conscious awareness. We will not change and grow until we consciously choose to release any primitive beliefs that hold us captive.

Our male energy is our physical energy and it is present in each and every human being living upon Earth. Our physical energy is the mirror image of our trinity of Spirit or God energy: the male, the female, and the spirit of us. As our spirit energy is reflected to Earth, it creates a shadow or image of our true self.

Our shadow self is our physical body, our intellect, and our ego. Our ego is designed from our belief systems. Our shadow self may be the only part of us that is acknowledged, allowing us to quickly be cast into our physical role. Our limited perception of self allows our concept of the physical world to become our accepted reality. But as we evolve through our soul growth the truth of our physical life becomes more apparent as our finite reality.

As our soul evolves, we will find that we have a conscious awareness of all parts of us, our male, our female, and our spirit energy. Growing into a full awareness of who we are changes our entire perception of ourself, other people, and the world. Our physical shadow self that feels supreme is the only finite energy within us. But our focus upon the external world as our reality allows us to live in our belief of the physical self as the only accepted reality of our physical being. We lose our focus on all but the physical reality anytime that the external influences of life capture us and we become their slave. When change begins to occur within us, we begin to change our overall perception of reality.

Change is the only method that allows us the freedom of growth within the internal energy of our soul. When we think of change, we immediately think of changing our location, our job, our friends, our lovers, or any other change that can be negotiated within the physical, external world that we see as reality. True change can only occur from within us as we change our beliefs and our perceptions of self, life, society, and the world.

Absolute change is an attitude adjustment. We must change the way that we think before we can change the words that we speak, or the actions of our life. Instead of our physical perception of living in a fearful world, we must begin to change our perception to focus upon the value that we find in our physical life. But when our concept of reality is directed only upon our shadow self, we will feel constant fear because shadows are always destroyed by full light.

Internally we know that our physical self is fragile. It is this realization that allows us to be compulsively concerned with our physical health. The ego is at all times conscious that if we become aware of who we are, change will have an effect upon our belief in our physical reality. The ego knows that it is as finite as our physical body and it fears for itself and the body in which it lives. It is from our intellectual view of reality that our beliefs are created from the primitive perceptions within our developing soul mind.

Our body that is our joy has been created by the slowing down of soul and spirit energy to magnetize physical matter. Each time that we choose to become physical, we design a physical body that will support us in our life design of lessons. We learned the pattern for our physical development during the first dimension of our creation, when we very methodically and with total freedom of choice chose the perfect elements for our human form.

We are an electromagnetic energy of spirit consciousness. When we began to slow down and magnetize matter, we polarized ourself into our personal pattern of evolution. We designed our physical pattern to integrate our mind and body with nature, allowing us to stay in a total harmony and rhythm with the evolution of Earth and the Universe.

We created the pattern of our physical body through the experience of *thought* moving through the natural elements of Earth. As we began as *thought,* we merged with the dust, minerals, plants, and animals of Earth, seeking the most complementary form in which to grow physically and mentally.

It was through the physical polarization of our divine energy that our potential for soul and spirit evolution was created. Polarization gave us the ability to create what we are, not in the separateness of our intellect and ego, but in the unity of all of our energy forces of self.

Our physical body provides us with the negative polarization that is essential to our staying upon earth. Our physical body, intellect, and our soul mind become our tools for soul and spirit expansion. We are seeking balance as our major goal of each physical life. In each life we are seeking to balance within our physical experience our male physical energy, our female soul energy, and our spirit energy.

Life is our learning process. We have not reached our full potential when we allow ourself to be totally polarized into the concept of our physical body, the intellect, and the ego. In this singular polarization we block out all memory of soul and spirit experience. Unless we have evolved far enough in our physical embodyment, we will not remember to leave our soul and spirit windows open. Keeping the windows of our mind open will allow us to consciously work with soul and spirit energy through our physical experiences.

When we experience memory in our life that is not a learned memory of this physical life, we are accessing the wisdom and ingenuity of our soul. If we understand how to be a carpenter, a plumber, a mechanic, a musician, a writer, a singer, a painter, a sculptor, or have a knack for any other activity that we have not consciously learned in this lifetime, we are using our soul memories. Everyone uses his soul memories to some degree. Our soul is our rational mind and it can assist us in figuring out complex, intellectual problems.

There are no accidents within the Universal system of energy. Therefore, as we have developed into our physical orientation, there will be advanced souls who have left the windows of their mind open and have integrated into their Universal consciousness. Our expansive Universal memory has been designed and created through the inspiration of our spirit and the motivation of our soul.

Our integrated mind is the library of the Universal consciousness, Earth consciousness, and our human consciousness. This has been our pattern from the beginning of time. It is only as we open the windows of the mind that we begin to become comfortable, aware, and open to information from within. In our spirit or Universal consciousness we have already stored all information.

When we learn something new we are simply remembering. A perfect example of the mind and its function is the computer system. Our computer understanding has been given to us as the caretakers of Earth as a symbol of the way our mind works. In the left side of the brain is the floppy disc of our mind computer. In our intellect we can store the facts, the figures, the concepts, the beliefs, that we are exposed to in this physical embodyment. In our floppy disc all of the information from an individual lifetime can be recorded.

In the right hemisphere of the brain is recorded all of our soul memory. All that we have ever been, ever will be, and are now is already known in soul memory. Our soul memory is the accumulation of information that is transferred to our soul mind from our intellectual mind at the time of transition into pure soul and spirit energy at the moment of our physical death. Our soul mind is equivalent to the hard drive of our computer.

The largest expansive memory bank within our internal computer system is the mainframe computer or server unit. Symbolically the server unit or mainframe of the computer represents our cerebellum, the nucleus of our intuitive spirit mind. Our intuitive mind is our Universal consciousness that includes the entire memory of creation and all of our soul lessons that have been learned with clarity. As our soul learns a lesson with love, truth, and perfection, that lesson is transferred into our Universal memory as an expansion energy for our spirit.

In our memory bank we understand our origin and the origin of the Universe. We understand our purposes and our goals. And we have a life design within our mind in which we have created alternate plans that will allow us to reach our goals and fulfill our purposes, regardless of our life experiences. We have unlimited time and space in the physical sense to learn what we must learn for our soul and spirit expansion.

Best of all, we do not have the entry code in our physical mind to change the energy of our soul and spirit minds. Therefore, no matter how bizarre our physical experiences are, they will all be to our ultimate, growth advantage. Our physical experiences will always be seen with the loving perception of our soul and spirit, and they will be healed through other physical experiences. There is no hell except for the life that we create as we are living with our singular, floppy-disc mentality of ourself and our reality.

If we acknowledge only our intellectual mind, we limit the information that we consciously store within our floppy disc in a single lifetime. Our beliefs build energy boundaries that we use as our intellect and ego veil of resistance to opening the windows to our soul and spirit memory. *Beliefs limit the information that we allow ourself to accumulate in one lifetime.* We can choose to accept more if we are willing to do the inner work to free our boundaries of beliefs that create the veil of resistance and denial between our intellect, the rational soul mind, and the intuitive spirit mind.

When we live our life through the physical orientation of our ego and intellect as our only source of knowledge, we create a box out of our body. Our self-imposed box compresses our knowledge, our mind, and our life into restrictive limits of reality. Our experiences become the manifestation of our confined and suppressed mind. *If our mind is limited by beliefs, we can only look backwards into our primitive beliefs for our physical experiences of growth. In front of us is a restrictive veil that we can't see beyond.*

We have enclosed our intellect and ego in this shell that protects us from an awareness of who we are. In our fear of change we deny that we could possibly be more than what our conscious awareness accepts. Change would require time-sharing between

our external and internal minds. Change from our external mind to our internal mind would require an acknowledgement of our internal mind's existence. Veiling our intellect from our soul and spirit memory is equivalent to refusing to use the hard drive and mainframe information of our computer.

When we use a network computer system in our business, it allows us to expand our business and its efficiency of operation. As humans we can expand our understanding and wisdom by using our intellect, our soul mind, and our spirit memory. When we are open to all that is within our mind, the mind can flow with a rhythm and a harmony that allows us to use our total power. Accepting the divine nature of our soul and spirit changes the fear that is so common within our mind to an energy of love and truth.

The male energy gives us multiple perceptions of physical reality. When the perception of life is limited to the external perception, we see, we judge, and we live in a world defined as separate from ourself. All of our acknowledged reality exists outside of ourself. We see ourself as separate and unconnected to others, which is a symbol of how we exist as an intellectual mind. *Our external perception of reality allows us to believe that we are fear, we are our money, our possessions, our greed, our judgement; that inequality exists between the male and female; and that the sum total of our physical possessions defines our worth.*

Our rule by competition is used to judge and control everyone upon Earth. It is a rule that has held us attached to the dark side of our soul for millions of years. This rule by competition has affected every aspect of Earth society from the beginning of time. *The superiority that man has felt over woman is the symbol of the superiority that the intellect and ego feels over the rational and intuitive minds.*

Our perception of being smarter and better than others is the most dramatic fantasy that man has perpetuated upon Earth, and it is the primary and constant example of our lessons of equality. Our competitive perception of others allows each and every experience of our life to be judged, blamed, and dissected for just physical cause. When our mindless impression of right and wrong is fully understood, the transition to the light side of the soul will occur for all of humanity. Understanding equality will dramatically change the judicial and penal systems as well as all other systems of society.

When the veil of the intellect is dissolved, the soul and the spirit will motivate and inspire us to new and dynamic heights of cooperation and achievement.

Blame and judgement are commonplace in every aspect of our personal life, in our society, and in the world. Massive amounts of time, money, pain, and emotion are spent on belaboring a source of blame. We constantly point our finger outward from self, not inward toward self. But we are responsible for our creation in every dimension of our reality. Blame and judgement that we create on the shadow side of our soul will be healed on the light side of the soul. *When we begin to accept the inner and higher virtues of our personality and character as our female energy, these values and virtues will be sought after to bring peace and joy into the reality of the world.*

Our inner and higher virtue, personality, and character traits provide our balance. The good parts of our thoughts and our behavior represent the God within us. The fear, doubt, and rejection of our inner and higher self are the acting out of the ego within our shadow self of the physical. Our society has interpreted, ruled against, defined, and judged from the basis of an external perception of reality. All of life is judged in relationship to our external standard of beliefs. Beliefs are not identical in any two individuals. With our external perception as the only acknowledged reality, we limit and resist the growth of all human beings upon Earth. The heart of a man or woman can't be defined by the clothes he or she wears or the status of his or her lifestyle. *Moral and virtuous living in love, truth, and perfection is being the spirit of God upon Earth.*

It is only when the physical perception can be combined with our intuition, from the inspiration of our spirit and the motivation and knowing of our soul, that we can look at an event and stay open to its true interpretation. Without an open and integrated flow within our minds, we cannot make an objective, open assessment of the event. Instead, the interpretation will originate from the perception of our own restrictive and limited beliefs.

If we look at the smallest event in our world, the tiniest experience of our life, and we view the event only through the judgement of our intellect and ego, we will perceive it according to the belief systems that we live through. Our external perception of reality allows fear to become a foreboding presence within our intellect. Because of the judgemental and competitive nature of the intellect and ego, the relationship of the circumstances to the ego's survival will outweigh and control all other perceptions.

Throughout history the ego fear has been dominant within the male energy and it has influenced every aspect of our society, especially the judgement and control of the female. To use our soul and spirit power we must remove the veil that separates our intellect from our soul and spirit. Our goal is to balance the intellect with the soul and the spirit. We are searching for an openness, a freedom, a perception of the love that exists within the three facets of our mind. We want to know who we are. We want to search out our individual potential. We want to use the power that is within us. We want our soul and spirit to be our friend. We are seeking our internal inspiration and motivation to guide our intellectual creativity. We are ready for individual, societal, and world change, and the shift in the consciousness of humanity has begun.

Each and every time the power of our soul and spirit is honored upon Earth, miraculous happenings become commonplace. There have been miraculous inventions and discoveries that were given through the spirit and soul wisdom to allow people to continue learning and growing. As a physical, male-oriented society, we are reaching the fullest potential of relative knowledge that is possible for our intellect.

All advancement of thoughts, words, and actions must now originate within the soul and spirit of our internal self. The stasis of the intellectual mind is firmly attached to the examination and reflection levels of our soul evolution by the ego.

Breakthroughs in any field of endeavor happen from the inspiration and motivation within the individual. The ego feels supreme and consciously suppresses the energy of our soul and spirit. The ego will reach its trajectory point into the light side of the soul, and when it cannot find its balance devolution becomes the solution. When the intellect and ego chooses to solve problems through violence, competition, judgement, and war, we will bring upon ourself multiple crises. Our thoughts, words, and actions always determine our activities and events within the physical world. In our physical beliefs there must always be someone to blame before we can satisfy the energy of our intellect and ego.

If we observe our society we will see that when an event occurs, judgement and blame are consciously sought to interpret the reality of what happened. With judgement we issue perceptions of right or wrong which can lead to repetitious behavior, fear expansion, war, and violence. With blame being consciously placed upon another, we remove the responsibility of the so-called victim. We also expand the negative, physical energy of the drama one step further by rewarding the aberrant behavior with an influx of media attention and money.

This is the acceptable intellectual approach to what is viewed as competition between right and wrong. This approach also provides the drama which is the vehicle for our lessons of being a savior or a victim to be played through in our life. Both the savior and victim lessons are the negative physical approach to the lesson of personal responsibility. But the negative approach expands the negative energy and creates a more dramatic wound to be healed throughout society. When our attention can be directed towards the positive events of life, change will occur. This is true at all levels of life as an individual, as a society, and as a world.

Our external perception of change creates the illusion of the solutions arising from the depth of our problems. War is a perfect example of seeking solutions from the depths of our problem, and it is doubly so when there is outside interference. This concept originates within our ego and intellect. Judgement expands itself and the solution repeats the events of our problem from a different image. The cooperation and peace of our soul and spirit, or female perception, can break this cycle of physical repetition through the insight and intuition of our mind.

This cycle of repetition can be found within us as individuals, and it is repeated within our society, nation, and the world. We must look at our family, community, and society to understand that we as individuals create our intimate relationships, our community, our state, our nation, our world, and our Universe.

Our power is a significant force that expands from our mind to our actions. If we are negative, our actions are negative. Our energy impacts everyone that we are in contact with in our life. We may not have a conscious awareness of the effect of our energy upon someone else, but that does not neutralize our impact.

Understanding this phenomenon will help us understand the inherent power that is within us. Understanding the power of fear and how negative beliefs and feelings are spread as surely as a contagious disease will encourage a change in the way that we speak, the way businesses are managed, and the way negotiations of world relationships are carried on. If we perceive our life only through the intellectual perception, we will live our life in judgement, fear, anger, and resentment. We will be a victim and we will reflect our unworthiness to others and victimize them.

The opposite energies of fear and love will exist until all of humankind has learned to live the actions of his physical nature through his divine nature of love, truth, and equality.

Control creates suppression in all circumstances because it creates fear. Control will initiate rebellion in the individual, the state, or the country that seeks freedom. When freedom is the way of life on all levels, we give our inspiration and motivation an opportunity to be activated and our intellect the freedom to be creative. When this cycle of creation is used in relationships, businesses, and with world events, the results are worthy of true celebration. Any relationship may appear as controlling, but when controlling behavior is no longer acceptable within our mind, freedom becomes the only solution.

Living in controlling energy allows the actors to play out their victim drama. In this way we learn what we don't want. By creating our world, our growth, and our education as positive forces through the physical polarization upon Earth, we will choose to participate in all relationships because of the joy of working together. Every dimension of our life—the microcosm, the mesocosm, and the macrocosm—is here to help us change and grow.

It has been useful for humanity to have experienced this intellectual, ego perception of life for many hundreds of thousands of lifetimes. We choose each life to continue with the karmic lessons that we must learn. In the same manner that we repeat the lesson over and over and over again in each lifetime, we repeat the lesson within each life until it is understood. This pattern can be seen throughout history and within our personal life. We will continue to be in fear, to be in violence, and to be separate until we learn to effectively use our soul and spirit energy. To hold our intellect separate from that part of our mind that nurtures, loves, protects, and expands our mind, dishonors our true magnificence.

When we were created by the Creator, we were given the loving power of our Creator. Therefore, we have innately within us the power of creation. We create each and every moment that we breathe as physical beings. When we die we continue with our power of creation as soul and spirit. We create through our free choice, free will, and free intention. If we create only from our intellectual, physical perception, we create through the energy of fear and our belief in our physical needs. A single fear, such as unworthiness, will lead us to other levels of fear such as victimization, control, suppression, inequality, and anger as one negative emotion expands into other negative emotions.

It is important to understand that our physical, male energy is inherent within all of us. It is through our physical, male energy that we usually identify who we are and how we relate to the external world. Fear has become a learned emotion of our physical mind. Fear is generated from our self-judgement in relationship to our self-consciousness, which we base upon our external, physical beliefs that we have accepted as truth. Our standard of judgement decides which beliefs our intellect and ego will accept to camouflage our soul and spirit influence from our aware consciousness. Our physical, male energy is the energy of our intellect and ego, and it lives through our emotions of fear and judgement.

We must be open to understanding how we program our minds with these beliefs before we will be willing to allow our internal power to be acknowledged. We choose to change and grow without fear when we understand the value of happiness, peace, expansion, freedom, and power that is good, useful, and productive in our life. Removing ourself from the repetitious cycles of fear, anger, rage, victimization, and control is our gift to ourself of a new life.

Throughout our life we will be actively or passively involved in multiple experiences. Each experience and event is of tremendous value to our soul growth. When we have a physical, male orientation in life we are choosing to understand the external world and its relationship to humanity. The male orientation is learning the lesson of love, truth, and equality. Physical experiences are polarized to the external perception by the negative energy of the Earth when we are living through our external energy.

When we choose to enter life with a physical intention of growth, we can choose to design our life to seek the opposite of what we appear to be. Therefore, our goal of life is to develop a conscious awareness of our soul and spirit, but we will approach our goal through our multiple levels of physical perception and attachments. This includes the entire spectrum of life and relationships.

Fear will be a major issue for anyone with a physical focus. Fear will exist as a fear of failure through greed, attachment to possessions, multiple dependencies, and most of all, a fear of commitment and responsibility in relationship to women and children. As human beings our focus is to merge our physical nature with our divine nature. Women and children are the symbols of our divinity, which we are actively rejecting within ourself. They manifest the need within the male to nurture and caregive, allowing the male to work with his lesson of commitment and responsibility to trigger his soul and spirit energy. It is in the love of family that we trigger our soul and spirit self as a reminder of its presence.

We will approach this challenge differently, depending upon the male or female gender of choice and the intricate design of our life lesson. We seek to live as humans through the love and truth that is inherent within us as spirit, and the wisdom and ingenuity that is the strength and courage of our soul. Choosing the physical perception of life is no accident. Our physical lessons are the way of approaching our life to learn in a very intellectual way what does not work in our society. The intellect is essential to our path of change and growth, especially to reaching the Cycle of Understanding. *It is with the use of our intellectual knowledge that we have the most efficient tool to rend the veil of our mind.*

The most significant lessons of our reality are the lessons of freedom, equality, integrity, balance, responsibility, commitment, and unconditional love. We approach our lesson of freedom by living with our perception of needing to control. Our society has a paternalistic belief in control. The control issues that exist within the male energy begin with an expansive vision of control that includes the individual, the family, the society, and the world. The perception of the male energy is "if it exists, it can be controlled."

Our "need" to control has expanded into our society and into the world. The more elaborate and war-like the control issues become, the less the family, as the nucleus of learning in life, is controlled. The family begins to mirror the energy of the society and the world as it too becomes war-like. This is the repetition of the breakdown in societies and cultures throughout history.

Control is the most predominant lesson within the male mind because it is the opposite of freedom. As we seek to learn, we first work with our lessons of the opposite to see what we don't want. In choosing control as a way of life, the male symbolizes the physical, intellectual control of his mind into his external life. When power is also a lesson, the control is seen from a different image than it is with someone who sees himself as powerless. Power is demonstrated on a societal or world level as war, but on an individual level power becomes physical, emotional, and psychological abuse. Despite the level of awareness from which the control emanates, the results are identical. Control and power together create the energy of discrimination and inequality when we control others through the assimilation of power.

Our power cannot be removed by another, but control allows the belief in our removal of power, which results in our sense of helplessness and our willingness to be controlled. When we fail to recognize that we have power, we willingly give our power away, which has happened in every facet of our life.

Both males and females live from the male focus of the external lessons of control, power, and judgement. We have been taught these beliefs for many thousands of years. If we remain a captive of our primitive perception, the multiple problems within our society will increase.

Our external search for control and power leads to discrimination, greed, graft, fear, crime, and war. We have the choice to free ourself from our fear or to remain in our perception of "need" for external power. As individuals we must explore the validity of our beliefs that are based upon superstition and myth. When our beliefs no longer serve us in our own change and growth, it is time to change our beliefs.

We are the world. When we each change as individuals, the nature of our world will change. We must live from our positive feelings of good, compassion, mercy, love, equality, and truth. Positive power acts as a catalyst to positive experiences in our daily life. Each person has a magnificence that is not understood. We have a magnificence, a power, an energy, that is expansive and glorious, and it is the energy of "Heaven upon Earth." The life experiences that we create through our negative, physical perception do not honor who we are.

In seeking freedom we live the lessons of control. In seeking equality we live the lessons of discrimination. In seeking integrity we live through the physical experiences of dishonesty and greed. In seeking the lesson of balance we will find ourself in the physical experiences of disease, greed, lust, fanaticism, discrimination, and gluttony. In seeking the lesson of responsibility we will find ourself vacillating between the roles of the victim and the savior. In seeking the lesson of commitment we will find ourself deserting and being deserted, being promiscuous, undependable, never being on time, and never keeping promises. In seeking the lesson of unconditional love we will be learning to love ourself and all other people without judgement or blame, and our physical experience will reflect the difficulty of the lesson by our feeling of constant judgement.

Each lesson can be learned by either passive or active participation. Lessons will be approached from multiple images as well as multiple cross-connections of lessons. We never devote one life to a single lesson but we will juggle multiple lessons at one time and weave each of them through every facet of our daily life. This allows the lessons to cross-connect repeatedly for greater emphasis to capture our attention.

During periods of multiple cross connections we feel that everything in our life is changing, going wrong, falling apart, or turning upside down. All of our physical life experiences are lessons of choice. We are never victims of life events or circumstances. Our freedom of choice is at all times honored and respected by our soul and spirit.

Each person will have a moment of awakening. The time of awakening from our physical perception may be triggered by a personal crisis of disease, trauma, or age. Many individuals will be triggered to look within themselves because of a sense that something is missing from their life. This can trigger an external search for a new relationship, bigger physical toys, a new physical body and image, a determination for success, or money.

As we begin to look within ourself, we become aware that we

are more than just an intellect and an ego existing within a vacuum. The ego with its external focus will reduce us to moments of extreme doubt and fear when this realization occurs. We can become angry, resistant, hostile, revengeful, unforgiving, violent, and/or heavily dependent on an emotion, relationship, alcohol, drugs, or experience that will suppress the emotions and feelings within us.

Do not be dismayed by these feelings. Negative thoughts have a finite life span in the same way that physical matter has a finite energy span. Change and growth are our way of life regardless of our ego resistance. As we perceive our life from a new awareness, the ego within us becomes frightened. The fear within our ego will resist any message that comes from our soul and spirit.

The ego and spirit tug-of-war is the internal conflict that we continually experience in life. Our ego becomes more intense when it is gripped in fear and it may seek to find a mirror image of itself. Supporting the ego with negative emotions when it is in a state of depression or self-abuse is not the way to change the energy.

The external ego perception is to fear for its survival. The ego always fears for its survival: it will never welcome unity. The ego believes in separateness. It will resist change. It will deny any need for change. The ego will kick and scream like a spoiled child as it reminds us of the possessions it has provided for us. It can trigger a sense of panic, telling us to move, change jobs, or find new friends. The ego can make us sick, directing attention to our physical body to bring us to our knees. Our ego can plan dramas within our life and disease within our body. But we have the power to choose who controls our life. We can say no to our ego and never feel guilty.

It is our choice to listen to our intellect and ego voice or to listen to the balanced and integrated voice of our soul, spirit, and intellect.

Our history documents the influence of our male-adapted society and the results of our lives when we live from our intellect and ego. Inequality, control, greed, dishonesty, war, and fear have never worked for us because they do not honor and respect our Higher Universal Mana of being HUMAN. It is time to reassess this life experiment and choose to change and grow into the loving unity of our mind and heart.

As our male-adapted society judges the female unequal in many ways, including the intellectual and emotional strength she possesses, the identical symbol of judgement and blame is occurring in our mind as the intellect and ego judge the soul and spirit unequal in every way. But the female has a longer physical lifespan because of her soul and spirit influence, which should be an indication of our soul and spirit power.

Women are symbolic of our soul and spirit energy, and they also possess the inherent power of physical creation. Our female power has instilled fear in the minds of the male from the beginning of time. As humans we have been living our lesson of equality. We are one mind. We are female, male, and spirit.

The power of creation does not render the female inferior to the male in any conceivable way. Eve created Adam through her androgynous energy. Mary created Jesus through her androgynous energy, later recorded as an immaculate conception. The symbols of our soul and spirit are there for us to honor. The soul and spirit has worked through the symbol of the female to reach an understanding of equality within the externally focused, physical mind.

The male resistance to equality is the acting out of the supreme ego of the external, intellectual mind that sees itself as superior.

When man sees himself not as separate in his intellect, ego, physical, male energy, but as one with the soul and spirit, evolution will begin shifting from its long period of knowledge stasis. *When we see ourself not as separate genders of male and female, but as both genders in one physical body, we will truly respect equality.* We are male, we are female. We are intellect, we are soul mind, and we are spirit consciousness. We are all that is. Our challenge is to learn how to live as whole people, while enjoying our magnificence.

When society interprets the male role one way and the female role another way, it establishes widespread beliefs in separateness, competition, and fear. These beliefs are understood as fact and are reflected in every aspect of our physical life. The beliefs become cyclic and are passed from generation to generation by our behavior, beliefs, and our laws. We are seeking unity internally and externally. But when we as individuals, societies, and nations live from superstition and myth we self-destruct our change and growth. We set ourself up for failure.

The actions of our life have to be consistent with our thoughts and our words or we create conflict. Our beginning, the creation of man, was interpreted by the male and that interpretation has captured the mind of man in fear, guilt, and sin. We have lived in our anger, our fear, our guilt, our sin, and our belief in judgement from the beginning of our soul evolution. It does not matter which physical role or identity we choose in terms of gender, career, or possessions, because our lessons are designed and learned despite our seemingly inappropriate life choices. And in our innocence we fail to see that change is the essence of our growth. We must have the courage to look at us and our life.

Lift your hand and make a tunnel. Close one eye and look through the tunnel of your hand. How far do you see? You have experienced the limited vision from which we live. Understanding that we are all that is will motivate and inspire us to love from the inherent power of our internal soul and spirit.

Say this affirmation several times each day: "I am. I am love. I am. I am love." Repeat these affirmations to yourself for the rest of your life to protect the loving energy within you.

Our intellect, when united with our soul memory and Universal consciousness, has the ability to be more powerful and more creative than we can begin to imagine. The magnitude of the potential of our integrated mind is not within our intellectual concept of understanding at this time.

The physical interpretation of our society and of our needs is leading us into a separation from nature. Nature is a symbol of God upon Earth. The Earth was provided for us as our source of physical energy. The sun, the moon, and the Earth move in harmony to provide a source of energy for us. When we remove ourself from the supporting nutrients and minerals of Earth, we deny the effect of the moon, the sun, and the Earth. We separate ourself into our cocoon, this veil of fearful energy that keeps us focused only upon our intellect and ego, which generates thought through fear not love.

Our pattern of life was provided by the Creator. Our physical body has been designed by us as our own creator. We are being nurtured and guided by the three major bodies of the Universal system. We are influenced by other planets within the Universe, but the sun, the moon, and the Earth are the symbols of our spirit, our soul, and our physical body. They provide a guiding force for us that affects our spiritual, emotional, and physical health. When we separate ourself from these energies of the natural Universe we will feel our spiritual, emotional, and physical deterioration. This does not happen instantly, but it occurs gradually with time. As we pull the veil tighter and tighter around ourself, creating a cocoon where we can hibernate, we will feel protected and have the appearance of survival but we are a crisis waiting to happen.

Our ego is creating a threatening misconception because we are being separated from God, from the Universe, and from Earth. We cannot physically survive without honoring the source of our creation. It is the ego that is being protected in this physical interpretation. The intellect is our method of creation within the physical world. The intellect is that part of our mind consciousness that is finite. Integrating a healthy body and mind with our soul and spirit can create our physical magnificence and a long and healthy life on Earth.

The ego, on the other hand, is worried only about its immediate, finite survival. It is a living element of fear. The ego is created through our survival belief systems that focus upon fear and anger. We accept the ego as a necessary part of our mind. But our ego is wrapped in its cocoon of fear and cannot survive in its present state in the energy of love, faith, and trust. These loving energies dissolve our shell of fear and the ego becomes humble in the love and wisdom of our soul and spirit. Our perception of life is then expanded beyond our linear view. *When the ego is merged with the divine nature it becomes humility.*

When we experience the energy of fear, we must understand that it is our ego fearing for its survival and not allow our ego to convince us that no other path is possible. *Understand that as eternal spirit created by God we cannot be destroyed, and that all things not created by God will not survive.* It is our fear of death that attaches us to the fear of change. We fear what we can't see and we can't see beyond the veil of beliefs that surrounds our intellect. Change is symbolic of the death of our old beliefs and behaviors.

Death of our soul and spirit energy can only happen if we fail to change. Energy must move and change to stay alive. We are energy. Change allows us to interact with new people, to learn new things, to open our mind and heart to love and giving. The increased exposure that we have to life from the very act of change raises our level of aware consciousness. Change expands the very essence of who we are. Each and every change that we experience in our conscious awareness allows us to have a new perception of ourself and other people.

Each change that we experience will naturally replace our old belief system with new beliefs and behaviors. It is this sense of eminent change happening within our minds that allows our intellect and ego to withdraw in total fear. Fear can capture our physical body in the same manner that it captures our intellect and ego. Fear is one way to create physical disease.

Our ego fear will create physical symptoms within the body because fear constricts the heart and blood vessels, which has an effect upon every cell within our physical body. Our heart is the point of power for our spirit. Anytime that the ego succeeds in constricting the heart, it is winning the tug-of-war with the spirit. This change takes place within our energy fields, which triggers our emotions, and which then triggers our physical body response.

Identical responses occur in our liver as a point of power for our soul. If we refuse to acknowledge our life lessons we can choose to create disease. Our lungs are the point of power for our physical life. If we are feeling suppressed or controlled physically, by ourself or someone else, we will develop breathing problems.

Each of these three important organs are connected to our spirit consciousness, soul mind, and intellect and ego, and they will reflect the control that we are creating from our mind restrictions. This is not a conscious action of our aware mind but it occurs at a subconscious, soul level and an unconscious, spirit level.

To the intellect and ego all change represents a new beginning, and a new beginning is understood symbolically as imminent death. Allowing the ego to control our physical action, reaction, and our emotional response is taking away our freedom, equality, integrity, balance, responsibility, commitment, and the unconditional love that we have for ourself.

There are many lessons that we are to learn as humans upon Earth. Our lessons are at all times learned through our relationships. When we do not speak from our love and truth in all relationships, we are consciously resisting our lessons of life and we are denying the power of love and truth that is within us.

Change is a challenge because our beliefs do not honor our power. We have allowed ourself to live from the beliefs of others. Living through the beliefs and behaviors of inequality, judgement, blame, fear, and expectations does not honor who we are.

When the behavior of the physical world is directed towards discrimination, judgement, and blame, the time for change should be accepted and rewarded in celebration of our opportunities to learn and grow. Yet in each physical crisis the masses of humanity continue to seek someone to blame. Life's crises are here to teach us change not blame. When the focus of the physical mind continues with an expectation of judgement and blame it is being controlled by the ego because the ego is afraid of change.

Our fear of assessing and changing beliefs that no longer serve us has allowed us to create a distortion in the energy upon Earth. Many believe in change, seek inner and higher changes of self, and want to explore methods of protecting Earth and the Universe. Others continue to fanatically protect the old beliefs that come from the primitive levels of our soul growth. This protection is the symbol that represents the ego and spirit tug-of-war in the mesocosmic level of society.

Our physical house can easily be destroyed. But the tree from which our house was built has been created by God and it will regrow. We can destroy our physical body, but we will live again. An understanding of the eternal life within us should give us the energy of hope, faith, and trust, because what God has created will live eternally. We are part of the Creator, we have been created by the intention of the Creator, and we are eternal. We bring the destruction of ourself, our society, and the world upon ourselves to serve as our lessons of change and growth.

When we judge and have the expectation that someone has to be blamed for every crisis within our life, we are overlooking the reality that our life is about us. Our responsibility in life is to live from our love, truth, and perfection. If one person or a group of people are not living from their soul and spirit, we compound their lesson by rewarding their destructive behavior and casting blame on a passive participant. Our savior lesson allows us to enhance our victim energy and misdirect our own feelings of guilt and fear.

As a society our behaviors and beliefs have not supported equality as an inalienable right of the HUMAN. We have not supported freedom, integrity, balance, responsibility, commitment, love, or truth by our actions.

Our support has been only within the delusion of support through our thoughts and words. The support of greed, dishonesty, discrimination, victimization, abuse, judgement, blame, and control has been the reality of our behavior and beliefs. Words of freedom and equality have been spoken, but the actions of our society have not been consistent with our words, actions, and our laws. We have created dishonesty not truth. In our dishonesty we create fear. Love, truth, and equality cannot be separate from our actions. They are one, as we are one.

Unequal behavior can be seen within the actions of individuals and society, as it reigns rampant. Our vision of support is of the right intention but from the imperfect reasoning of the intellect and ego mind, which fails to respect the intention by valuing it with our actions. *When our individual actions are initiated from the energy of control and fear, the results will be coming from the convoluted energy that is being created.*

This convoluted energy supports our greed, discrimination, victimization, abuse, and control because negative energy attaches itself to negative energy and the expansion of fear continues. The results of this convoluted negative energy are clearly visible in our government, schools, health care, businesses, finances, corporations, religions, and within many individual relationships.

All aspects of society are formed from the individual contribution and cooperation of our thoughts, words, and actions. If love, truth, and perfection is not present within the individual, it will not be reflected within our society. Love, truth, and perfection can only be present when our personal energy is coming from our soul and spirit. This is our lesson of responsibility.

Our lessons of responsibility are becoming glaringly obvious as we observe the reactions and crises that we confront on all levels of society. Our sense of inadequacy for our own personal accountability and responsibility began with the religious belief that a Messiah was coming to save the Hebrew nation. Believing that someone else is responsible for saving us creates society and the world as our victims as we fail to help ourself.

When Jesus arrived on Earth his teachings were that man must save himself by living from his internal love, truth, and equality in his daily actions. Jesus was very clear that each and every man must accept accountability and responsibility for his own actions, which would allow him to merge his divine nature with his physical nature. Because of Jesus's internal understanding of his own soul and spirit self, he denied that he was the Messiah who had come to save humanity. Jesus did not feel that the teachings of Moses were the teachings that were appropriate for the day. He knew that God was love, not wrath. He knew that God was truth, not greed. He knew that all of humanity was equal and that all should be treated equally.

The Hebrews and the Romans were not happy about Jesus's refusal to accept the responsibility and accountability for all of humanity. They were fearful and angry because his teachings were the opposite of their beliefs, and therefore they planned his death. But in their belief in his death, they were free to follow and teach their own beliefs that Jesus was the Messiah and would save humanity. Jesus had the power to save himself and others, but it was never his intention to use that power indiscriminately. He wanted each and every person to discover the power of his own divine nature and to live and to die from his own internal power.

Jesus never taught what man wanted to hear. And Jesus knew that man would live his lessons one at a time through his life experiences, because man refused to hear his words. The beliefs about Jesus became revered by many with the perception of his death. But Jesus was revered by only a few in his physical lifetime.

Today's belief that if we believe in Jesus we will be saved is a continuation of the ego belief that allows control, discrimination, crime, greed, abuse, fear, hate, and multiple other atrocities to be committed in the name of religion. The only true religion focuses upon the love, truth, and equality of humanity and lives according to those thoughts, words, and actions. Man's perception of giving the responsibility of being saved to Jesus rather than accepting it himself has allowed the individual and society to experience the lesson of individual responsibility in all other aspects of life.

We expect the physician to be responsible for our health and if he fails to save us we will legally blame and judge him. We relinquish our personal responsibility to search and to learn as free thinkers to a school system that blindly adheres to accepted belief. If we find ourself in financial crisis, we expect someone else to be responsible for saving us. If we commit a crime, we expect the government to be responsible for protecting us. If we are greedy and controlling, we expect others to be responsible for giving us love despite our behavior.

Throughout the ages we have resisted accepting the responsibility for our thoughts, words, and actions. Yet our expectations of reward have expanded through our greed. Restricting the balance and equality of the female mind in all aspects of society has allowed discrimination, inequality, greed, control, and all of the negative aspects of the intellect and ego energy of our male mind to control our family life, our society, and the world. The results of our beliefs can be found in the history of religions, cultures, and nations.

The only way to restore balance within the world today is to balance the contribution of the female soul and spirit mind with the male mind of the intellect and ego. Our female mind is the energy of love and truth. Our male mind is the energy of fear and control. This is our lesson in balance.

For many thousands of years, all conflict has been settled with war, murder, and imprisonment. This is the male mind that competes by using fear and control as its defense. The female mind will restore the art of communication and cooperation in settling disputes. Love and truth will be the inspiration and motivation that will guide all interaction. It behooves us to always act in compassion, love, truth, and humility; energy is contagious. We have walked the path that others are now walking. It does not serve our own growth to be pulled down to a lower path of reality.

As our collective consciousness shifts to a new perception of individual responsibility, freedom of thought and expression, equality, integrity, balance, commitment, and unconditional love, we will begin to build a new and beautiful society that will allow us unlimited growth.

Homosexuality is one way for the individual to actively seek to balance the soul and spirit of self with the intellect and ego of self. It is a lesson in our path of evolution as we learn balance. The denial of the power of the female energy has been apparent within society and within the individual. If we find ourself living a dual nature, it becomes evident that both natures are a part of us. Homosexuality frequently follows a life of homophobia. Protesting any activity with anger and fear in our heart attaches us to the karmic energy of future lifetimes, where we will seek to understand by being what we so protest we don't want.

Our denial of the lesson of balance is seen through discrimination, greed, savior beliefs, victimization, control, abuse, dishonesty, and fear. Balance will continue to be a lesson within the individual, the society, and the world until it is learned with total clarity. As more individuals are challenged to create balance, we will see homosexuality and disease expanding.

Judgement has become an integrated structure of our life, expanding our fear and controlling our activities and worthwhile intentions. Judgement and blame become our first thoughts upon hearing, seeing, thinking, feeling, touching, tasting, and smelling. We have designed our life and our physical world from the energy of our judgemental thoughts, words, and actions. Judgement is a weighing of events to create conflict, competition, and fear through the relativity of emotions and events. It is a belief in all aspects of life being right or wrong, black or white, good or bad. Judgement is the intellect and ego in action.

Living in judgement is our way of learning our lesson of unconditional love. All judgement is living life in the lesson of the opposites. Judgement is the way of reflecting our fear to the external world around us. When we are judging others, we are in reality judging ourself. The standard beliefs and behaviors that we use as our personal reality checklist, we also use to judge others. Therefore, all judgement of others is identical to our judgement of self and is being mirrored back to us.

We may be challenged to share the love and truth of our heart with others, but we will freely and gladly share our judgement. This allows us to see that judgement is our physical nature and is familiar to us. The love and truth within our hearts is our divine nature and may be unfamiliar to us. Anytime that we are asked to share our thoughts, we will automatically share those that are familiar and acceptable to our perception of self within our intellect.

We unwittingly expose our true personality and character

traits through the energy of our thoughts, words, and actions each time that we communicate.

Communication occurs through the energy of all of our senses, our physical body, our thoughts, our words, and our actions. Truth is the consistency of our thoughts, words, and actions. If we think one thing, say something else, and act in yet another way, we have shown the falsity of ourself. We have shown the self-judgement that exists within us. We have shown our own state of doubt, confusion, fragmentation, dishonesty, self-abuse, imbalance, discrimination, inequality, and ego control. If we are disrespectful, angry, nasty, abusive, judgemental, argumentative, or critical, we are wearing our personality and our fear as a cloak to mask the true us. And many times we will be unaware of the message that we send to others through our behavior.

Understanding that we live and experience different images of our life lessons in every facet of our life will expand our aware consciousness and change our perception of reality. Communication at all levels of sensing is our way of changing self by changing our level of awareness of our reality.

The male is more willing to change his external, physical possessions than his internal perceptions of awareness and reality. Man has designed a physical world that is symbolic of our need to change. Our world is a trigger to help us understand that if we can change our external world, we can change our internal world. If we can go from carving words into stone and sand to working with words electronically, we can see our capabilities. If we look at what we can do intellectually with machines, we can understand that we too can change into one mind that is magnificent.

It is through our inspirations, motivations, industrial development, and intellectual expansion that we have been continuously bombarded with triggers to unite ourself. Finding ourself behind an emotional veil subjects us to a continual electronic storm that keeps pounding and punching at the veil. The soul and spirit is consistent in its determination to rend our veil and to help us expand into the true power of our one mind.

Within time, tiny pinholes begin to appear in our veil. Next, there are rips and tears that create bigger and bigger openings. When we look through a pinhole, our vision of the outside is seen through a tunnel of perception. As the veil is more heavily damaged, our vision allows us to view the terrain on the other side with a different perception. The constancy of the electrical onslaught against our protective shell of the ego will in time rend our veil once and for all time.

The mind energy that is the most important to us is our female mind. Our mind consciousness is seen within our personality, character traits, everyday actions, thoughts, words that are spoken, and the multiple experiences and events that we become involved with in life. The female mind is loving, truthful, caring, sharing, cooperative, and nurturing. The female mind can be found in both males and females. When we look at our life, we can see the symbols of our lessons being acted out within our physical experiences. Each experience, when it is understood as a lesson, becomes a diamond paving our path of soul growth. The female mind evaluates life experiences differently than the male mind.

Our male mind is seen through our intellectual interpretation of life, the organization of societies and communities, the laws that are made within the judicial system, the religious organizations, the health care system, the educational system, the banking system, the government, and within private corporations. The way that life is carried on within a family, a society, and a nation reflects the energy of those who are making the decisions, the rules, and the judgements. The male mind can be found in both females and males. When we assess the conditions of our families, societies, and the world, it becomes apparent that change is long overdue. The male assessment of reality no longer works in our society by itself, and we must balance our life by seeking the female influence.

It is our mind and the level of perception of our mind that determines the functioning energy of life. When the perception of life is one of fear, that is the nature of the personality of the organization. We have males that function in female energy and females that function in male energy. The personality of any business can be determined by the happiness and creativity of the people involved. If there is love, truth, and integrity within the work place, female energy is being exercised.

If the business operates fairly, with compassion, mercy, truth, equality, and love as its guidelines, it is being operated by female energy. If a business is unfair to employees, based upon greed and ego-fulfillment, if it discriminates, harasses employees or clients, if everyone wants to quit and fear and insecurity are prevalent, it is being operated by male energy.

As the shifting from the male to the female consciousness begins to occur within society, there will be mass confusion until a balance is reached. This confusion rests within the mind and can be a source of anger and fear because the identity of roles is defined by our interpretation of gender. Manipulation can be judged as female energy. Inconsistent behavior can be judged as female energy. Any blame or judgement that can be directed at the female specifically or the gender collectively will be used as a resistance technique to avoid releasing old beliefs. This judgement should not be supported as significant, as the shift is essential to the health of our society. Additional confusion can occur if the mind energy is not consistent with the physical gender role.

Family and societal changes are not easy for us to accept unless we understand the necessary reasons for the change. Each of us has a divine nature which can be brought forth into our daily life if we can release our fear.

Our divine nature is the hero within us. The ego is the demon dragon, spitting fire, creating havoc, eating people alive as we are condemned to hellfire and damnation. But the hero, the hero of our spirit, will win the tug-of-war eventually because the rage and the anger of our ego is a finite energy and our spirit is eternal. Our spirit never gives up. Our spirit will continue its symbolic triggers within the mind of humanity until humanity is ready to hear and ready to see. But we must see, not through our tunnel vision and not with the male, intellectual interpretation of life, but with both of our eyes wide open as we learn to bask in the humility of our ego.

Our tug-of-war did not just begin with our aware consciousness of today's change. It began in the days of Jesus of Nazareth, the days of Adam and Eve, the days of the ancient continents that have been lost with their physically, intellectually focused cultures, such as Atlantis, Lemuria, and Plesaideius. These cultures evolved into intellectual societies, but they denied the influence of their female soul and spirit. When it is time to change and grow, the female energy must always be honored. The female has always been the creator of life, the mother, the hunter, the caretaker, the nurturer, the teacher, the doctor, and the provider.

There were many great women of wisdom and ingenuity that are not recorded in history because of the ego fear and beliefs of the male mind. It is time for the female power to become active in our world. The female mind is the perfect energy to interpret challenges and solutions for our society and the Universe.

In the world of Buddha the female, the yin, was seen as cool, closed, and contracting, and the yang, the male, was interpreted as open, free, and expanding, which described their understanding of life as a description of the sexual organs. This was the ego image of self that has created a lasting perception for man and one which continues to control us today. The male mind and ego lives from the fear of life that is perceived from behind its veil of beliefs. The beliefs of the male mind have created separation within our mind, our body, our family, and our society. Few of those beliefs have validity in our rapidly changing soul. It is the female mind that is providing the inspiration and motivation to allow us to change, because the female mind has the wisdom and ingenuity to understand the importance of our change and growth.

As each of us change from the male interpretation of life, we are going to change the definition of yin and yang. We are going to change the definition of male and female. We are going to replace our fear with love. We are going to live in a balanced freedom of unconditional love that will elevate us into a "Heaven upon Earth."

We will change our society from being a male-dominated and interpreted society to being a unified energy of equality from the trinity of our one mind. It is by our eternal unity that we are inspired and motivated to live from our love, truth, and perfection.

Working to expand our internal self is the first step toward change. Changing self is the only change that creates results within the Universe. If we allow our intellect and ego to overwhelm us by bringing old primitive beliefs into our conscious mind, we will shake in terror at the slightest perception of change. Change requires that we look at ourself with strength and courage, knowing that change is our responsibility and our soul purpose. It was through the force of One that the Universe was created. It is through the force of one that it will change and evolve.

We create our miracles of being in the way that we live. If we deny or resist our dual energy of self, it is our choice to limit who we are. It is our choice and our opportunity to live by the expansiveness, the openness, and the love that is within. When we resist living in "Heaven on Earth," but choose to remain in the hell of our physical creation it is our choice. When we understand and seek success, it is there within us. It is our responsibility to reach out and grab the golden ring of life as our miracle.

4.

Our Soul
*M*ind

◊

"The ascent of the human soul to the supreme Spirit is that soul's highest aim and necessity, for that is the supreme reality; but there can be too the descent of the Spirit and its powers into the world and that would justify the existence of the material world also, give a meaning, a divine purpose to the creation and solve its riddle."

Sri Aurobindo, On Himself

Our soul is the self-reflective internal memory within us that is eternally spirit-connected and is forever striving to discern truth and love within our mind that is evident in our physical nature.

Our soul is the connecting bridge between our physical self and our spirit self. It receives the reflection of love and truth from our spirit and consciously seeks to relay that spirit reflection into our physical nature.

Our soul is the accumulation of lessons from all physical experiences within our eternal life cycle. The soul is our infinite memory of our physical experience and an eternal energy of our divine nature.

Becoming aware of our inherent truth and love inspires us to rise above the lower nature of our physical senses. Our soul is our bridge to growing and changing our physical perception from fear for survival to love and truth. Becoming consciously aware of our spirit allows our soul to reflect truth and love into our physical life experiences.

The self-consciousness that we develop as physical beings is not the soul of us. Our physical self-consciousness is the reflection of our beliefs that we have woven into the fiber of a veil that surrounds our intellect to become our ego. Our ego image of self-consciousness reflects into our intellect, controlling our physical behavior.

The reflection of our ego self-image allows us to judge ourself as inadequate or unworthy physically and intellectually. Our ego reflection then becomes the belief of the intellect. The ego wants the intellect to accept the reflected image of itself as the soul. Through this reflected image of our ego, our self-consciousness becomes the behavior of our physical nature. As our self-consciousness grows and changes within the ego, the ego image can change from a feeling of unworthiness and inadequacy to a feeling of superiority. At all levels of change the ego continues to pass its own reflected image off to the intellect as our soul.

When the ego reaches the heights of its feelings of infallibility, it will try to firmly establish itself within the intellect as our spirit. This self-consciousness of the ego that believes itself to be the soul and spirit happens when the soul and spirit is tugging at the veil of the ego for acknowledgement. The ego is a chameleon because it will masquerade, using many disguises to play different roles, while holding its position of confining and reflecting the intellect.

Our daily life experience always reflects the ego-controlling behavior of our self-consciousness towards the intellect. It is the feelings of self-consciousness that allow the ego to fear judgement. Judgement is feared because the ego is in judgement. Anytime that judgement is feared, the intellect finds it challenging to speak the truth. We are being controlled by our ego's self-conscious fear of discovery, which allows the events of our life to feel traumatic. If we are asked to be self-expressive, we will have a morbid fear of being judged because we are reflecting our judgement of everyone else. Our intellectual mind thinks in judgement without a conscious awareness of judging.

Many times we attempt to control our self-consciousness by separating ourself from other people and events, but the ego can choose obsessive involvement as well as separation. Our fear of judgement can begin to dramatically control our lives in relationships and careers.

Speaking to small or large crowds will cause a physical panic for some. And others may speak incessantly about nothing, which is the opposite ego response to the fear of speaking as the chatter masks our real feelings. This is a way of ego distraction as it forces attention to its mindless behavior, which is focused upon meaningless thoughts and words but no action. The ego likes to hear the sound of its voice because it provides one more physical sense barrier between it and the soul and spirit. The ego is a non-productive, controlling mind force because it creates stagnation through fear and fragmentation. The ego can effectively short-circuit the intellect and prevent any help from the soul mind through the soul memory.

Our soul memory is a comprehensive record of our life experiences from the moment that we were created as *thought* energy. Our soul mind is our subconscious mind. The information that is stored within our subconscious mind will frequently begin to be remembered as we rend the veil of the ego and free the intellect. Those memories that flash into our mind will be images of the lessons that we are now experiencing. Since we learn our lessons through the negative experiences first, our memories of past physical experiences may be negative.

If we are involved in the lesson of learning to love ourself in this lifetime, we may suddenly remember episodes in past lifetimes of physical, emotional, or sexual abuse. Abuse is the opposite of the lesson of loving self. Our karmic soul memory can be perceived as a memory of this lifetime until we are open to understanding that we have memory available to us that goes far beyond the reality of this lifetime. Our past life memories are triggered by the soul and spirit to remind us through passive memory, which helps us avoid active participation in the negative aspects of abuse in this lifetime.

Part of the lesson of loving self is learning to accept the responsibility for our personal life design. Until we can freely and knowingly accept full responsibility for our reality, there will be the temptation to blame and judge other people whom we perceive as being responsible for our multiple lessons. The intellect and ego will not necessarily perceive the difference between past life memory and present life memory because there is no awareness in the intellect and ego of infinity since they are finite.

Without this differentiation being understood, multiple dramas of our past lives can and will be remembered and judged as having happened in this lifetime as old karmic lessons are ready for completion. Understanding this soul and spirit memory will provide us with the insight to accept the lesson of loving who we are in this moment. If we can't understand the lesson, we will allow ourself to create new negative experiences of abuse to support us in seeing what we don't want. Attaching ourself to the negative memories of this life or a past life is not appropriate to our soul growth. Forcing ourself to relive a drama of negative experience that may be 1,000 years old is self-abuse. Self-abuse is the negative approach to learning to love ourself.

As an example, the experience of sexual abuse that is unknowingly stored in soul memory may be perceived to have occurred within this lifetime. Relatives who are completely innocent of the abuse will be blamed because the difference between past life memory and current life memory is not understood. The karmic experience cannot be learned as the lesson of love if we attach ourself to the perception of present abuse.

As our growth continues, more and more examples of this

phenomenon will be apparent within our society and will cover a broad spectrum of experiences. As the soul and spirit move closer to the intellect, past memories become more available to the conscious mind. Belaboring or wallowing in any negative experience will not allow us to experience soul growth. Acceptance of our lessons will allow us to move forward and release old karmic ties.

Using our moral consciousness acknowledges the presence of our soul and spirit as the magnificence of our internal mind. The realization that our intellect and ego is reacting in fear to our soul and spirit consciousness will be an acceptance of our internal female power.

Our soul cannot exist as part of our intellect without moral thinking and virtuous actions. We must accept the responsibility for our moral assessment of our own activities and our own memory. All of our good thoughts, words, and actions come from the love and truth of our spirit being reflected from our soul into the reality of our daily life.

When the intellect denies the existence of our soul and spirit, confusion will be rampant within the intellectual ego mind as past memories begin to surface. When the subconscious memories of our soul mind are believed to be memories from our current lifetime, we set our crisis drama in motion. When the memories of our past lives are not recognized for what they are, anger, denial, and total emotional chaos can be our physical reaction within this lifetime and we will spend our beautiful life being unhappy and depressed as we cast blame to others.

A soul that is intellectually denied is a persistent and courageous soul, which challenges the ego and intellect. Intellectual denial of our soul and spirit is the physical manifestation of the internal war that exists between the soul and spirit and the intellect and ego. Emotional conflict mirrors the loss of harmony that is being reflected between the soul and spirit consciousness of our divine nature and the strictly focused intellect and ego self-consciousness of our physical nature. Our physical nature will adamantly resist the presence of our divine nature because it is a threat to our ego.

Our purpose of life is to learn to live from the inspiration and motivation of our soul and spirit while in our physical reality. Our soul and spirit cannot be documented by scientific testing. Yet each of us fully understands that we have a soul and a spirit within us. We feel the presence of the love and truth reflecting from our soul and spirit but our physical experience has not prepared us to acknowledge our soul and spirit influence. If our recognition of God is accepted as external to us, we are not prepared to understand the good that is within us.

The consciousness of our divine nature is an internal understanding of the magnificence within us, whether or not we acknowledge and accept that special power intellectually. Without an intellectual knowledge of the source of love and truth that we feel, we search for love and truth in another person. Our external search then creates self-judgement of our own worth when we feel that our need for love and truth is not forthcoming from another.

We consistently mirror our own energy to others. Therefore, if we do not love ourself, we will never attract true love because we will not know in our heart what true love is. When we are consciously aware that we are living our truth and love in our physical lives, we find ourself with an inner peace and joy that far surpasses any "need" that can be fulfilled by others in our physical experiences. Knowing that love and truth are reflections of our own internal soul and spirit helps us to understand that we cannot receive love and truth until we can give our love and truth.

Becoming aware of our soul consciousness is a gradual happening within us. Our awareness is triggered by our soul reflection of love and truth within our daily, external, physical living. We begin to have a greater appreciation for life and ourself. We awaken in the morning with enthusiasm and excitement. The day becomes a glorious opportunity to live. Nature begins to be perceived with more intensity and appreciation. Colors are more vivid. Food becomes an eating experience, where the natural flavors trigger all of our senses. Foods with chemicals become unreal and unacceptable in our life. Clothes suddenly become an issue when we find our body unable to tolerate anything but natural fabrics. Relationships with friends become more important, and lovers are chosen from a new value system.

The three dimensions of us—the physical, the soul, and the spirit—are intricately interwoven within the multiple levels of growth that we experience within our physical life. Each dimension of our energy is constantly present within us but not constantly acknowledged. Our soul and spirit seeks acknowledgement. We can only give and receive that which we are conscious of as real within ourself and our life.

If our perception of reality is limited to the external, physical world, that is all we will be able to give and to receive from our family, lovers, friends, and career. We will give money, status, education, and possessions to those we love, but we will not be able to give the love and truth from our heart or the wisdom from our soul. Embarrassed to share our true feelings, ideas, imagination, and emotion, we will keep our love, truth, and wisdom separate and hidden from everyone, including ourself.

We learn from our perception of each moment of our physical experience. If our conscious awareness is suppressed by the control of our physical senses, our perception of life is severely handicapped. Our physical senses are our path of acceptance for our soul. Our senses allow us to feel internally.

If we feel that another person is responsible for loving us, we are denying the love of self that is being reflected from our soul and spirit within. As we deny the truth of our own loving self, we deny the reflection of love and truth from other people. If we deny the love and truth of others, we will hide the love and truth within ourself. We are suppressing our ability to feel the love within us and within others.

As we totally understand each level of our soul and its relationship to each level of each dimension of our growth, we experience soul evolution. Our conscious understanding of growth begins gradually as we move closer to the Cycle of Understanding within our dimension of soul. We have lived through many levels of evolution without a conscious awareness of our soul growth. But as the soul moves through the Cycle of Awareness, we become more aware. The beginning level of knowledge in our soul growth focuses our search within the external level of our intellectual mind as it develops our conscious awareness. Our awareness of self as a physical being must be learned before we can understand ourself as a soul being.

To discover our personal wisdom and truth we must be open to understanding our inner soul and to living from the moral character and personality of our spirit self.

Acknowledging and accepting the inspiration and motivation within us as the inherent energies of our spirit and soul is our first step to understanding in the second cycle of soul growth. The inspiration and motivation of the spirit and soul are *thought* energies that must then be integrated into us physically through the creativity of our intellect.

If we respond to our ideas, imagination, and dreams, we are acknowledging the inspiration of our spirit. If we respond to our inner knowing that tells us how to make an idea work, we are acknowledging the motivation of our soul. If our ideas and our knowing are brought to fruition as a reality of our life, we are acknowledging our physical ability to create. This is the way to use our intellect, soul, and spirit as our integrated mind. This is how we create our reality from the merging of our divine nature with our physical nature.

Understanding the power of our integrated mind as our inherent human consciousness of one mind is the path to learning how to heal our body and mind, our society, and our world.

We can only perceive our life experiences from our level of conscious awareness. Without an active awareness of the way that we create our life and our experiences, we will continue to repeat our experiences with an escalating level of drama. We frequently live multiple repetitions of the same life experience before we become conscious of our need to be totally aware of what we are creating. We always create physical experiences to symbolize our soul lessons.

When we create only from our intellect we perceive creation, intention, and freedom of choice from the basis of physical gain not creativity. Physical gain is judged by the intellect in terms of quantity: how many lovers, how much money, how many possessions, etc. Creativity is acknowledged by the soul in terms of the quality: the love, the truth, the beauty, the magnificence, the service, the caring, the sharing, etc. Without a conscious awareness of the power within our mind, we will continue to create our life experiences from the intellect and ego as the negative images of our soul lessons.

We have been taught that our intellect has the capability of learning, remembering, and analyzing. Our intellect is only one small part of our mind but it is the externally focused part that we choose to separate and focus upon. With time we learn to accept that we have a rational mind and an intuitive mind, although we usually question their thought communications with our intellect and refuse to follow them. Our rational mind is our subconscious soul mind. Our intuitive mind is our unconscious spirit mind.

It is our personal responsibility to search for our soul truth and our spirit love that is within us. A determined search will awaken us to the knowledge and understanding that we are more than our external image of intellect. Searching expands our consciously aware mind to its greatest potential. Searching within gives us the opportunity to discover the beauty and magnificence of who we are as a unity of self, externally and internally. No one else can make our search for us.

Change is inherent within us as individuals, society, and the world. We are energy, the Earth is energy, and the Universe is energy. Energy by its very nature must move and change. Despite our intellectual resistance to physical or mental change, change is a given in our life. We change from infancy to childhood, to puberty, to adolescence, to adulthood, to mid-life, to later-life, and we continue on after that. From the moment of conception we begin our path of physical change, and it continues until our moment of death as our choice for a new beginning.

We do not have the power to interfere with change, except on a temporary basis. As our body and life change, our mind and soul change. We experience soul evolution whether or not we are consciously aware of the change that is occurring in our soul growth. The changes that occur in our physical life are symbols of the changes that occur in our soul life. Change is being initiated within our soul consciousness to facilitate a shift in our collective consciousness. It is our collective consciousness that will change and expand society into the next level of soul evolution for the mesocosm.

If we are going to be worthy of imminent change, it is time to look at ourself with a broader perspective of our mind. We must go beyond the ability of the intellect to gather knowledge as fact and begin to understand our purpose of being, changing, and growing as a Higher Universal Mana upon Earth. We cannot rest complacently upon what we know, but we must seek to understand why we have the ability to learn, to think, to speak, and to bring about change within the Universe.

We must grow into an understanding of who we are, how our trinity of one mind works, why we have been given such a magnificent mind, and how the mind can heal us as individuals, a society, and as a world.

Change is what the human consciousness has been about since we first began as *thoughtforms*. All energy, including physical matter, must continue to change and grow to prevent decay. When fruit has reached its maximum growth, it falls from the tree and the decay begins that returns it to dust. We are also a fruit of God's tree, and we have the ability to grow again and again. We are different than fruit from a tree because we have the ability to think, to speak, and to experience dramatic change and growth in each lifetime. Without change within us inertia creates stasis of our mind, body, society, and the world, and we return to dust.

We are our soul mind, physical body, and spirit essence. We are the community, the society, the nation, and the world. What we believe, we create as our personal life, our social life, and our political action. If we choose not to be active in life, then life will begin its process of decay. This holds true for us as individuals, for society, for government, and for all businesses. The combination of our beliefs becomes the actions that we live through the physical experiences of our life.

It is through our beliefs that we create who we are. If our beliefs are rigid and unchanging, we create the repetition of past events. And as we live in our repetitive state, we resist change in every aspect of our mind. We become like a dog attached to a rope and tied to a stake. We run around and around the stake, at the end of our rope, repeating the same experiences over and over again. After a few revolutions around the stake, the rope begins to shorten and we are on a downward spiral of devolution. This constant repetition begins to make us feel like a victim, and we begin to blame others for tying us to the stake.

But we aren't animals. We are the thinkers of the world, and we have been given the power of creation, free choice, free will, and free intention. Our beliefs create our ego which becomes the veil that separates us from our soul and spirit. If we resist changing our beliefs, we will resist acknowledging that we have a soul and spirit. Our religious beliefs do not always honor the soul and spirit that is within us, because the belief directs us to a God external to us. The belief that God is external to us was created by the ego of ancient man because of fear and ignorance during the reflection level of our soul growth.

It is this separation from the reflection of our soul and spirit that allows us to see ourself as a victim. Our belief in the separation of ourself from God separates us from our internal magnificence and attaches us to the beliefs of the past, which we have grown beyond. It is this separation of our minds that holds us captive in fear. The ego continues to fear change because it has no respect or value for the unfamiliar, which it cannot understand. The ego is determined to survive as our protective veil of beliefs to prevent any change from occurring.

Our mind is pure energy. Our body is the energy of matter. If we stop using our body or our mind, decay begins as disease. If we believe that our intellect is all there is to our mind and we deny our soul and spirit mind, decay or disease will result. Decay does not affect the soul and spirit mind; it will only affect the intellectual mind and the physical body as our finite energy. Disease creates the opportunity for us to change our perception of life or to choose death as a new beginning.

In earlier times of our growth when the soul and spirit were being used more fully, many individuals lived very long lives and *chose* death as a new beginning. Because our focus is now intensely directed within the intellect, we limit our ability to live long and productive lives. Our lifespan can be changed as we learn to use the power of our soul mind. *The enigma of scientific knowledge is its consistent search within the physical, external world to find ways of prolonging human life. Life will be prolonged upon Earth when our intellect is integrated and the understanding of our one mind is expanded.*

After birth, the first three levels of the Law of Sevens are consumed with the development of our physical body and our intellectual mind. This is the period of human development when the development of beliefs also plays a significant role in the development of the ego. During the second, third, fourth, and fifth levels of the Law of Sevens, the ego is busily trying to shut out the soul and spirit energy within our mind.

From age seven until age forty-two, our belief system grows from the exposure that we have in our physical experiences. Our perception of the experience allows us to absorb beliefs from that level of perception. Our perception at age seven would be different from our perception at age thirty. Therefore, a child and a parent will have two different perceptions of the same event, which becomes an important issue of communication between grown children and parents and dramatically affects our soul growth.

During the first level of the Law of Sevens the infant and child is pure soul and spirit until the merging of beliefs with the physical mind, which begins around age seven. Keeping our mind open will prevent our attachment to obstructive beliefs. But staying open becomes the challenge for the soul and spirit during this period of developing perceptions. The family environment has not supported our soul growth with a conscious acceptance of our soul existence. The religious foundations that teach about God as a wrathful, judgemental force external to us deny the presence of our internal soul and spirit as a powerful, supporting energy force. Our external perception of God creates our fear of internal possession by unknown spirits and closes the mind to our true magnificence.

The challenge to keep our mind open will frequently be addressed by the soul and spirit in our life design. Lessons are woven into our life design to expose us to our soul and spirit as it protects us. Two lessons that are frequently used to keep the mind open are the experiences of childhood disease and child abuse. When the pain of physical life is critical in childhood the child stays fully in soul and spirit, using its powerful supporting energy force, which protects the intellect while giving the soul freedom to work with the soul lesson.

In the adult life of this child the mind will never be able to focus only on the intellect because the veil is open to the influence of soul and spirit. If the physical support is not there to support the child in understanding the soul and spirit, a phenomenon can occur of living subconsciously in past memory, which would be considered mental illness by science.

When we are actively working with the lesson of loving

ourself, we will design experiences of abuse into our life. The abuse will challenge us with our freedom of choice to love, respect, and value ourself and not to reward the abuse. Abuse can take the form of self-abuse, mental, psychological, physical, verbal, or sexual abuse, and it can be perceived in all relationships at some level. If the lesson has not been learned, we will continue exposing ourself to abuse until we understand that the lesson no longer serves us. The perception that we have of the abuse will control our belief and our attachment to the drama. When we no longer accept abuse, we are learning the lesson of loving ourself.

Our perception of events, which we present to the mind as fact, creates our veil of beliefs that surrounds our intellect as ego and blocks out the memory of our divine nature. Our perceptions can trigger or block old beliefs by the manner in which they are seen. For example, many people that are reared in the Jewish faith may not consciously feel an attachment to the belief in original sin and its emotional energy of unworthiness and victimization. But original sin has become a collective consciousness that all of humanity has experienced, in the same way that all of humanity has experienced abuse. Unworthiness and victimization are profound emotions of many in the Jewish faith which they are dramatically attached to and which they live as normal emotions of life.

The belief in original sin is a form of self-abuse. If our conscious memory denies either of these emotional experiences of original sin or abuse, the ego will block the memory longer than usual as we work with our lessons in the physical experience. There is no stigma attached to the experience of these lessons for the soul. Abusing self in any way is the opposite of loving self.

Abuse and the belief in original sin are both lessons of the soul and the stigma is only created through our own judgement of having committed sins or having been abused. Our intellect and ego believes that someone must be judged and blamed for these events. The ego seeks revenge, not learning. In reality, our soul and spirit designs each life based upon the lessons that we choose to learn. Sometimes we challenge ourself more in some lives than we do in others, but each soul lesson is cleverly thought out and designed by our soul and spirit.

When we learn to live in the moment, we begin to understand that this life and our past lives are important only in terms of our soul growth. The drama of our physical experiences is simply our soul method of learning. It is our ego that thinks we should belabor, from birth until death, each and every negative perception of our physical dramas. If we believe that we must blame and judge someone for every word they speak and every act they commit, we will never have time to live our own life productively or happily. Most important, we cannot learn when we are living in fear and judgement, whether our fear and judgement originates in our present life or in our historical past.

The ego remains a driving force in the restriction of our human consciousness until we can see that we are totally responsible for who we are and make the decision to begin changing ourself, our life, and our beliefs.

The beliefs from which we formulate our perceptions in early life may not serve us effectively in our later years. When we can look within ourself, we can examine our outmoded beliefs and release our attachment to them. Physical growth in each lifetime becomes an escalated pattern of the evolutionary growth of all three dimensions of self. Our physical life is a mirror image of our chosen lessons for soul growth. If our conscious awareness does not change and include our soul and spirit, our physical dramas escalate and we will find ourself with physical and mental disease.

As we move through the Law of Sevens in our physical development, we are symbolizing by our growth the entire Cycle of Development and that part of the Cycle of Awareness that we have traveled in our soul evolution. Our lessons will be quickly reviewed by the body and mind. We will challenge ourself with all lessons that we have yet to complete. These challenges will be designed and woven into our relationships throughout our life. If we camouflage the soul and spirit during this review period, we will challenge ourself with physical crises designed to trigger our soul memory. *Our soul is not comfortable when we live in a state of physical mindlessness corrosive from the sands of time.*

Our beliefs that develop the veil around our intellect to block the reflection of the soul and spirit can be worked out in our physical exposures to family, society, and education, or they can remain karmic lessons for future Earth lives of the soul.

All ego beliefs resist change. Beliefs that become obsessive, fanatical, egotistical, or self-serving are the biggest challenges for the soul to overcome and change. Each of these levels of beliefs will allow the opportunity for physical or emotional crisis as a way of changing the focus of the mind from the external to the internal perspective.

Some of us choose to change our wardrobe every season, buy a new car every year, a new boat every two years, new furniture and appliances every five years. Yet when it comes to changing our beliefs, we feel compelled to hang on to what we think we know. We are terrified at the very concept of changing our physical, male beliefs. But it is through changing our beliefs that we have the power to shift our consciousness to our female soul and spirit.

Isn't it perfect that women have always been known to change their minds, but somehow men seem to find it unacceptable to change their minds? The soul and spirit of our female energy is a champion of change. The intellect and ego of our male energy is a stubborn resistor of the slightest change.

The fear of changing our mind is a belief that changing the mind is a sign of weakness. For centuries changing the mind has been permissible for women, identified as the weaker sex, and unacceptable for men, who revel in their image of physical strength and a strong mind. The reason that women find it easier to change their mind than men is because women are the physical symbol of the internal world of soul and spirit energy upon Earth. Men are the physical symbol of the external world, which is intellect- and ego-directed. Soul and spirit welcomes change and our ego resists change.

When we focus only upon the one facet of our mind and exclude all other facets, we are denying the unity of ourself as male, female, and spirit. This separation tends to identify us with the beliefs of our roles as they are defined by society, and it removes us from a consciousness of our own unity as well as from our true path of soul growth. *The soul and spirit female energy is the mother of life. Life is the mother of change. Eve, as the mother of life, gave birth to Adam.*

We were taught, and it is the belief of many, that Adam was created by God from dust and then God created Eve from Adam's rib. This belief defies the entire knowledge and understanding of human creation, but during Biblical times human creation was not understood. When the intellect has no knowledge of why, how, and for what reason an event occurred, the mind perceives the experience and defines it from the limited information that it has available. The examination and reflection upon our creation were all perceptions of our minds that were in the early stages of growth. The parable of Adam and Eve is a perfect example of a perception that ends in an interpretation and continues into the accepted belief of our human consciousness.

Adam and Eve were by no means the first humans that lived upon Earth. This parable was handed down as superstition and myth for many thousands of years before it was recorded. It was recorded as it was perceived by the scribe and it was interpreted many times over as it was perceived by the interpreter. Many intellectuals have dealt with this parable throughout the years and have been faithful to their own beliefs, allowing further changes to occur in the ancient interpretations.

Eve came to Earth as a Christ energy and created Adam as her twin soul energy. Adam was the perfect division of Eve and in the physical form they were opposites. The purpose of Eve and Adam upon Earth was to help man understand his human sexuality and procreation by showing him the joy, pleasure, and family life of the male and female when they join together. Eve and Adam had many children together, and many with other males and females as the lesson of sexuality continued. Eve also experienced the immaculate birth of Seth, who was called the son of Adam. Despite the teachings of Eve and Adam by their example, the lesson of human sexuality and procreation has lasted for millions of years and man continues working with the same lessons today.

Man had no concept of how or why sexual activity was important. He feared woman and for many thousands of years he considered sex with males or animals preferable to intimate interaction with women. This fear of sex also initiated genital mutilation as a common practice. Approaching sex and women from fear has challenged the extinction of the human race multiple times since the beginning of creation. Sex itself was not understood, but conjugal relationships were feared in the mind of the male with even more intensity because it brought with it the lessons of commitment, responsibility, and unity.

In ancient times man did not understand the phenomenon of birth, or why women had this strange capability and men did not. Man created gender roles of control over women in an attempt to control what he could not understand, and those teachings have continued into today's society as remnants of our primitive beliefs and behaviors.

It is the perception of the male as the symbol of physical life that has defined and interpreted life. The male influence created the design because in learning how to be HUMAN, we must first learn how to be physical. The physical, male role of life is symbolized by the rebellious child who has no intention of learning or sharing because he prefers to be separate, angry, and fearful. The soul and spirit, female role of life is symbolized by the nurturing mother, teacher, and lover who stays in her truth with patience and compassion, until her hour has come.

Eve and Adam's visit to Earth was misunderstood in the same way that the visit of the Christ consciousness was misunderstood when she came to Earth the last time as Mary and Jesus. In both instances the beliefs and perceptions of man were not changed, because man was not ready for the step forward in his soul growth that the Christ consciousness was teaching.

Birth was a spirit message to the ancients that was grossly misunderstood from man's level of conscious awareness. His perception and definition of birth, women, and life have resulted in multiple superstitions, including the inequality of the female, human sacrifice, and castration, that have continued into the present century.

The power of the female ability to bring forth new life was viewed through the superstitious perceptions of an ego mind. This acknowledged power within the female allowed the physically self-conscious male to declare the female unclean, inferior, and of unequal status with the male, casting the female into the role of servicing the male sexual appetite, which continues to exist today.

Males did not accept the responsibility for the bringing forth of children into the world, and therefore the love, respect, and value of children was absent from the male heart. Sex was an instinctive physical reaction that was fulfilled without a knowledge or understanding of the purpose or outcome. Man continuously fathered children he never saw and so he had no sense of connection within his mind between the act of sex and human birth. Responsibility, commitment, respect, and value towards the female were not even considered, as the female was primarily considered a possession and therefore was seen as a liability and even a sexual duty for the male in some cultures.

Sex and birth were not connected within the mind as being dependent upon each other. Human life that began as an androgynous reaction became through the division of the twin soul a shared action and a responsibility for procreation. But it has taken the male perception millions of years to understand the connection and to begin to perceive the power and equality of the female.

In reality the female is superior to the male in the same way that the soul and spirit energy is superior in power to the physical energy.

The beliefs in female inequality, inferiority, and uncleanliness were established within the religious foundations of many sects and tribes from the Hebrew nation. This was also a superstitious belief, but not a religious belief, in the early days of our passage into soul growth as human form. Inequality, inferiority, and uncleanliness have become perfect examples of karmic beliefs that are acted out within the physical nature of humanity and must be part of the experiences of life until such time as life can be fully understood. These ancient beliefs created false perceptions of the female that continue to be practiced in society and by many religions. These ancient, misdirected fears set the stage for the life designed by our soul and spirit.

The accepted separation between the male and the female is the symbol of the separation of our physical nature from our divine nature. We, as male and female, must reach a physical and intellectual understanding before we can be of one mind.

We each choose lives as male and as female, creating our own suppression and control in our lessons of each lifetime. Suppression and control is our own personal example of the intellect and ego moving into full gear as our physical nature seeks to protect us from our divine nature. As we act out suppression and control of others in our life experience, we are creating the symbol of our own suppression and control of our soul and spirit, which we will experience in another embodiment if we fail to understand the lesson in this lifetime.

When our male energy is focused upon controlling everything and everybody around it, we are actively symbolizing the suppression and control of our female mind of soul and spirit by our intellect and ego. This represents the control of our love and truth by our fear and judgement, and if we look at our life we will find living examples of our behavior in all of our relationships despite our outward perceptions.

Each and every human being is male as physical energy, female as soul and spirit energy, and God as our perfection of spirit consciousness. We choose our gender consciousness and our physical gender in each embodiment based upon the lessons that we have designed into our physical experience. Therefore, males can have a gender consciousness of their female energy, and females can have a gender consciousness of their male energy, which is different from their physical gender.

Gender lessons are designed as physical life experiences to allow our soul to evolve. The more evolved the soul becomes, the less separation there will be in the gender personalities in human form. As we seek to unite our physical nature as a male consciousness with our divine nature as a female consciousness, we will discover an equality and freedom in our gender unity.

The multiple levels of sexuality within us symbolize our path of soul growth. It is through the sexual focus of our human form that we have designed our lessons of soul evolution. It is our way of learning our freedom of intention, freedom of choice, and freedom of will in always honoring, respecting, and valuing ourself. We are learning to remove sex from our focus on the biologic reaction of physical response and freely choose to honor and celebrate our love and truth. Our beliefs, perceptions, and intention toward our sex life symbolize the internal relationship of our intellect and ego to our soul and spirit. As we are growing on the shadow side of our soul, we will find ourself attached to examination, reflection, and at times the primitive levels of soul growth. Each attachment and each drama has a purpose of teaching us through our physical experience.

The merging of our male and female natures is seeking to create once again the androgynous nature of our spirit. Human life began as androgynous energy and it must return to androgynous energy through our physical experience as a lesson of soul growth. Primitive beliefs and perceptions about sex that do not honor ourself or our mate are strongly attached to the primitive levels of our soul evolution. Heterosexuality and homosexuality both have primitive strings attached if they are practiced promiscuously or in an abusive manner.

As the soul lessons are expanded, the male and female nature will be seen in all of us despite our choice of physical gender. Our merging natures will create many physical dramas for the individuals that believe in role identity and are in denial of their soul and spirit. As the soul evolves through the primitive level, examination level, reflective level, and the knowledge level of soul growth, strings will be attached to the levels they have passed through. These are the karmic streams of energy that represent lessons not yet completed. This will allow abusive acts, confusion, and experimentation to occur as we relive mirror images of lessons that we experienced in our levels of the primitive, examination, and reflection periods of our growth.

The symbol of the physical consciousness within us is manifested as our sexual orientation. We began as a unity of our divine nature of androgyny. As our divine nature was separated from our physical nature, the human was created as male and female. To return to the unity of our divine nature, we must live through the lessons of our physical experience and open our minds beyond the heretical beliefs of history. As our divine nature unites with our physical nature our male and female energies will become one androgynous energy again. We will function as one magnificent mind in our whole physical body from the openness of all our physical senses.

Immaculate conceptions were androgynous births of an advanced soul and spirit creating physical form as an example of a passive lesson for mankind. We are a repetition of the Universal pattern of energy and our mind is the perfect representation of that pattern. The intellect is the microcosm of the energy of physical perception focused within the left lobe of the brain, the soul memory is the mesocosm of soul energy focused within the right lobe of the brain, and the Universal consciousness is the macrocosm of spirit energy focused within the center and back of the brain.

The energy of the macrocosm of our intuitive mind is the point of power of our spirit consciousness which makes us unique as humans. It is this specific point of power that is our Higher Universal Mana. It is the spirit consciousness that bestows upon us the gift of being HUMAN. HUMAN became the first anagram within language.

By accepting our spirit consciousness as our physical self, we elevate our growth through our soul experience into eternal spirit.

We, as humans, are the chosen ones to carry on the expansion of the spirit consciousness of love, truth, and perfection. We are the thinkers of Earth. We are the speakers of Earth. We have the power and the freedom of choice to become the Gods of Earth. We are the symbol of the second coming of the Christ consciousness upon Earth. When we are totally conscious of who we are and why we are here, we will be the second coming of the Christ consciousness upon Earth.

When the interpretation was made that the Jewish people were the "chosen ones," it was an interpretation that became a belief for the Hebrew nation. The Biblical history of the Old Testament was interpreted and set down primarily by Jewish scribes. "We" referred to all of HUMANity and not to the exclusiveness or separateness of those of the Jewish beliefs. The Christ influence is seen in the behavior of individuals, societies, and nations. Those whose souls reflect fear and anger through war and abuse are still tied to the primitive stages of growth. Living consistently with the influence of a primitive belief strengthens the ties to early evolution and limits soul growth.

All of history is written from the perception of the mind and its beliefs, using the level of aware consciousness that the mind has reached. All scribes, as male, were focused upon the physical perception and beliefs of the primitive levels of soul evolution. We are evolving through many levels of learning as we seek to understand ourself. When we understand ourself, we will understand the Universe. All that is above, is below.

Our mind, when used as a superconscious mind of integrated energy, gives us the power of love from which we can live our physical experiences in health, joy, and happiness. Our soul and spirit as love is the opposite energy of the physical, intellectual mind that lives in fear and perceives life in anger, judgement, disease, and despair.

Spirit consciousness was created as *thoughtform* from the seed of the *thoughts* of the Creator. Our creation began at the specific moment the Creator began creation as pure *thought*. Our thought is used to create within our lives in the identical way that we were created by the Creator. The Creator's first intention of *thought* was to create life through the experience of being in physical matter. *Thought* then began its evolution through the evolving elements of ether to create the physical matter of the Universe. As *thought* gathered together the stardust of the Universe, it began to create physical Earth.

Nothing was missed in this evolutionary process. *Thought* developed the patterns within Earth from the pattern of the Universe, each becoming a fractal of the pattern of the earlier creation. *Thought* searched for the perfect elements to create the perfect physical form that would serve as a temple of spirit consciousness upon Earth.

The pattern for the physical body was created during the first Cycle of Development of our physical evolution. The continuing task of refining the physical body and the growth of the soul began in the second Cycle of Awareness at the beginning of our soul growth and refinement. Today as we reach the midpoint of our soul evolution we will merge into the Cycle of Understanding if we refine our souls to that level. For humanity to shift from its present Cycle of Awareness to the next Cycle of Understanding in our soul dimension, the veil must be rent and we must awaken to our own magnificence. This requires that our examination and reflection periods of growth have allowed us to grasp the present level of knowledge. With knowledge we begin to see that the stasis of primitive beliefs is not conducive to the refinement and growth of our soul. We begin to see that we must move beyond the earlier levels of examination and reflection if we want to rend our veil of beliefs.

The spirit consciousness saw immediately that the path of evolution would not be swift or easy for the physical form that it had created. But the Spirit knew that the physical form that was now embedded with spirit consciousness would have perfect intention, love, and truth to guide the intellect if it would listen. Seeing the significant differences that existed between the physical and the spirit realities, the spirit knew that a bridge had to be established. With that thought, the soul was created as an attachment to the spirit. Our soul became the bridge that would bring the physical nature of the human into harmony with the divine nature of the HUMAN.

The creation of the physical body, soul mind, and spirit consciousness as a functioning, refined whole has required more aeons of years than our intellectual linear mind can grasp. As evolution has progressed we have moved forward into the mesocosm of our soul evolution. The second dimension of our soul growth is symbolized by our society as it has evolved from our own development as functioning human beings. We have completed the development of the human form as our first dimension of growth, and in the second dimension of our growth we are creating our soul mind as our bridge of memory to our spirit. The bridge of our soul mind designs all of our physical experiences to help us understand our whole self as body, mind, and spirit.

Our spirit and soul consciousness have enfinite patience with our seemingly slow progression through our physical development and our soul evolution. Time is unknown within the spirit consciousness. Time is a method of measurement between two events that has served the physical world. Our soul and spirit lives aeons in the time it takes our physical body to pass through one day. Polarizing physical matter on Earth, as a vehicle for our soul and spirit, has slowed the soul and spirit to provide the opportunity for us to understand and integrate ourself as a whole being.

As we sleep, our soul and spirit energies move from the dimension of our physical body and work with the timelessness and spacelessness of our spirit dimension. This allows the soul to rest fully in the energy of spirit, which restores the energy drain that is inherent in our physical body. When we do not eat the proper foods, drink pure water and breathe pure air, we need the sleep time to provide physical restoration as well. If we use chemicals, drugs, alcohol, or electrical equipment at our time of sleep, we will interfere with the ability of the soul and spirit to restore balance within our physical body.

Our physical life is not predetermined or predestined. We have the ability with our soul and spirit influence to change any aspect of our life design, despite the multiple alternatives that are already designed into our soul plan. The soul is seeking a conscious awareness and understanding within the intellect of the purpose for life. Once our physical mind merges in absolute truth with our soul mind, we will begin the expansion into our spirit consciousness of Universal memory.

The work of the soul and spirit is always moving forward as it designs new experiences, new lessons, new changes, and new lives to be acted out in our physical nature. These messages of the soul are frequently passed on to the intellect as dreams. Each message is given to the intellect in symbols of physical reality to aid the intellectual mind in understanding. Each dream is symbolized uniquely for the mind of the dreamer, using our accepted realities to symbolize the suggested growth and change for us and specific symbols that are relevant to our individual soul path of experiences.

Each of our dimensions of growth are divided according to the Universal pattern of the Law of Sevens. Our physical form developed according to the pattern of seven levels relative to seven into infinity. Our soul mind is now developing according to the Universal fractal pattern of seven levels relative to seven into infinity. And with our evolution into the light side of our soul we begin our intention of expanding our spirit consciousness according to the pattern of seven levels relative to seven into enfinity.

As a society we are now living the various levels of the mesocosmic Law of Sevens of the soul dimension, which involves the evolution of our intellect into the light side of our soul mind. The old and advanced souls who are living the fourth level of soul evolution are within the completion of the Cycle of Awareness in the shadow side of our soul. This cycle alone has taken tens of thousands of lives for each soul to experience the stasis of knowledge within the intellect. There are some souls upon Earth that have already reached the Cycle of Integration in the third dimension of our HUMAN energy of consciousness.

The intellect was created as a physical tool to develop insight into the physical experiences of our life as our lessons, and therefore assist in the evolution of the soul into spirit consciousness.

The difference in our levels of soul evolution can only be seen in our physical life by the way that we use our intellectual mind, our beliefs, and our physical behaviors. If the intellect is the focus of our ego attention, we have not passed through the veil. If we are living in fear and judgement, we have not passed through the veil. If our intention of life is focused upon greed, possessions, vanity, or consists of any behaviors of the primitive level, examination level, or reflection level, we have not passed through the veil. But life itself is an indication that we are seriously working with our soul growth, and in time we will rend the veil. Comparing our individual life today with earlier levels of our soul evolution allows us to become aware of our progress. Looking back into history at the individual lifestyles, cultures, religions, and governments, allows us to view our own growth. Our lifestyles, attitudes, and knowledge have evolved and are continuing to evolve.

Levels of Soul Evolution

The first level of our second dimension of soul evolution focuses on the primitive cycle of lessons for humanity that was consumed with the need to survive upon Earth.

Survival itself was a mystery that had to be understood and mastered. The body was not understood. Life was not understood. This was a time of learning the basics of our relationship to nature as we experimented with air, water, food, and shelter to sustain our life.

The relationship of our natural consciousness levels began to interact with our five primary physical senses. As our physical senses became activated in relationship to nature, the effect upon the body and our comfort became more obvious. The more attunement we developed with our senses, the more attunement we developed with nature, allowing us to survive from the fruits of the Earth. As humans we were reflected in the harmony of our behavior towards nature and each other. The relationships that developed between man, Earth, and the Universe began to mold the human awareness of self and life.

The physical consciousness was following the instincts of our newly developed soul and the intuition of our spirit, but it was faced with the task of learning what to eat, how to eat, what sleep was all about, and the multiple challenges of how to survive in the nature of Earth.

Survival was seen only as physical survival within the elements of nature. A self-centered approach of personal survival prevailed. The physical form had not yet become concerned about anyone but self. But as each level of growth was experienced, the mind was inspired and motivated to search out the infinite levels not yet experienced and strive to learn by creating that experience. The mind of the primitive being created a web effect of its nature awareness that strengthened the basics of life, tying them together into an energy of survival in the soul mind.

As the disparity of beliefs between our soul levels becomes intense, fear becomes a reaction to our sense of loss of old beliefs, of going forward, and of change. Our primitive level of soul growth became a part of our soul memory, and it also became a fear for physical survival that will continue to manipulate our lives until we begin to understand the meaning and purpose of our eternal life.

As we complete one physical life and begin another, we bring those lessons that we did not learn back into our present life with us. Each lesson creates its own stream of consciousness that stays attached to the level where it began. The lesson will continue throughout our path of physical lives until the energy stream of the lesson is released by our understanding the lesson with total clarity.

Envision these energy streams of lessons as rubber bands stretched around an egg which symbolizes our intellect. As we work with the lessons the rubber bands can squeeze the egg, sometimes cracking its shell. Once a lesson is learned, the single rubber band will snap and break. As all of the rubber bands are broken, the egg is free and clear in its own beauty with all of the cracks visible for the shell to be removed. When the shell is removed from the developing embryo of our intellect, the intellect is free once again to change, grow, and expand.

Our continuous lessons of soul memory become more disparate, and therefore more conflicting with each level of growth. Our old, outgrown beliefs that hang around in our new levels of growth become our lessons of conflict and competition. Our karmic lessons of physical life allow the entire spectrum of human experience on the shadow side of our soul to be present at one time upon Earth.

If we are attached to the perception of "fighting for survival," we will approach the conflict of our own emotions with tools of survival such as guns, knives, rocks, clubs, anger, and fear, each being dependent upon the primitive belief. Murder, war, and cannibalism are all symbolic of primitive beliefs that exist within the minds of some humans today.

Cults that practice control of beliefs, human sacrifice, or mental, physical, and sexual abuse, symbolize primitive beliefs that are disparate in relationship to the current level of our soul evolution. When we live in a society that functions from one level of soul evolution but we as an individual continue to be attached to the primitive levels of soul evolution, we will create chaos. These different levels of soul growth produce internal conflict, fear, anger, and unworthiness within us as self-judgement concerning our difference in beliefs and behaviors to the rest of humanity. Our self-judgement is then reflected outwardly as judgement of others. Competition, conflict, and separateness will follow as those with one belief strive to become superior over those with different beliefs. This is how civil wars are created within families, societies, and within nations. Each group attached to the belief system is seeking validation of its superiority in claiming to be right, and seeking to make everyone else wrong.

Disparity between levels of soul evolution can be symbolized as time warps, where individuals resist change and become stagnant in their beliefs, allowing soul revolution and devolution by denying their ability to change. Time warps can be seen in the personality and character of their lives as they create conflicts for society that threaten the growth structure by challenging current beliefs. Examples of the different levels of soul evolution are rampant in the multiple beliefs and behaviors throughout the world. Wars, civil chaos, disease, starvation, drugs, and religious cults are thriving everywhere. All religions are cults, if they seek control over the beliefs and lives of their followers. Most conflicts are originating from the foundations of various religious cults and are being acted out within society.

Past lives that we have lived can be repeated in a nearly identical design, if the challenges of the lesson were grossly misunderstood and misdirected. The choice to repeat a lesson at another time in society's growth would emphasize the events of the lesson more dramatically because of the additional disparity between the relationship of the individual's belief and perception and the beliefs of humanity at a more advanced level of soul growth.

Many people continue to act out their daily lives focused upon the primitive actions of hate, fear, anger, and survival. These beliefs result in murder, rape, abuse, greed, and terrorism. These revolving souls are captured by their ego which becomes their personal rope, tethering them as they run in circles repeating their lessons of life, totally unaware of their emotional investment in learning. As they run in their revolutions without learning their lessons, devolution sets in as their ropes tighten and their beliefs become more intense.

The second level in the second dimension of soul evolution is the development of our physical comfort zone through the examination of our physical senses.

Being comfortable and at ease with ourself is learning to use our physical senses comfortably and in a productive way. Our physical senses have been given to us as a purposeful way of protecting, enhancing, celebrating our life, and continuing our growth into the expanded dimensions of our soul and spirit energy. We must use all of our senses to fulfill our purpose of life, although we have not yet learned to use our physical senses effectively because of our resistance and denial that accompanies our fear.

When we understand and use all seven of our physical senses fully, and our soul senses, we will be ready for civilization. As we have grown we have separated our physical senses in the same way that we created our senses one at a time. Bringing our physical senses together in unity is symbolizing the bringing together of our minds in unity.

It is from the level of examination that we first began to think and reason with our intellectual mind. Thinking, when combined with our other physical senses, begins to arouse new perceptions from our still-primitive physical nature. As humans, thinking is our level of physical sensing that removes us from other levels of life upon Earth. Thinking was essential in our second soul level of growth so that we could effectively examine our beliefs and behaviors of the primitive level through our sense reactions.

Our supreme physical sense is the combination of our first five physical senses, which forms the supreme sexual sense.

The sexual sense was acted out in aberrations of sexual activity and in physical competitions that brought the five primary physical senses into conscious memory for our mind to examine. This sexual focus was our way of trying to become comfortable with the power of our physical sense response, which we translate into sexuality and competitiveness as physical reality.

These two activities frequently compounded each other as we examined our physical experiences. During this period the society focused upon flaunting sex and competition through sports, greed, and self-indulgence in sexual aberrations in the same way that the individual focused upon sex, competition, and greed. Despite their long period of examination, our early societies of man did not discover the soul purpose of sex in their examination. Their thoughts regarding the senses focused upon their superstitions and myths which allowed them to see evil in themselves and in their behaviors.

Our period of examination required many millions of years to evolve, and this level of evolution has major streams of karmic energy that attach us firmly to its level of energy today. The symbol of our attachment to the level of examination is seen in every facet of our life as life itself is microscopically examined ad infinitum through our scientific, intellectual, and negative energy perception. Our approach through examination defies and denies the soul energy of trust and faith.

All aspects of sex, competition, and greed were prevalent within the individual, the society, and the world during this second level of soul evolution. This was found more excessively within the male than the female of society, although greed, competition, and sexual exploitation can capture the female that is living in her male nature. When the lessons of soul examination or any level of soul evolution are not learned with clarity, the life experiences will be brought forward into the next level of soul growth to be lived in a different image.

Sexuality and competition are discovered in the microcosm of individual life during our second Law of Sevens in the same pattern in which they are found in our second level of soul evolution of examination in the mesocosm. If the energy of sexuality and competition becomes stagnant, it can remain until death within any single embodyment. Change will be avoided at all costs, because in the examination of the beliefs and behaviors the perception of need for change has not been accepted. Our entire perception of life will be based upon the controlling energy of these two concepts until the connecting energy streams can be released.

In the mesocosm of life, the physical lesson is found when the main focus of society is upon sex, business, and sports. Society will be manipulated by sexual desires and exploitations. The physical body will be worshiped, and the intellect will be worshiped. The balance that is being sought in body, mind, and spirit will be forgotten. The experiences of our physical life must be examined at all levels of soul growth to release the energy streams that bind us to this second level of our soul evolution. Our lessons are learned through the fiber of our relationships, which requires frequent internal examination to be understood.

Society will experience sexual promiscuity, sexual aberrations, homosexuality, bisexuality, heterosexuality, and multiple forms of sexual control through abuse and disease. Worshiping of knowledge, money, greed, and success will also be the way of society. Our worship can be perceived as a symbol of physical examination for the ego, but it will tether the energy to our growing soul using a firm bond for control.

Searching for the physical comfort zone allows physical control to be rampant within the individual mind and within the collective mind of society. Physical control replaced the joy of our senses in seeking our comfort zone, and it has become a massive lesson of our soul evolution as symbolized in our controlling relationships and addictions. Many people in our society are living within this level of examination in soul evolution, and others are firmly attached to major energy streams of karmic energy from this level of examination. Each individual's soul evolution is unique to self, and reflects the image of our physical life from the mirror of our ego. In the level of examination our awareness level has not yet reached a level of true conscious awareness. We are living through only a few of our physical senses in our second level of growth, although we are seeking to examine them.

The third level in our second dimension of soul evolution is reflection, which is acted out within our physical reality as socialization. This began the early structure of joining together as nations, governments, religions, and families.

In this level we become aware of what other people mean to us. We begin to see socialization as a means of growth. We begin to look upon our relationships as a means of growth. We begin to seek others of like mind that we can relate to individually, socially, and intellectually. We begin to think, to speak, and to communicate with a different level of conscious awareness. *We seek mirror images of ourself in careers, play, sexual activity, intellectual pursuits, and in our perception of status, education, identities, and roles.*

In the level of reflection, as in all levels of evolution, there are seven levels relative to seven into infinity. Because of this we will see ourself moving through different levels of socialization in the same way we move through different levels of sexual interest, competition, greed, and fear. In this level of reflection our personalities, beliefs, and character traits reflect and attract socialization with other people, and we truly begin to seek answers relating to ourself to help us discover who we are.

In socialization we will find ourself searching to understand ourself, relationships, communities, societies, states, nations, and the world. We will begin to compare ourself and our abilities to our friends, to other family members, to the information that we gather about others, society, and the world. This is the beginning level of relating to and attracting other subconsciously and unconsciously recognized soul and spirit support into our life. Our sense of self-image begins to change and we relate to others on a more advanced level of conscious awareness.

Each step of the way in our growth, we develop a standard system of judgement for ourself from the perception that we get from our reflection from others. The challenge for us to remember is that the reflection we receive is the reflection that we send. We are at all times looking at our own image in other people. And we see our image from our level of conscious awareness, which is dependent upon the degree of development and use of each of our physical senses.

Socialization begins in the individual when we begin life within a family. It continues as we begin playing with playmates that are the mirror image of ourself, in school relationships, career relationships, intimate or sexual relationships, and marriage relationships. As we move through our Law of Sevens our relationships will change and grow as we change and grow, always reflecting from our own ego mirror. This reflection gives us a feeling of being appreciated and loved as we interact with the changing environment of our relationships.

When we find ourself coming into life without a supportive and loving family, we are actively working upon an image of the level of soul growth that is socialization. We are challenging ourself to find our own supporting energy from within our own reflection and within our own mind source.

This may be a review of the lesson of socialization which we will clarify rapidly and continue with loving souls other than our parents. We may also see ourself acting out conflict with friends, business associates, or any number of social relationships. Those actors on our stage of life are from our soul and spirit families and they are in our life design to support us in our lesson. Our physical expectation of the manner in which they support us may not be the same as our soul design.

Conflict shows the karmic energy streams that connect us to our primitive level of soul evolution. Reflecting our primitive lessons can manifest itself in our behavior as isolation or in extreme superficial socialization, where all communication relates to the external world and never to the internal events of our soul life. Reflecting our level of examination can manifest itself in our behavior as obsessive concentration on minute details or other obsessive compulsive behavior. We can also reflect any or all of our lessons from one level into the next level.

Socialization is the beginning of searching for our inner and higher energies by seeking acceptance of ourself within our perception of the social world of other people. Searching for our own soul and spirit internally is being symbolized by searching externally for others to be a part of our physical experience of life. If we have not released our attachment to the primitive and examination levels of growth, we will judge ourself and those we seek to become part of our life by our physical concept of need. Our physical concept of need can cover the gamut of survival, money, status, sex, image, and socialization.

The concept of need that we attach ourself to in the primitive level of our soul growth becomes a demanding karmic lesson as we move forward in our soul evolution. Our need to be needed reflects a dramatic sense of inadequacy and unworthiness within us. Need then becomes a declaration of "love" from our ego in its intention to control and manipulate the social environment into meeting our unique needs.

When these attachments that tether us to the primitive and physical-sense, examination levels of soul evolution are in place, we are not at peace with ourself. We find ourself living in fear, judgement, depression, and anger. As we judge ourself we judge everyone else through our reflection. The emotions that we feel within ourself will be examined and reflected into our relationships and will be assumed to be traits of the other individual. Our ego manipulates the image reflected to keep us from recognizing our own image.

As we reflect our own traits back to self and judge other people in relationship to our own image, we convolute our energy and create a self-judgement that acts as a veil to seeing ourself with clarity. Our convolution of judgement begins a cycle that expands and expands into every facet of our life, without our being able to see beyond the veil that we have created. This veil that we are creating from our beliefs becomes thicker and harder, forming an impenetrable shield around our intellect that increases the intensity of our mirror reflection.

The degree of conflict within all relationships will be determined by the disparity found within our separate levels of soul growth and the density of our ego. Each individual perception of the relationship will originate from the single perception of each person, and these perceptions will be totally different if the levels of soul growth are different. Our physical senses allow different perceptions and awareness within our senses, from which we examine and reflect the information from our different levels of consciousness.

Our religious beliefs and our homosexuality and bisexuality are all lessons of reflection. Each has created its own level of socialization through the reflection.

Relationship challenges can only be solved by two or more individuals when love and truth prevail in an open interchange of feelings and communication where freedom of choice is understood and valued. Despite a difference in soul levels, the love of one soul for another soul never wavers. The physical relationship can end, but the soul relationship will continue.

Communication in socialization allows our ties to the examination and primitive level of beliefs to be released and our level of perception to become expanded as our aware consciousness expands. We work through our karmic lessons by communicating our soul feelings through our physical senses.

The fourth level of intellectual knowledge begins the middle level of our soul growth. It is this mid-level of soul evolution that offers us our first opportunity to fully awaken to our soul and spirit memory.

The fourth level of soul evolution as knowledge is the stasis level of the soul and the transition level of our shifting consciousness. Knowledge is the most expansive level that we experience in this dimension of soul growth. When we find ourself at this level of growth, the ego has reached such a state of assured complacency that the veil of our ego is thick and satisfied. From this vantage point, our ego is self-fulfilled and self-satisfied in its attachments and its control. Our ego is firmly encased in this veil that allows it to judge all that is from its reflected image.

Our challenge is to penetrate the veil of our ego, which is at its maximum strength. The veil is stronger than it has ever been and the ego knows that it is on the line and fighting for its survival. At this midpoint of knowledge, we feel that we know all there is to know. We are self-satisfied and egotistically superior in our mind to all other people because the ego is creating resistance to further growth. Maximum maturity has been obtained by the ego: it has reached its destination.

Life is a journey not a destination, but our ego does not have the same perception because it has fulfilled its role. The ego is a temporary protection zone that is created to act as a buffer to the sensitivity of the intellect, while keeping the beliefs that must be dealt with uppermost in the mind. The ego is more finite than the physical body and when its veil can be rent, the physical survival of the body is dramatically increased.

All of our soul evolution is dynamically directed with the full intention of rending the veil to transition the physical, intellectual mind to work in harmony and integration with the soul mind and spirit consciousness.

When the intellect that is focused upon knowledge expands or opens enough to become aware of soul and spirit energy within the mind, cross-fertilization begins. In the beginning of our transition the seepage of our soul and spirit energy begins to infiltrate the intellect through the multiple cracks and holes within the veil.

The soul and spirit has full intention of cross-fertilizing the energy of the mind as a means of rendering the veil useless. This gradual onslaught of our divine energy punches holes in our belief system and prevents the ego shock that could occur with a full-fledged frontal attack. This is a war between the ego as an old, outmoded fear belief system and the positive love and truth within our soul and spirit mind. The intellect becomes a formidable opponent as it joins forces with the ego, but once the love and truth begins to filter in, the veil explodes and is rent into nothingness. The chicken embryo of our intellect has just smashed the shell of the cosmic egg.

Rending the veil allows the soul mind to awaken to the magnificence and beauty of its total energy force field. Removing the veil allows the electromagnetic energy field to flow from the right side of the brain to the left side of the brain and to the cerebellum in total freedom.

The ego acts as a shield to the energy transmission within the mind. Rending the veil leaves the mind open to the free flow of energy and thought can then be initiated from any part of the mind. Once the ego barrier has been removed, the intellect welcomes change. The intellect that has been used as a library with a limited number of books now finds itself in a library with an unlimited number of books. At first it seems a little overwhelming, but the intellect is capable of the challenge because it has the freedom to choose one book at a time.

The boundaries that were created by our primitive, physical, social, and intellectual beliefs are suddenly gone. Life takes on a new excitement and enthusiasm that is glorious. The ego was the last bastion of fear within the mind. When fear is gone we begin to see life with a new perception. We no longer see limitations, we see opportunities. We no longer see problems, we see challenges.

Rending the veil of our intellectual mind is the symbol of the "big bang" theory as the moment of creation. Once the veil has been dissolved into nothingness, true creation begins for the integrated mind. We no longer find ourself with the perception of *can't, won't, don't* that is attached to fear. The judgement of ourself disappears. We begin to appreciate our life, who we are, why we are here, and we begin to live in the moment, being creative and productive in our physical reality through the loving ingenuity of our inspiration and motivation.

When the ego is in its final tug-of-war with the soul and spirit, we may feel paralyzed. We can't work, we can't think, we can't be creative. We feel stuck in the mire of life, unable to make a decision to change. We may feel like we are in a state of slow motion, waiting for the days to pass, waiting for the seasons to change, waiting to grow old, waiting for deliverance, waiting for life to shock us out of our lethargy.

Our sense of stasis in the passing of time becomes obvious because it is the complacency of the ego waiting with full expectations for something to happen to save it. As the ego waits, the energy of the failed expectations will be transferred into our physical life and into society as a sense of nothing working right. We must be willing to make changes at this time to deliver ourself into another state of mind.

We must become active in the living, the doing of the physical world, to experience the levels of growth that will be evident within other people. As we become active we gain insight into ourself as we see other people in their energy, and we will see ourself reflected in their energy. We will find ourself challenged with some of the most seemingly thoughtless people of our life. This is a true reflection of our own inability to think, to move, to become engaged with life when we are captured in fear.

Once the veil is rent, intellectual knowledge will release all attachments to the primitive, examination, and reflective levels of soul evolution and our point of power will be directed toward understanding what we know. In the microcosm of the individual, we will see the ego begin with an all-knowing attitude that is totally surrounded by fear of new thought. Old beliefs represent security and survival for the ego and intellect. Releasing our belief in the supremacy of the intellect is an ego-shattering experience for us.

It is just as well. As the ego is gently shattered it recognizes that it does not know all there is to know after all, and it immediately becomes humble as it is faced with this new spectrum of knowledge. Our ego acts as a boundary to new thought by weaving together old beliefs, superstitions, and myths as our accepted reality. Once the veil is gone, the ego becomes our humility and our perception of reality changes.

Humility allows us to remain open to change, never feeling supreme or all knowing. The love and truth of the spirit will be immediately recognized by the wisdom and ingenuity of the soul, and the fear that is continually harbored by the ego will no longer exist as the intellect is flooded in spirit love.

As we change from ego to humility, our beliefs will begin to change and our mind will be open to hearing new ideas, reading books with new thoughts, reading history and religion to see them in relationship to our new perception of awareness, and we will find ourself reaching for those self-help books on the bookstore shelves. It is important to search for and to find a source of help to support us in our shifting consciousness.

Explore thought and knowledge in the same manner that you would explore a forest or a castle. Look within the crevices of thought. Work with it in your own mind, letting your inspiration guide you. Never blindly accept the words of another person but search to find your own feelings and your own thoughts in relationship to the concepts. *Never give away your power.* You have freedom of choice, freedom of intention, and freedom of your will. This is your gift that gives you the power of creation. Never mindlessly follow anyone. You are a leader. Never get involved in negative approaches to growth. These are conflicting energies, as growth is positive.

Creating your own conclusions about life is accepting your responsibility for self. People that have integrated their minds will search for knowledge but they will not accept the control of another person. You can work together as a team player, but you do not allow yourself to be controlled. Maintain your inalienable right to equality and freedom in all circumstances.

Knowledge as the fourth level of soul evolution is also the level of stasis. It is the level of our greatest resistance to change. Knowledge is the ultimate level of ego self-centeredness.

Our intellectual mind and ego find all of their power challenged in a life-or-death struggle with the soul and spirit minds. Our ego, spirit tug-of-war continues until the veil is completely dissolved and frees our soul memory and spirit. The intellect and ego must be faced with beliefs on an individual basis at times, until the love and truth of soul and spirit are respected and valued as the primary energy force of our mind.

When the veil has been rent and the ego changed into humility, the physical experiences of life will always reflect humility, love, and truth. As we make this change into humility we will continue to find challenges in our life that will test our strength and courage. We are testing our ability to cope with our physical life through the strength and courage of our divine nature.

There will be no attachment to the primitive physical, social, or intellectual levels of growth. Thoughts, words, and actions will reflect the consistency of truth and love at all times. The physical experiences of our life will change to reflect the love and truth of our soul and spirit.

Survival, sex, competition, and greed will no longer be an issue because once the ego is living in humility all fear is gone. The energy of fear is the strength behind the concepts of need that create survival fear, sexual fear, fear of failure, and fear of not being loved.

The ethical awakening of the intellect to the presence of our soul and spirit mind is the fifth level of understanding in our soul evolution.

This becomes a moment in time when we realize that our life is about us and no one else can accept that responsibility; physical "things" have no relevance in life except in our belief system; once we have a comfortable quality of life all else falls into the realm of greed; truth is a living energy of our aware consciousness that must become the reality of all of life's actions; internal love is our source of happiness; and all judgement is in reality a judgement of self.

Once reality is understood from an integrated intellectual and soul mind level, balance will become the intention of our life on a daily basis. We are created through an intricate balance, Earth is created through an intricate balance, and the Universe is created through an intricate balance. We have disease because we indulge in excesses and deficiencies of our mind and body. We pollute Earth and the Universe with our mind and body excesses and deficiencies.

Balance is the secret to our life and it must be maintained in both our mind and body. Our dependencies of thought, physical need, and emotional need are the methods that we use to stay attached to our ego fear and unworthiness. When we understand that our life is changing daily and we must be in harmony with our change, we have accepted our power of creation. We will feel the freedom, balance, commitment, integrity, and truth all around us. Our search for truth will totally absorb us as we seek to understand ourself, Earth, and the Universe.

Our challenge is to keep our search in the order of the microcosm, mesocosm, and macrocosm, because we cannot understand Earth or the Universe until we understand us and our relationship to our support system. Exploring what we do not understand, before we have an understanding of who we are, can destroy our support system. Understanding is the symbol of our growth and it must follow a natural order of progression. Look at nature and you will see that the fruit does not grow before the tree. Exploring reality in any other order is looking external to ourself as an ego perception of our ability. Living in our humility, we know that we do not have to use every ability that we have, to know that we have it.

We will see our choice of activities, reading, movies, and all media changing. And we will find our friends changing. We will suddenly want to be with those who understand us and with whom we can communicate freely and openly without judgement. We will live from the enthusiasm, inspiration, and joy that is expanding within us. All of our physical actions will be guided by the inspiration of our spirit and the motivation of our soul.

The sixth level of our soul evolution is found in our wisdom as we discover the unity of all things.

We are taught in our culture to focus upon living in competition. We are taught competition in education, religion, sports, marriage, friendships, business, and the list could continue endlessly. Competition creates a natural order of separation. I won, you lost. I am good, you are bad. I am smart, you are dumb. I am right, you are wrong. I am management, you are labor. I am the boss, you are the slave. I am rich, you are poor. I am male, you are female. I am strong, you are weak. I am educated, you are dumb. I am white, you are black. I am healthy, you are sick. When we learn unity in our wisdom of growth, we begin to see life as a team action because we experience our soul equality.

Our beliefs affect the politics of our mind. We are taught that the intellect is supreme, that the intellect is the only mind that we possess, that we are unworthy unless our intellect is judged at a superior level. We have separated the intellect into intelligence quotients, defined by numbers, and we judge each other accordingly. We evaluate our intellect by our judgement of education. In turn, our judgement of our education becomes our judgement of self.

When our mind is integrated we work through the politics of unified cooperation, where each facet of the mind has an equal input. The intellect is not ignored for the soul, the soul is not ignored for the spirit, and the soul and spirit are not ignored for the intellect. As the energy of the mind integrates it becomes politically wise in its function as a team, or one mind. Political wisdom sees nothing as separate but recognizes only one unified mind that is an artful, ingenious whole that functions as a wise, prudent, compassionate, and merciful energy force.

As we can see, we have many beliefs within our intellect defining, identifying, and judging our life into separate and competitive views. None of them are valid. The political wisdom of our integrated mind teaches us about integration, equality, balance, love, integrity, and truth, and it allows us to see the fallacy of our competitive beliefs when we rend our ego veil. The wisdom of the integrated mind is cooperation and unity; it is love and truth that is lived with a balanced equality.

Competition, conflict, and separateness are seen as the primitive and physical growth of a young soul. Our minds have the clear intention of a team energy, or a trinity of three minds working as one. When we understand the political wisdom of our integrated mind we will practice that wisdom within our individual life, our community, our nation, and within our political world.

The seventh level of our soul evolution is truth.

Our truth is inherent within our spirit consciousness, the source of our eternal life. Our truth is the reality of our physical creation, soul evolution, and spirit consciousness as a unified system of energy existing within the physical world as three dimensions or three layers of thought energy. This trinity of our mind and physical body creates us within our eternal life cycle.

Our eternal life cycle in human form consists of these three primary layers or dimensions of energy that we must grow within and learn from in multiple lifetimes. Each layer is divided into seven primary levels, but it also has an infinite number of levels if we need more to understand a lesson. As we complete our soul evolution, we complete the second primary dimension of our eternal life cycle. As we finalize our understanding of absolute truth of who we are, we will be ready to enter the third dimension of our spirit energy.

From our moment of rending the veil that surrounds our intellect in the level of knowledge, our intention becomes focused upon understanding, because the remaining levels of soul evolution exist in the Cycle of Understanding. It is within our moment of awakening from our veil of the ego that we enter into the light side of our soul evolution. This is our opportunity to create a "Heaven upon Earth."

Living a "Heaven upon Earth" is living the love, truth, and perfection of our spirit consciousness in every facet of our life: the microcosm of our physical life which symbolizes us, the mesocosm of our soul life that is symbolized by society, and the macrocosm of our spiritual life that is symbolized by the world.

Living our truth must begin in our daily life, as we allow ourself to function from the inspiration and motivation that is within us. Our soul and spirit energy will create enthusiasm, excitement, happiness, joy, peace, equality, harmony, and freedom within our physical life. We will be living from our one mind and we will be at peace. We will quickly forget the depression, fear, conflict, anger, competition, and judgement that were our ruling forces in our physical separateness of intellect and ego.

Our society is now at various stages of soul evolution. Some people are now entering the higher levels of soul and spirit consciousness where responsibility, truth, and love are being understood. Others are struggling at various levels of our soul path, determined on a subconscious and unconscious level to reach the peak experience of change from the shadow side to the light side of the soul. The majority of humanity is flush against the ego veil and feeling the pressures this position creates in our life. This level of intellectual spiritualism is the ego and spirit in its tug-of-war. Have faith in your ability to move through this level with ease and purity of intention.

In the higher levels of soul consciousness, evolution is understood: the relationship of our physical body to Earth and to the Universe is totally clear; the integration of the trilocular minds exists in harmony and rhythm; the inner child of the soul loves the fun and laughter of being young; and the spirit loves self, the Creator, and all of creation as one in complete happiness and joy. Those who are now living in soul and spirit consciousness have no fear. Change is welcomed and they are absorbed by truth as they search to understand. There is an understanding that eternal life is truly eternal and that the physical body is a tool that gives the spirit an opportunity to learn and grow through the lessons of Earth. Growth and change are "the way" of evolution and each are pursued with excitement and enthusiasm.

To understand evolution we need only to look at our history and understand the growth and change of humanity in physical time. Change has occurred on all three levels of us as individuals, as our society, and as our world. All change within the Universe follows the same pattern. Once again, when we understand ourself, we will understand the Universe.

Our history is invaluable to us. When we understand history, we can clearly understand our path of growth through what we have already experienced. We can also look carefully at history to learn the lesson of what we choose not to repeat. History can show us the destruction of societies and cultures. It can show us the path of disease. It can show us the misdirected perceptions of beliefs that were created through ignorance and fear. It is important to examine history for these lessons so that we can release our need to repeat the experience again by actively living the lesson.

We can learn more by studying the past than we can learn from dwelling on the future. Our past explains the lessons that we are now living as individuals, as society, and as a world. We must not be afraid to look within ourself, within our society, and within the world to discover what we do not want to live again. We must not worship the past as being better than now. We created the past during other lifetimes, but we should have no need to repeat it again if we are changing and growing. We must always live in the moment with total conscious awareness.

Each and every experience of our life is a jewel in the memory of our soul. We have our levels of examination and reflection as part of our growth path to encourage us to see our path of learning. We have our physical senses from which to evaluate and feel. We are living the present, and objectivity becomes lost in the judgement of our intellect if we have no understanding of the depth and patience of our soul.

The intellect is veiled from the mind energy of our soul and spirit. The ego becomes our veil to resist change and to hold us in the repetition of revolutionary cycles of physical experience. It is our responsibility to seek the truth that is hidden beyond the beliefs of our ego, which will allow us to live in the love of our divine nature. Our repetitions are there to be explored, learned from, and released with grace and love.

These repetitions can easily be seen throughout history in the revolutionary wars, the support of superstitious beliefs, and the attachment to destructive behaviors. As individuals, we can see our own repetitions of life as we look back at our present life experiences. As a society and as a world, we can historically view the multiple levels of the soul that we have experienced as physical reality since events were recorded.

Our individual experiences can best be seen through the examination of our relationships. The relationships we have with our families, lovers, friends, and acquaintances give us the perfect reflection of our lessons on the microcosmic level. The relationships of communities, cultures, ethnic groups, genders, races, and religions are the mesocosmic relationships that reflect our beliefs through our collective experience. The relationships of nations, countries, and the world are the macrocosmic relationships that reflect our behaviors through our collective experience. The same lessons will be apparent to us within all relationships, from family relationships to international relationships. The only difference will be through our way of relating in our physical life.

The revolutionary cycles of our government in this country have been evident now for over 200 years, but we have not yet learned to stop repeating our cycles. Our political system itself is no longer functioning from the original political wisdom of cooperation and unity, but it is now focused upon separateness, conflict, and competition which is being generated by the individual egos.

Two parties competing against each other instead of communicating about issues is the symbol of the primitive level of soul evolution for us, society, and the world. This is our political system as the mesocosm, and our intimate relationships as the microcosm of our life. When we change, we will change every facet of our life. We are society.

When we hear someone say, "But we have always done it this way," we must become conscious that our evolution as growth is being resisted. Our mind analyzes best when we can balance one image with another and see the relationship that each has to the other. Seeing what does not work in our personal life, our family life, our society, and our world, gives us the opportunity and challenge that we need to change. We are here upon Earth to make history, not to repeat history.

History is life in retrospect because history is our past and living can only occur within the moment, but life can be consciously approached with truth, love, enthusiasm, inspiration, and motivation as our way of being. No one ever makes new and important historical change by repeating work that is already known, understood, and documented. Our intellectual mind is always reviewing the trivia and daily events of our life. Our spirit provides us with ideas, imagination, and dreams to help us change and grow in our good thoughts.

Our intellectual, trivia-review technique is there in our mind to motivate us to look deeper within our experience of relationships that are securely connected to the primitive, examination, and reflection levels of our soul growth. Relationships at all levels of our life create the fiber that is the design of our soul lessons. The design of our life can be found by looking at the way we interact with others, and we then symbolize our relationship with others into the way our physical organs and cells interact with each other in our body. Our body then becomes the reflection of our mind. There is nothing new within the Universe.

As we learn to help ourself by understanding us, we will learn to heal ourself. Healing our physical body is a soul and spirit function that is normal and patterned into our spirit consciousness. Only our mind can truly heal us. Any other healing will be temporary if it happens at all. In not believing in our own divine nature we deny our personal responsibility for our actions as we impatiently wait for someone to save us and to heal us.

When we learn to heal ourself individually we will also be healing our society and our world. We are all connected by streams of collective consciousness that have the power to heal us, the Earth, and the Universe. When we complete our shift to a collective consciousness of love instead of fear, the healing that takes place within our world will be a miracle for all of us to see. Man continues to wait and pray for miracles within the external world. *Life is not about miracles to be performed, life is the miracle to be lived.*

At last we can joyfully acknowledge our spirit consciousness which we have been since the beginning of time. We are truly spirits walking our path on Earth as we learn to be HUMAN. Humans struggle to live with their love, truth, and perfection because they cannot believe they are worthy of such divine virtue.

There will be rejoicing within the Creator when all of humanity begins to understand self because He will have succeeded in His purpose of sending eternal cells of Spirit consciousness from Himself to Earth to learn how to be human. At that moment we will be HUMAN.

5

*L*ove

"The motive power of all is Love. If this Love manifests itself as Desire for things of Matter, the Lover stays in Darkness wandering; if it becomes the Will to know Light, the Lover becomes the Knower of himself, and so eventually at-one with Good."

*G.R.S. Mead, Thrice Greatest Hermes,
Book II Sermons, Poemandres, The Shepherd of Men*

*O*h, sweet mystery of life at last I've found you, ah love let us be true, alas how love can trifle one, all for love and nothing for reward, are ancient platitudes of love spoken from different perceptions. Each of us sees love from our personal perception of what love means to us. And as we can so readily perceive in these examples, our search for love is inclined to be more to satisfy our physical senses than our emotional senses. Frequently, the search and conquest is as important to the ego as the relationship itself.

Love is spoken, felt, searched for, and yet hardly ever considered perfect as the heart seeks something special that our intellectual mind does not understand. The love that we physically search for within our life is there as a symbol of our spirit love that we have eternally searched for from the beginning of our creation.

Feeling unloved leaves us with an overwhelming sadness, depression, and an intense sense of unworthiness. When we feel unloved, we judge ourself unworthy of love. Our sense of being unloved cannot be fulfilled by physical love, yet the intellect feels temporarily worthy of love if we are physically attractive to another person.

Our feelings of fear of being unloved are connected to the primitive memory of separation that is the symbol of the internal separation that occurred between our physical, intellectual mind and our spirit consciousness when the ego first began to veil our intellect. When our beliefs began to create the barrier of the veil between our intellect and spirit, our fear, our loss, and our grief began. With the beginning of our fear, loss, and grief, we determined within our soul to reunite our intellect with our spirit.

Our creation of the veil began our eternal search to reunite with our loving spirit and it also began our symbolic physical love experiences of life to trigger our memory. When we physically experience dramatic loss and grief, we turn to God, seeking the comfort and love that we sense he will give us. Although we see God as external to us, we begin to speak to the spirit within us. Our beliefs have created the separation between our intellect and spirit and now view God as external to them, because our spirit is externally behind the veil.

Our sense of an external God has continued because we have

not yet reached the level of understanding that will allow us to remove our ego veil. It is our ego which separates our spirit externally from the consciousness of our intellect and gives the illusion of an external God. Once our veil is removed we will clearly see that our Spirit is God and He has not separated from us and does not exist outside of us except within the perception of our ego.

If we continue to live behind our ego veil of beliefs, God will be perceived in an external position to our intellect because it cannot see beyond the veil. The intellect and ego does not admit that a soul and spirit exists within us. These memories are all within us, but the intellect continues to perceive our spirit and its symbol of love with unexplainable confusion. The intellect recognizes its confusion and continues to search, knowing that the love it has lost is hiding behind something, somewhere, and in the ego mind love will be found external to self.

God represents love and love represents God which the ego sees as external to self. The ego is the opposite of our God or Spirit self and represents fear. Keeping the God energy external to the ego assures the ego survival. In our intellectual approach to finding the love of our life in a relationship, we have the same sense that our perfect mate is out there, external to us, just waiting for us. We do not comprehend intellectually that our love and our perfect mate is the spirit within us.

Anytime that we physically lose something, we feel inexplicably confused by our loss and annoyed with ourself. It is hard for us to believe that we can lose our car, our jewelry, our clothes, our money, our keys, and sometimes our honor with total unawareness. It is hard, too, for the intellect to think that it cannot find the perfect person to give it the love for which it is desperately searching. The ego feels this special need to be united with the love it seeks as it continues to look for its lost love external to self in another person or an obsession. Our ego has not caught on that our love is there waiting to be found within us.

The intellect and ego is judging itself in relationship to its ability to be loved by others. But being loved by another eases the sadness, pain, and longing only temporarily before our loss is again triggered by the soul and spirit mind saying, "you still haven't found me" as our soul and spirit seeks to become one with the intellectual mind. The more desperately we seek to rend our veil, the more obsessively we search for physical love, which strengthens our veil.

This is one reason for the multiple breakups that have been seen within society in both heterosexual and homosexual relationships since the shift in consciousness began more than three decades ago. For many individuals who have continued their unexplainable search for true love, there is no logical explanation within their mind to explain the motivation for their actions. They simply feel an overwhelming need to continue their search and they follow their sense of "need." The external love that we seek is the physical symbol of our internal path as our intellect seeks to unite with the love of our spirit.

But we will forever seek to fulfill our unquenchable thirst for the beauty of love, because love is the hidden power of our life. When we can rend the veil of our ego and discover our spirit as our love, we will realize that we have always been seeking to love ourself. The spirit within us is the eternal self that we seek to understand before we can know who we are. *We are one as eternal spirit and we are love.* We will continue to seek our love as ourself forever into infinity, until we find it.

It does not matter from what level we perceive love because innately we know that love is essential to life. Our knowing, which comes from our soul influence, provides us with the motivation to continue searching. We do not perceive that the love which we physically seek is in truth the love of ourself and our life. Our perception of love is accepted from the reflection of our self-image that is reflected back to us from the veil of the ego. Our self-image is reflected back to us as our fearful, physical self. The vision that we see of ourself is what we will seek. If we see ourself as physical, we will seek physical love. Our reflection of self may not appear the same emotionally as physically, which creates homosexuality as well as heterosexuality.

Our intellect cannot see through the density of the veil to perceive the love that is being sent from within us by our spirit. Therefore, our perception of love is understood by the intellect as coming from someone external to us. With this image of the source of our love firm within our intellect and ego mind, we desperately search for love, totally enthralled with the mystery of the unknown.

We will seek the truth of our love into enfinity, at first focusing on the love that is external to us and at last knowing that love is forever internal to us. The love that we so diligently seek external to us is the mirror image of ourself, reflected outward for all to see. The emotions that we feel toward ourself will always be our definition of the love that we feel for another. Our loves will be attracted from our own energy and reflect our own energy, although the behavior that is acted out in the relationship may differ dramatically. In soul and spirit energy, like attracts like. In physical energy opposites are frequently attracted to each other. When we are attracted by soul and spirit energy, we will feel a "high" that may last forever. When we are attracted by physical energy, our attraction can be very fleeting.

Love becomes our dream, the mystery of living, the jewel that is worth the endless search. Love is the essence of all human consciousness. Love is our eternal spirit self. Love is the part of us that is hidden behind our veil of fear. It has no physical, tangible matter that can be clasped in our hand like a small bird or a golden coin. Love is the lesson of our physical life, the path of our soul, and the true perfection of our spirit. Life is ours to use as a tool, allowing us to experience our love in relationships for the purpose of seeing a behavior within us that is good and fulfilling for at least a moment in time.

Within all of our physical relationships there are elements of love. The love that is reflected from ourself connects us with the soul and spirit love of the other person, or we can be attracted to and feel love for the physical image of the other person. We are all connected within our spirit consciousness and the spirit never fails to honor that love.

But in our physical behavior we frequently fail to show honor, respect, or value for the other person. Our resistance to loving other people with total respect and value is our resistance to loving the soul and spirit within us with total respect and value. The stronger the soul and spirit connection, the more disdain the physical ego will show toward the relationship. This phenomenon of opposites is frequently evident in the physical personalities and character traits that attract each other in intimate relationships. This is why twin souls don't come together in recognition until they both are open to their soul and spirit as their physical life energy.

As we reflect our love, we will also reflect the emotional and physical baggage of our soul memory that we are seeking to heal and cleanse through the relationship. Because of the reflection of our karmic lessons of the soul, we may find our fear energy attracting more relationships within our life than our spirit love energy. In repeating the experiences of karmic lessons, we once again submerge ourself in the emotional baggage that has become the physical symbols of our love.

With each physical repetition of our dramas, we expand our challenge and our opportunity to learn the magnificence of our spirit and allow our love to become the essence of our life. In choosing to live our love, we profoundly trigger our spirit, and we live our commitment to self and others in a happier and more peaceful life.

Our spirit love exists as a feeling without physical matter and it can only be experienced through the actions and behavior of our physical body that we have designed for that very purpose. It is our choice to choose to relate through our spirit love or through the dramas of our physical nature in any relationship. Until we pass through the veil of our ego, we will not have respect, honor, and value for a loving, spirit relationship. We will relate to our mate from the reflection of how we feel about ourself, and our relationship will reflect our own fearful search or our own loving peace.

In the beginning we were created as love in the energy of spirit. In the beginning of each physical life, we are born as infants in the purity of our spirit love. It is in the living that our love becomes veiled from our life and lies forgotten under the rubble of beliefs and fear. Our life is the literal embodiment of our unacknowledged love, covered over with our own avalanche of intellectual beliefs, fear, and endless searching. Each fear that we are working with internally will be expressed through a physical action or behavior externally.

Love is recognized as an essential component for us, but it occupies the same position as our God and is seen only as an external object to attract and capture. Without an acceptance of our internal love, a gut feeling of emptiness and loss overwhelms us. If we are emotionally and physically separated from the love of our spirit, we will feel separate from all of humanity. This feeling of emptiness and loss agitates and excites us to search for our missing love in examples of physical behavior that reflect into our primitive days of growth.

Because of our learned belief that gratification can only be found outside of us, we begin to look to others, to careers, or to possessions, to give us the love we feel we so desperately need. The more we search the more insatiable our need becomes. The beliefs that direct us to external love are based upon the fear of the unknown inner soul and higher spirit. When we begin to realize that we have found false hope and not the real thing, desperation can truly set itself firmly into our minds and we once again set about another frantic search for another person or thing. *Beliefs that are based upon fear are the result of myths, superstitions, inaccurate perceptions, control, manipulations, and fear itself.*

Love and fear are not compatible in the same mind space. Therefore, when we are living in fear we are denying the love of our soul and spirit, while many times we continue to believe that we are living in our soul and spirit. Our intellectual spiritualism becomes the illusive ghost of our spirit flirting with us as we flirt with others that we meet.

We have an intellectual knowledge of our need to be acknowledged by God. This intellectual perception of spirituality has captured many people who are seeking to "rend the veil" of beliefs that hold them attached to fear. We may travel through many lifetimes thinking and speaking as spiritual people, but our actions will not support our words. This can easily be seen in the greed, abusive behaviors, control, judgement, guilt, sin, and fear of many religious leaders as well as avowed religious followers.

Intellectual spiritualism, or merely following the dogma of religious beliefs, will not show the consistency of life being lived in love and truth. There will be an intense judgement, fear, and inconsistency between thoughts, words, and actions. As we search for love within ourself, our internal search is symbolized by our intellectual desperation as we look for love in relationships, religion, education, and science. Failing to acknowledge the one place within us that is always love and truth allows our external fear behavior to resort to fanaticism, fragmentation, and fallacy.

When we are captured in intellectual spiritualism we have the sense of knowing about the spiritual, but our physical judgement will send us reeling from lover to lover. When we are in love, all problems within the relationship will automatically be judged as belonging to our partner. We will not be open to seeing our personal lessons, because we will believe that we are the spiritual party. Our intellectual beliefs will not accept that we could be responsible for the destruction of the relationship because our ego characterizes our physical presence as being our love commitment despite our physical actions.

Love can only be found within you. Look within yourself to see if you have a fear of never finding someone to love you, or someone for you to love. If this is your belief, it is time for you to examine your relationship with your internal self.

Feeling the emptiness of a lost love brings us face to face with our unhappiness, grief, physical needs, unworthiness, loneliness, loss, rejection, inadequacies, and fear. Knowing no other way to find fulfillment in love, we begin a desperate search in the external, physical world. The primary intention within our search is to have our sense of physical needs fulfilled by another. We see our needs only in terms of having someone to love who loves us, having a bed partner, finding financial security, having another to be responsible for us, having someone to spend time with, and feeling that closeness of love that relieves our sense of loss, grief, and fear. Each individual physical need represents the emotional need within us to love ourself.

We will rush into relationships knowing not what we will find, knowing not what love truly is, but feeling the pain and sorrow of our own sense of loss and isolation from love. Our needs become a source of physical and emotional pain because of our sense of separation from love. In our desperation, we have a sense that just having someone to hold us and give us physical love will ease our loss, pain, and fear. Instead it begins a new perception of our love as we attract from our negative energy of loss, pain, and fear.

Life is our spirit tool of physical process that we designed to give the soul an opportunity to learn its lessons of love through our physical experiences. The lessons of our soul are learned through the interaction of our relationship experiences. Learning the lessons of the soul allows us to grow into the love, truth, and perfection of our spirit. The energy of our soul is seeking the perfection of our spirit by living the lessons of love and truth through our physical experiences.

When love and truth are understood in the wisdom and ingenuity of the soul, they expand into the perfection of the unconditional love of our spirit. When the love and truth of our soul reaches a state of living spiritual perfection within our physical life, we balance ourself as body, mind, and spirit.

At that moment we clearly understand that love is within us and it cannot be found in its true purity external to us. Until our internal love becomes our external love we search for love in the fantasy of our external physical attractions.

Spirit can only be recognized on Earth as the physical actions and behaviors of love that we express through our daily activities of life. Our Spirit has designed and created our physical bodies as a way of manifesting soul and spirit love in the physical world. The true expression of physical love is expressed in the nurturing of our physical body with freedom, food, air, and water. This understanding has been physically expressed as "a way to a man's heart is through his stomach."

The social expression of sharing food and drink is the true expression of love that begins with the mother-love nursing the infant. The art of cooking and sharing food remains the true expression of spiritual love manifested as physical love. To say "I don't know how to cook" is to say "I don't know how to love." Throughout history cooking, as the symbol of love, has been left to the female. A female or male who can't cook is captured in her/his physical energy and is unwilling to learn to nurture self and others.

We have defined our love through the fantasy of sexual attraction. Sexual attraction is a primitive level of soul experience that has yet to release the physical attachments of fear and judgement. The energy of fear grew from the early primitive focus upon competition for survival. Sex is a biological function designed for procreation that does not necessitate nurturing as an integral part of the act.

Judgement has grown within us as we compare ourself and compete with the standards of judgement established by others. This comparative and competitive judgement abounds in genders, races, religions, ethnic groups, education, and between age groups in our perception of status and money, and a multitude of other factors.

The primitive fear that was common to our evolution in

another time and space continues to be prevalent as a driving force within us today. Competition for survival continues to be acted out within every facet of our life. Fear has captured the heart and mind of our human consciousness. In our all-consuming fear, physical love and sexual attraction can only be a vision of our mind. Love and fear are incompatible within us.

Our soul is the wisdom and ingenuity that we accumulate as we live the experiences of our physical life. Part of our soul wisdom and ingenuity is in knowing when a belief is no longer supportive of our growth as human beings. If we continue to believe in fear and judgement, we continue to live in the dark side of our soul. The dark side of our soul lives in the shadow of our ego beliefs that have created a shell around our intellect.

Fear and judgement are a physical indication that we have not yet reached the peak of knowledge to rend the veil that separates us from the spirit within. The soul uses each event, each experience of our daily life, to gather together the wisdom and ingenuity that is required to understand the lessons of love and truth. If our love is defined totally through our perception of physical need, we will find that violence, anger, fear, unworthiness, inadequacy, judgement, control, or dependencies will design the interaction of our relationships, until we change.

Soul is the true mind of man. Soul is energy in the same sense that spirit is energy. Both the soul and the spirit have individual electromagnetic energy force fields that function at different levels of consciousness than the intellectual mind. The soul is our subconscious mind. The spirit is our unconscious mind.

Our lack of awareness of our soul and spirit mind is due to our ignorance of their influence upon us. Ignorance is the stasis that we create when we attach ourself to our perception of intellectual knowledge and choose to ignore that which is not understood.

The intellectual mind is attached to the external, physical energy forces of the body. The intellectual mind is the basis of our aware consciousness. Our intellect is limited by us in the knowledge that it can accumulate in any one lifetime, but it acts as an epiphysis to the true mind of our soul and the soul is an epiphysis to our spirit mind.

When we believe that the intellect is the only mind that we

have, we again limit ourself. The symbol of the mind is represented throughout the physical body. Imagine yourself with feet but no legs, with hands but no arms. Denying the extensions of our mind is equal to either phenomenon. Imagine yourself with fear but no chance to ever experience love because it does not exist.

Soul and spirit can only be physically active by using the physical matter of our body. Our feet would be limited in their scope without the use of our lower and upper legs. Our hands would have a limited reach without the benefit of our fore and upper arms. Soul and spirit are an integrated part of our mind energy. They can be denied, ignored, feared, or hated, but they never abandon us. But if our soul mind and our spirit mind are not consciously used, we limit the power of our mind. If we consciously work to strengthen our arms and legs, we increase our ability to work with our hands and feet. We can lift more weight using our arms than we can if we use only our hands. We can run faster, ski better, bicycle longer if our legs are stronger. In working to balance the strength within our physical body, we must also balance the strength in our intellect, soul, and spirit minds.

Our soul and spirit are to our intellectual mind as our arms are to our hands, or as our legs are to our feet. They work as one in total unity. All of our body is designed in units of three separate parts working as a whole to remind us to honor, respect, and unify our soul and spirit. We restore our physical body with food, air, and water. We restore our soul and spirit with love, truth, and equality.

It is within the magnificent energy of soul and spirit that our true power lives. The power of spirit is symbolized in our life as joy, inspiration, imagination, enthusiasm, and ideas. The power of the soul is symbolized in our life as motivation, wisdom, ingenuity, and peace.

The intellect receives its power from the facts and figures it stores as knowledge, its willingness to create from inspiration and motivation, and its openness to exercise its freedom to change and grow. When drugs, chemicals, or alcohol are used to promote sleep, the connection is broken to the soul and spirit, draining the restorative power of the intellect and blocking the restorative power of the soul and spirit.

This integration of power between our intellect, soul, and spirit minds can be defined by the joy, peace, and happiness of our life. This is how we live from the love and truth of ourself. If we are living from our love and truth, we will have no fear. We will have tremendous amounts of faith, trust, respect, and honor, and we will challenge ourself to maintain our faith, trust, respect, and honor in all circumstances. We will challenge our own ability to love ourself and to withstand the judgement of others with morality and virtue.

When our belief system denies the presence of the soul and spirit energy of the mind, the intellect and ego will search for a shadow of that lost energy within relationships or possessions. This search will be pursued external to self within the external understanding of love as physical attraction for another person, money, possessions, status, and on and on. The body of self or another will be loved with the same intention as possessions, money, power, greed, control, and self-gratification, which controls the emotions of love and caring.

The sense of loss that is being felt within the intellect is being acted out in the physical world as a symbol of needing love. As we seek to balance the internal mind, we manifest our love search within physical relationships as misdirected energy.

The drama of our relationships captures our attention by using the physical experience of love as our trigger. In this way we expand our knowledge of love by living our physical lives through the drama of sexual love. When our mind is distracted by physical love, we remain unaware of our need for soul and spirit love. Our physical focus attaches us to the external consciousness and suppresses the internal consciousness, which misdirects our magnificent power into insatiable confusion and sexual desire.

Since the symbol of loving self is worked out through the fiber of all relationships, we will focus our fear and judgement primarily upon those that we love the most. They will be targets of blame and abuse. Our blame will heap the responsibility for our pain, fear, and judgement upon any shoulders but ours. In our intimate relationships, we will find our need for love accelerated. The first image of love is acceptance. When we begin to accept our soul and spirit, sex will slip from our mind.

True love will not be found within physical relationships until we learn to balance the internal love within us with the external love that we seek. As we open to the love of our soul and spirit and balance it with our physical love, we will begin to celebrate love, acknowledging the beauty and magnificence of our female energy.

We must love ourself before we can truly love another. Because our external need for love is galvanized physically and experienced as sexual arousal, we find many of our physical attempts to find love resulting in the negative dramas of life. Negative dramas of broken relationships provide an opportunity for us to see how we are living our soul design and our challenge to learn from our soul design. The negative experiences of life are a more dramatic stimulus to the intellect and ego, because we will go to any physical extreme to get our attention.

We have innocently belabored our negative experiences for many lifetimes without allowing our understanding of the lesson to filter into our conscious awareness. All experiences of life are repeated until they are fully understood within our aware consciousness. The lessons that we choose do not matter. We will experience sexual love, love of money, loss of possessions, and disease, and each experience will have multiple lessons interwoven into the physical circumstances of the event. All lessons of embodiment are repeated and repeated until they are fully understood within our aware consciousness.

What we fail to understand we will repeat until the lesson is of such magnitude that the drama of the experience will be one of crisis or chaos within our life. Disease has become a lesson of crisis and chaos, as it affects every facet of our life while allowing us to live our loss on different levels of awareness. Disease can affect our life, business, finances, family, and friends, but we hold our power of life in the hope and happiness of our loving spirit.

Crisis and chaos as a way of life triggers the intellect and ego to remember that we have a spirit energy, or God, that can be of help in times of need. At such moments we are programmed to pray to a higher power for help. We don't need to be in a church or down on our knees to pray. Prayer is natural to our thinking as *thought* energy. We may not accept or acknowledge that a higher power exists, until we are challenged with a crisis. Our crisis becomes the symbol of the ego and spirit tug-of-war that is going on within our minds. Crisis is our own two-by-four that we have inflicted upon ourself to get our attention.

Our life is about us. Other people are only actors upon our stage. We have invited each actor to participate in our drama of life. Our life is our stage. We write the script, produce, direct, and act in our own dramatic creation.

When fear is the predominant energy of our life, we have no awareness of how we create our own intense dramas. We have no awareness that life is free choice. We have no awareness that we have the power to change our life experience if it does not work for us anymore. We refuse to look at the many repetitions that have happened before to help us with the exact same lesson of this lifetime. Our crises will continue until we awaken to ourself. *The soul has total memory of all repetitions throughout our multiple lifetimes as we work through our physical experiences to learn the lessons of today.*

When lessons become a crisis in our life, we are reminding ourself that we have been working on the same lesson repeatedly. Crisis lessons are always accompanied with karmic energy, which shows that the lesson is not new. A karmic lesson is one that has been studied from many different levels through many different lifetimes. Creating a crisis in life is equivalent to hiring a tutor to pass a test in college. Many crises will involve a change of relationship with another person. The crisis can be a relationship ending, divorce, death, the loss of money, a career, or the loss of physical health, that will bring us face to face with a drama of loss and grief that we cannot avoid feeling.

We create a web of relationships that allows us to experience life on many levels of interaction. We have the freedom of choice and the power to change any interaction at any time during the drama, unless we are the passive observer who is learning our lesson by supporting another soul and spirit in their lesson. If we are attached to fear, we will challenge ourself to find a beautiful way to change the drama by using the love and truth that is within us to accept the lesson. In our acceptance of what is, we acknowledge our own strength, courage, and love.

If fear is the predominant energy of our life, we will blame other people for the situation, we will judge ourself, we will feel captured in the drama, and we will feel paralyzed, unable to exercise our freedom of choice and our inherent power of love and truth to free ourself. We will believe ourself to be a victim of the experience. *Because of fear, we will deny our power, our love, our truth, and our freedom of choice to change. Because of fear, we will deny the love of our soul and spirit which is the source of our wisdom, love, and truth.*

Fear is the opposite energy of love. Negative is the opposite of positive. Fear is negative energy and love is positive energy. If we are living in fear energy, we will expand our feelings of fear to every facet of our daily life. If we are living in loving energy, we will expand our feelings of love to every facet of our daily life.

The energy that we are becomes the energy of our life. Our energy as an individual affects us, and we in turn affect the energy of our society and our culture. The energy of our society and our culture in turn affects the energy of the world. Each of us has a far-reaching responsibility to live the loving, positive energy of our soul and spirit.

Finding ourself captive in an experience that produces fear, pain, and unworthiness is our opportunity to learn the lessons of love and truth. This is our trigger to change. We have created the experience within our life as an opportunity to learn. When we are open to accepting responsibility for our crisis, we will be accepting our responsibility and our commitment to change. *Until we change we will continue to challenge ourself with the same experiences of life, each time providing ourself with a new opportunity to change and grow.*

Breaking the habit of beliefs and behaviors that hold us captive in fear is the beginning of change for us, our society, and our world. Being willing to change our beliefs and behaviors is the first gigantic step in using our power to change our habits that are programmed into our mind. It will take some time to become conscious of our thoughts, words, and actions that react to our life experiences from habit. Once the first step has been achieved, our path of growth becomes illuminated.

Change is the symbol of our acceptance that our intellect and ego is not our ultimate mind.

Being on our path of self-growth through exploring the intellectual beliefs that create our behavior becomes a commitment to our growth and change. It becomes a commitment and an intention to live from our internal power of love and truth. Having the courage to study our own reaction to challenges is the first step. The experiences of our life are not as important as how we cope with them. When we can look at all events of our life through love and acceptance, seeing the lesson that we have learned, we will know that we are living from spirit. This does not mean that we reward inappropriate behavior, but that we do what needs to be done with a loving intention of helping the other party to learn their lesson. Coping with drama from a loving intention, rather than anger and revenge, allows us to learn from our experience.

Living from our internal power of love and truth requires that we give up all attachments to fear, and willingly pursue the clear understanding of self. Looking at ourself requires that we also accept that our inappropriate behavior must be changed. Denial of the behavior sends a message of reward to the ego and allows change to be rejected. Rejecting change sets the stage to repeat the drama.

At this moment in our life we will be tempted to attach ourself to a physical process as a way of understanding. This is because the ego in its need to survive will lead us to believe that focusing upon primitive soul memories will help us change. It does not help us change but it attaches us to a primitive memory of the soul that our intellect accepts as understanding.

We must focus within the moment to understand our soul and spirit love and to repattern our life in that love. If we are living in an ancient culture, our lesson is to be found in that culture. If we are living in a modern culture, our lesson is to be found in that culture. We can't find our answers by living in the past or transcending into other cultural beliefs. This continues the past life focus as a way of retreat, not growth. We must be internally who we chose to be at birth, with our freedom to grow and change through our physical experiences. We must always be willing to change and grow internally and not allow ourself to become attached to physical, external processes and controlling beliefs.

Understanding self is the level of soul growth that is beyond intellectual knowing. It reaches into the depth of the soul mind and shows us not only how the mind works, but why we have designed our energy in this spiral path of learning. Understanding allows us to accept what the goal and purpose of our life on Earth is all about. When we understand ourself, we will love ourself.

Knowledge is the fourth level of soul evolution. It is a level of stasis that allows us to react to change from our ego belief in the infallibility of our accepted fact. Our knowledge is the linear programming of our intellectual mind that remains ignorant to the understanding of who we are and why we have an intellect. At the intellectual level of soul growth there are multiple levels of denial of soul and spirit from the ego, and all levels of the intellect and ego react from fear, not love.

The intellect remains attached to its belief in supremacy because it fears the loss of its power and control. Ignorance is the action of the root word "ignore," and for many it becomes easier to ignore the intangible than to search for truth within ourself to support any explanation of its source.

Cycle of Change

When the intellectual mind that is attached to knowledge is choosing to ignore the changes it must make to grow into the Cycle of Understanding, it is reinforcing the pattern of its shell. Ignorance of the human mind that captures the ego in fear is an expensive lesson within our society. Changing from reactionary fear to open-minded love is a necessary step in the equal growth of us as individuals, as a society, and as a world.

We can initiate this Universal change by beginning to change our understanding of self and repatterning our thoughts, words, and actions from fear to love. Each level of growth is defined by a cycle of change that allows us to shift the focus of our consciousness and to move through our seven levels of fear into a change cycle of seven levels of love. It is through changing our beliefs and our behaviors that we create change in our life and in society.

The emotions that we use to help transport us from one level of awareness to another are the fractals of our electromagnetic energy force fields of learning. Our patterns of growth follow these fractal patterns of energy that are integrated within each and every physical cell and energy cell within us.

The cycle of change from fear to love will move through seven levels that are attached to fear and seven levels that are moving into the being of love. Many humans are living the final levels of their cycle of fear and are beginning to understand that love is beyond the veil and love is willing to support them in their growth.

Cycle of Fear

Fear begins with a belief.

Belief, as the first level of the cycle, can exist for multiple lifetimes and cover millions of years of our time, allowing the pattern created by the belief to be an intense path in our life. When a belief is intense it has karmic origins and it is not easily changed.

A perfect example of belief is the collective belief in the judgement of God toward man. We are not being judged by God. We are being judged by ourself as we reflect our own need to judge. Our need to judge us is reflected external to us as our belief in judgement as the behavior of God is reflected internal to us. By taking on the behavior that we believe to be the behavior of God, we are reminding our intellect that God exists within us. Our belief in the judgement of God began in the primitive cycle of soul evolution and continues as our fear belief and our reactionary behavior today. Multiple beliefs such as original sin, guilt, fear, demons, devils, sex, possessions, victimization, inequality, and supremacy, lie pregnant within our minds to be nurtured by our ego for its strength and power.

The second level of our cycle of fear is our fear behavior. When the belief is acted out in the physical world on a daily basis it creates a deeper pattern within our soul mind to become the karmic lesson of many lifetimes.

We have been taught to believe that we are sinful and guilty, and because of that belief our behavior will follow the path that we identify as sinful and guilty within our mind. We will intentionally choose behaviors to act out that will fulfill our belief. If our belief is strong enough the intellect will also believe that it does not matter what our behavior is, because guilt will always be there even when we do not follow through in our behavior. If you covet another man's wife you may feel guilty of adulterous thoughts without the physical behavior.

This crime will escalate into behavior because it allows punishment to be delivered for the sin and guilt that is felt. Punishment is sought to deliver us from sin and guilt, and punishment must be acknowledged by the world as being delivered for the specific behavior. Therefore, when people feel they must be punished because they are living as sinful and guilty creatures, they will commit criminal behavior to be apprehended and to receive recognition and punishment for their sins. Even behavior that is not criminal will be acted out in a self-defeating method to assure discovery and recognition of the behavior, which allows for punishment by another entity. Punishment fulfills our belief in the need for redemption and forgiveness.

Suddenly we will become conscious that we are setting ourself up with experiences to challenge the validity of our behaviors and beliefs. At first we will deny the validity of this trigger, because the logic of defeating ourself is remote within our mind. But our soul design will seek exposure to make us consciously aware of our beliefs and behaviors.

Denial becomes the third level in our cycle of fear.

We do not want to have an awareness of the trigger that is suggesting the coming of change for us. Our denial can become excessive as we try to reason out our behaviors and our beliefs into a logical perception to justify our self-destructive behavior. Highly intellectual individuals will deny the soul and spirit within them, because to accept the love of the internal self requires change from a well-grounded denial system, which they feel is based upon documented "facts." A mind with this intense pattern of denial will repeat the same lesson many times in one lifetime and for many lifetimes, proving that old habits die hard.

Facts are at all times relative to the perception of the person establishing the fact, just as they were during the time when the Earth was considered flat. The perception that the Earth was flat was a relative fact based upon the level of perception and knowledge that was available at the time the "fact" was determined, and the belief was a challenge of denial for many people when new facts were presented.

When the trigger of denial continues to be acted out in our daily experiences, we will reach the next level of emotion required for change and that is anger.

Anger is the fourth emotion of the seven levels in the cycle of fear, and it is the stasis level expanding the challenge of change.

The anger level is the stasis level and can take many dramas in life to fully overcome. When we ignore the small angers, we allow a gigantic anger to develop and take control of our life.

Anger becomes the emotion of self-judgement. Our self-judgement is also reflected external to ourself and will be directed at anyone who can remotely be blamed for the original belief. The anger will also be captured in confusion, and will swing back and forth from ourself to others, as well as from one perception to another. Anger is a declaration that change is not welcome, and as the stasis level of change in the fear cycle it will take time to move beyond this emotion. Time and a determined commitment will breed success at every level of growth, and although anger can become a way of life, spanning multiple lifetimes, anger too will change when we see the futility of the emotion.

Anger will bring us face to face with our beliefs, our behaviors, and our denial. If it is our choice to move beyond anger, we must not be fearful of looking at ourself. When we reach the level of anger in our path of change, we are seeking within ourself to release the perceptions that have served us for a lifetime and deal directly with the reality of our life on a moment by moment basis. We are seeking to release our attachment to anger as we are living it and to experience life as growth and change. Releasing the cocoon of habit that we have crawled into to protect ourself from change is our primary challenge. But we cannot change until we change the fear of our emotions and behaviors.

Anger allows us to live in passive-aggressive emotions, showing our agitation and anger one moment and being closed and unresponsive to life in the next moment. We will see our emotions as safe and familiar, and we will resist the next important step in the cycle of change.

Even anger can be seen as safe and familiar. The ego identifies anger as security and survival and it will deny the need to change. *Learning and growing is impossible in this level of emotion if the mind sees the image of self as the perfection of spirit, mistaking the passiveness as perfection and the aggressiveness as performance and change.*

Anger will always be present as it is mirrored into life from the earlier levels of fear, until we pass through the veil and merge with our soul and spirit love. The mystery for the person will occur because they feel change from the internal anger which is not showing externally in creative and productive actions. Crisis will force change and is many times essential to shock us into seeing the wisdom of looking at our beliefs, behaviors, and denials as we confront our anger. Once we see that we have no alternative but change, we begin to grieve.

Grief is the fifth level of fear change in our level of knowledge.

Grief will move us through many levels of exploration as we seek to understand the event. If we are ready to move forward and to face growth we may find our mind vacillating and consumed with doubt as our ego becomes desperate in its tug-of-war. In our vacillating emotions of grief and releasing anger, we will find ourself sliding back and forth as we feel the friction our behavior is creating for us. Our passive-aggressive behavior will escalate and become more evident in our normal behavior as our emotions rise and fall with the grief.

We will begin to feel saddened and begin to wallow in self-pity, relying upon our feelings of anger and defensiveness to protect us from our grief. When we reach this state of grief, we will feel overcome with inadequacy, unworthiness, self-blame, judgement, and victimization. This level of change can trigger the choice of death for the soul and spirit if the intellect and ego is waging a stronger battle.

It is common to continue our focus upon blame and judgement as we live through the emotions of grief. Grief will dwell on what could have been—the perfect marriage, the perfect life, the perfect career, the wealth that could have been, and on and on ad infinitum. The soul and spirit can become bored listening to this refusal to grow and accept responsibility for self. It may create another crisis during this grieving period simply to show that the cycle of fear must be understood and not belabored if change is truly being sought. We are grieving only from the expectations of our ego, but our soul and spirit prefers joy and happiness rather than grief.

The sixth level we experience in changing from fear to love is our sense of loss.

We begin to feel an emptiness as the loss of our beliefs and behaviors becomes apparent to us. At this time the mind begins to feel the energy of change and either attaches itself to loss or releases all attachment to all levels of fear. It is at this level that the temptation arises to seek a past experience or a new experience to substitute for the reality of the moment.

The ego is on guard to protect itself from the reality of change. Seeing change as loss, the ego will strive to cut its losses as thinly as possible by continuing with its determination to ignore what is going on inside the emotions. This fear of loss will initiate other circumstances in our life to replace those which appear in our mind to be lost. And this fear has the power to return us to our passive-aggressive beliefs and behaviors to start the cycle repeating again.

The result of this phenomenon is the "time warp" reality, where we resort to a return in memory to a past life experience or the immediate experience of the loss, where we can feel a relationship of safety and security. This "time warp" energy returns us to old beliefs and behaviors in which we felt safe and allows us to begin our cycle of fear again.

As the cycle of fear occurs to move us from intellectual spiritualism to living spiritualism, many individuals will be tempted to return to times of the past and to lives of the past. Others will find themselves in cycles of revolution. This becomes the ultimate challenge to the truth of our soul growth and change.

A fascination will develop for the behaviors of the culture, the beliefs of the culture, the dress, the jewelry, the customs, and many times the culture's living conditions, if we revert to past memories. Or the exact circumstances of the loss that is being felt will be reenacted to the best of our ability in a nearly identical situation that will keep us in our cocoon. Loss is a frequent perception that is felt in the replacement of one mother for another mother throughout our life. Our replacement needs will be fulfilled in our perception of our relationships and our beliefs and behavior.

Loss can be the behavior that we are living as the fear of change captures us while we are developing in childhood. If we fear becoming an adult and being responsible for self, we will seek a surrogate mother to allow us to stay in the role of the child, being physically cared for and nurtured with safety, food, and love. This phenomenon is frequently found in males and in females living in their physical, male energy. When our male and female energy is more balanced, we will experience fewer emotional ups and downs as we move through our cycle of change. If we are captured in the cycle of fear, we will expect all of our survival needs to be met by the mother, or female image. We will feel emotionally and intellectually handicapped in our physical life, because our loss will be very real to us.

If our perception of loss is released, we will begin to realize that our fear is being created from our perception of beliefs and it really doesn't matter because we need to change and grow. We will see our own inner power and we will rejoyce as we realize there is no loss, there is only change and growth.

The seventh emotion in the cycle of fear is apathy.

Having a clear understanding that it does not matter if we change allows the apathy to begin. We suddenly understand that change does not threaten our survival and we feel good about detaching ourself from our fear. We begin to see change as a positive transition, one that contains hope and happiness. We stop our fear completely and we no longer blame, or judge, or concern ourself with what other people think. The anxiety, confusion, depression, and hysteria that may have gripped us as we moved through our earlier levels of the cycle of fear are laid to rest. At last we can see that our life is about us, not anyone else, and we have an equal right to love and truth as the driving force of our life.

At first we will be challenged to maintain our new beliefs, and we will find ourself experiencing all of the previous six levels of fear as the ego struggles to win. But if we can get in touch with our positive inspirations, we will allow this stage to pass quickly and we will have a conscious awareness of the levels as we experience them.

Suddenly we realize that our life *is* about us. We must be who we are, not who someone else wants us to be. We begin to see that our identity lives within us and is always unique to us. We cannot live a life based upon another person's ideals, beliefs, or behaviors. We must use our spirit inspiration and our soul wisdom and ingenuity.

At last we will understand that growing is an internal change of self: it is not attaching ourself as a physical appendage of another, and it is not dependency upon another. This understanding is the beginning of our acceptance of our own sense of internal freedom. By seeking external freedom, we are learning internal freedom. When this lesson is learned we are willing to stop looking outside of ourself for love, and we are willing to accept that love has always been within us. At this time our physical relationships acquire a new meaning and our interactions are from a new behavior of self-confidence and love.

Cycle of Love

Apathy is the bridge that we have transcended to complete the cycle of change from fear to love. But to capture the love energy, our intellect must completely and equally replace the pattern of the seven levels of fear with the seven levels of love. This requires many years of internal exploration and physical challenges as we work through our multiple understandings with strength and courage.

Once the new energy has been accepted, one level at a time, it must become an integrated part of our life by establishing new beliefs and new behaviors from our love energy. Our new beliefs and behaviors can only transcend into our physical experience when we have the strength and the courage to live them in our daily life.

The first level on the path of our new cycle of love is our total acceptance that living through our love is our chosen goal.

Once we accept that we are seeking love within ourself, we begin a new and different search. Our search is a search for self as we are in this moment. Using all that the intellect can provide, we begin to seek validation that love is in there waiting to be fully understood.

Acceptance begins within our own mind and heart. We may not be prepared to share our feelings at that particular time. We may find ourself pursuing our new search through the absorption of knowledge. We will need private time to be alone, to read, to get to know ourself, and to become comfortable with our decision to change our perception of life. But we will begin to live from our inspiration and our motivation. The attachment to rote behavior, to task structure, to the common performance of work, and to a closed mind will be gone. We will no longer feel the judgement, fear, anger, denial, and resistance of our fear of change capturing us.

Our change will not be confined to our thoughts and our words, but it will become our actions. Our behavior will undergo a dramatic change. All resentment, resistance, self-pity, unworthiness, and inadequacy will have disappeared. We will know that ideas are to be tossed out and tried on. We won't be attached to them as life-saving, or ego-saving. We will have no fear of exposing our thoughts, our words, or our actions to public scrutiny. We will know that to err is human, and to forgive is divine. We will freely live our love without any fear of feeling rejected. We will accept ourself, and others will accept us. We will live with the intention of total equality, integrity, compassion, and mercy.

We will begin to feel a sense of freedom and excitement as the second step arrives and we know that we can acknowledge our newfound freedom and inspiration.

The second step is to acknowledge the love that we feel.

As we acknowledge the change in ourself, we will find a new energy of enthusiasm. Our acknowledgement initiates a new level of communication. We will seek out others of like mind, and many times we will be challenged to let go of old friends who no longer understand our new goals in life. In our detachment we will feel the freedom of our unconditional love for them and their path.

We will find new priorities appearing in our daily life. We may want to have silence around us for many hours at a time. We will turn inward to our own thoughts and begin the sorting out process. We will begin selecting our words as carefully as we select our thoughts. We will seek to make our actions consistent with our thoughts and words. Our commitment to change will move us forward to a new level of respect for the growth that we feel.

As we reach this new level of acknowledgement, we will not hesitate to acknowledge our inspiration and motivation. Our loving energy will be willingly spoken of at all times, and we will live our love through our behavior at all times. Our emotions will be full of enthusiasm and excitement. We will clearly see the opportunities for action and for sharing our enthusiasm. We will be motivated to help others learn by speaking of our feelings without embarrassment or fear.

It is at this level of change that we become a disciple for the beauty of our new beliefs and behaviors. Our enthusiasm will be so profound that we will not be able to contain our happiness within us, but we will want to reach out and to share it with everyone. Our excitement and our behavior will turn us into a living example of change as we seek to help others grow in the same way that we have grown and changed.

As we become comfortable and fluent in sharing our new beliefs and living our new behavior, we will attract others to us who are searching. Our ability to attract those who are seeking change will enrich and expand our life. They will have respect for who we are and they will see the wisdom of change within their life.

Respect becomes our third level of emotion in our cycle of love as we change and grow.

Respect requires that we support our newfound energy and work to expand the understanding within us of the change that we are experiencing. When we begin to respect ourself, we will not accept behavior that is emotionally, psychologically, or physically abusive to us. We will insist upon respect in our life, because we will respect ourself. We will not allow others to invalidate our right to be respected for living our truth.

At this time we may find ourself wavering and unsure. Respect is the true beginning of loving ourself by living the truth that is within us. The old memory of self-gratification will begin to look very much like self-love, and we may begin to wonder if our ego is truly humble and working in harmony with our spirit. This is the time for us to forge ahead with power, strength, and courage, knowing that as we change, the ego is becoming humble and will provide an added strength of humility.

When we respect ourself, we no longer allow others to be disrespectful. We listen to our body and our mind. We hear the messages of all of our physical senses. We stay open to feeling, to caring, to sharing, and to our inspiration and motivation. We respect the magnitude of our soul and spirit, and we know and respect what it can do to heal us in both our mind and our body. *When we respect ourself, we know that the only miracles in our life must be the ones that we create. We begin to respect our life as our miracle and our opportunity to make a difference in our family, our society, and the world.*

As we experience a growing respect for our change, we will become conscious of the immediate value this change of energy has in our daily life experiences. This sense of value as it is defined by our daily life experiences brings us to a new level of awareness.

We will reach the peak of the emotional level of value in our cycle of love. Value is the fourth and stasis level of our change into love.

Reaching the level of value will give us a new perspective of our life. Value as the fourth emotional level of our growth in love will be the most expansive level because it is the peak of the emotional wave of change energy. As the peak of the energy wave, it carries the most powerful and magnificent force that can hold us captive as we seek to see the true value of our change and respect for ourself.

The stasis of the peak in the level of value is equivalent to the stasis of the peak in the level of knowledge in our soul evolution. As we begin to understand the value of change we become very complacent and feel that we have completed the cycle of change. This repeats the energy of the level of knowledge as we become paralyzed and feel that we have reached the supreme level of soul growth. It is a challenge for us to understand that the best is yet to come.

We will find ourself cycling through each and every facet of our memory at this point in our growth. We will challenge ourself with triggers to examine each experience individually. Each experience allows us to see our acceptance, acknowledgement, and respect, and we will search for the value to us of our choice of experience. It is the challenge of the lessons within us that will bring our change into total clarity. The value of our change becomes the value we feel for ourself.

At this level of our growth and change we must find the value in who we are to be inspired to continue with who we are. If we do not see the value, we are living the fantasy of change and not truly changing. This can become our illusion through the strings attached to intellectual spiritualism, where we create the facade of change. Once we reach the level of value, we must be honest with ourself. We cannot believe that we have value without living the value that we are. We can challenge ourself with a reality test to see if we have any fears lurking inside of our mind.

Are we judging? Are we blaming? Do we feel rejected? Do we feel a lack of love and truth in other people? Are we listening, hearing, thinking, speaking, and seeing the reality of life around us? Are we able to touch, taste, and smell from our soul and spirit senses of emotion and feeling, as well as our physical senses? Do we feel free? Do we feel joyful and happy that we awaken each morning? Do we awaken with excitement and enthusiasm because we are gifted with a new day? Do we look within ourself to find ways to share and care about other people? Do we feel that we are taken advantage of by other people? Are we excited about communicating our dreams, ideas, and inspirations?

Challenging ourself to release all of the strings that may continue to be attached to our cycle of fear and to our early cycle of love will be useful to our growth. The events of our life will create physical opportunities to live our love by changing our perception of solutions to events. The physical circumstances of life will not change, but we will change the way that we perceive them and the effect they can have upon our life. This will begin our behavior of valuing ourself. *In valuing ourself, we never become a victim of circumstances but we become a master of challenge.* In valuing ourself we never accept behavior that does not value us.

As we explore our mind to find and trigger each memory we will become conscious of the cycle moving faster and with more harmony. Once all of our experiences are exposed within our mind and subjected to our loving energy of spirit, the value of living our change is accepted and all experiences of today and all other embodiments are healed by our mind. There will be no need to belabor the pain that was perceived with the experience. Only the lesson will be of value to the soul memory and to our intellect. Each lesson of each experience will become a diamond paving the path of our soul growth.

When the value of love in life is clearly understood, we begin to move forward, to the level of integrating new and positive beliefs and behaviors from our soul and spirit energy into our physical lifestyle and attitude.

Integration becomes the fifth level of our emotional change in the cycle of love.

As our new beliefs find courage and power as a way of life, we begin to integrate them into our daily behavior. This next cycle of personal growth enthusiastically weaves our new behavior into the everyday physical life that we live. As our changed behavior becomes an active part of our daily life, we begin to see the constant validations within our relationships, career, family, and activities. We begin to have a good time in life, enjoying people, events, and experiences with a new wonder and insight.

Our new beliefs and behaviors become the flip side of the coin. Instead of viewing our beliefs and behaviors with fear and anger, we begin to see the lesson that is hidden within each belief and behavior and we view the experience from the positive view of love rather than fear. This gives us the strength to release old beliefs and behaviors that no longer serve us, and we release each one with love, thanking it for having supported us in our lesson.

We begin to see that when we judged, we were judged. When we accept others for the perfection of their soul and spirit, they will accept us in the identical energy. We consciously change our speech from the can't to the can, from the won't to the will, from the don't to the do.

Our change of perception allows us to fully open to our soul and spirit energy of motivation and inspiration. We begin to bless our ideas, our imagination, our dreams, and our ability to create from our intellect within our physical reality. Life begins to flow with a harmony and rhythm that has never been known before.

At times we may feel that life is a magnificent scientific experiment as we gain insight and understanding of the levels of soul growth on our level, on the level of society, and on the level of the world. We will watch others in amazement as we see them working through their life issues as fearful, physical experiences. This vision is given to us as a validation of the value of change. Seeing the steps with clarity validates our choice of change, and it allows us to see the integration that occurs within us, society, and the world as one magnificent whole.

As integration flows through us with a new harmony and rhythm, we can sense, see, hear, and feel our minds working as one mind. We no longer feel the separateness of life, but we feel the unity of life and we find joy in living that unity. Our senses become acute as our physical senses integrate with our soul and spirit senses. As our senses integrate, their merging allows the energy of our soul and spirit, as well as the energy of other souls and spirits, to become a living part of our reality. Integration allows us to accept communication at any level of energy from ourself and others.

As the positive value of the integration of our changed beliefs and behaviors begins to reflect their image back to us, we begin to marvel at the abundance that we see within our life.

Abundance becomes the sixth level of emotional change that we experience as we change within the cycle of love energy.

Suddenly we become aware of the abundance that love has brought into our life. We see our loving family, friends, and close associates. We become conscious of the abundance of love, life, health, and experiences, and we begin to rearrange our priorities for abundance. We find that we no longer place the same value on money, possessions, careers, status, and greed.

We begin to find value in the simple life that connects us to the roots of the Earth and the energy of the Universe. Our perception of ourself begins to acquire a new image of wholeness. Our perception of time and space is open and flowing. We have no sense of control or suppression. We fully understand that the only moment of physical reality for us is this very moment that we are living. We no longer fragment our energy by thinking about yesterday or tomorrow. We live only in the abundance of the moment.

We see our connection to all people, nature, and planets. We release every sense within us of separateness, loneliness, and fear. We see ourself in total unity with the Earth, the Universe, and the Cosmos. We see ourself as one with the Creator and one with nature. *We see ourself with one magnificent mind that is always open and flowing in a harmony and rhythm. We see ourself as love and truth.*

We begin to understand that it is the balance of everything around us that supports us and our life. We begin to understand that maintaining nature's balance in a harmony and rhythm is the way we maintain our health and our happiness. *Our perception of abundance begins to expand and we see that which we are connected to as our abundance.* Nature, family, friends, love, health, and happiness become the fiber of our life and the foundation of our relationships, and we suddenly realize that we truly cannot have abundance without them.

In recognizing this new abundance, our priorities begin to change. Money and possessions are no longer our top priority. We see that in our natural abundance is our health and happiness, our connection to nature, and the people we love are all that we truly need in life. With this realization we understand our power of creation, our freedom of choice, our freedom of will, and our freedom of intention with absolute clarity.

As our recognition of life and self begin to expand, we enter into the last cycle of love and that is the level of celebration of love and truth.

Celebration is the seventh and last level in our cycle of love to create change within us.

Our seventh level of change gives us the freedom of choice, will, and intention to celebrate the energy of our love. Our internal sense of peace and joy expands our feeling of power and creation within us. Our new level of energy and understanding inspires and motivates us to enthusiastically create our inspired ideas into physical action. Life becomes an ongoing celebration of creation and joy.

We willingly accept the inspiration of our spirit and the motivation of our soul as part of our inherent energy force. Once we accept this inherent power within us, we understand with total clarity how to use our soul and spirit power to create within our reality. We honor, respect, and value the power of our loving energy. Using the loving energy of our soul and spirit becomes a joyful celebration of our life.

Our joy allows us to live in the moment, being in our power, and celebrating a deep and overwhelming happiness with our life.

As our cycle of change is complete and we find ourself living the love that we feel, our commitment to our personal expansion continues. Our awareness at each level grows, and in living our awareness we create self-expansion. As we expand into the full spectrum of our electromagnetic energy field, our life is no longer the same. Our expansion connects us to the harmony and balance of the Universal consciousness and the Earth consciousness. We see that as a HUMAN consciousness we are an integrated part of the whole consciousness system. Our love, compassion, truth, integrity, and honor qualify our every action, belief, and behavior. Our actions become intensely conscious, and reaction is lost forever with our fear.

As our integration connection begins, we become conscious of the various streams of electromagnetic energy and their effect upon us, nature, and the world. As we perceive the multiple levels of growth within ourself, we also perceive the vision of our whole mind as one integrated unit. Our view allows us to see the levels where stasis occurs, where we are attached to the various levels by our beliefs, and the lessons that we learn in our path of evolution. As this lesson of the cycle of love is completed, we finish our level of knowledge and move forward to our level of understanding, which is the freedom of our ethical awakening into the light side of our soul.

At last we can fully understand that life is a journey, not a destination.

Our power in living our journey is unlimited, except for the obstructions that we create within our own intellect and ego mind. Our failure to understand our female power and our wisdom is the only limitation that we meet. We create our life from our individual perception of our life's reality. No one creates anything for us. We have total freedom of choice as we create and as we change. It is our freedom of choice, will, and intention that directs each action of our life and thus creates our physical reality.

As understanding becomes our way of life, we find our communication changing, and our giving and receiving takes on a new rhythm and harmony. We find ourself viewing others in total nonjudgement, knowing they are working with their own growth and it is perfect for them. With this understanding, we remove any temptation to compare ourself to or to compete with another. At last we understand the wholeness of us, and we celebrate self in our purity and happiness. Cooperation and achievement becomes our purpose as we detach ourself completely from the competition and conflict.

At each and every level of our growth as we live the experiences of life in our specific level of evolution, we attract energy to us from our own electromagnetic force field of energy. Our energy supports us at whatever level of energy we are intimately involved in living.

If we are living in fear and are working through our life experiences at any one of the seven levels of fear that we have just discussed, we will attract people who are working with images of that same energy.

If we are living in love energy and are working through any one of the seven levels of love energy that we have just discussed, we will attract people to us who are working with images of that same energy.

In both instances the specific secondary level of change does not have to be identical, but the primary level of our soul evolution should be identical if our relationship is going to be productive for our growth. Therefore, those friends, lovers, and colleagues that we attract will appear to us in different images of the same energy force field. Many times the small difference that is present within the secondary levels will not trigger our understanding of the difference. Challenging ourself with growth from two very different levels of soul evolution can neutralize our energy.

We will find comfort and intimacy within some familiar energy fields, but energy fields that are focused upon levels other than our own have the ability to develop stasis within us rather quickly if we adjust to a lower field of energy. The more advanced our energy field is, the more challenging it is to accept a static or stagnant energy field. Staying within either energy field can be detrimental to our health because it allows deterioration to begin within our mind and our body.

The most important aspect of being in a loving, intimate relationship is our ability to grow and to help our intimate partner enthusiastically expand his or her own potential for growth.

This does not create one partner as always being the teacher in the relationship but it allows us to inspire each other, which can be an intriguing mind game that is limitless. As it creates an even exchange of giving and receiving of ideas through communication and living, we gain new insights into ourself and the Universe.

When each partner can live through the understanding of his or her power of creation, the ideas, inspirations, dreams, imagination, and motivation will create a constant flow of productive and creative energy that initiates growth.

Without both partners understanding their own abilities and power, the relationship will be reduced to a physical intention for survival and can allow the advanced party to be overwhelmed with boredom. If neither individual is advanced in his or her soul growth, the lessons will be learned by both parties at the physical survival level, which is perfect for them in equal levels of growth.

These are explanations of how and why intimate relationships thrive more efficiently in their growth if the levels begin at about the same scale and their path of growth continues to grow and change together. Staying in balance with each other allows for thought to be shared and understood as growth continues to inspire creativity.

Each idea emanating from one spirit mind can trigger inspiration from the loving spirit mind of the partner, transporting each individual to new heights of understanding as they indulge in mental games of inspiration with total enthusiasm.

When lovers are within the electromagnetic energy field of soul and spirit love, they have the ability to fly on each other's wings. Their growth becomes charged with the expanded energy of two souls and spirits working in a harmony and rhythm of energy that is beautiful and evolving. There are no boundaries in these relationships. As the friendship and the understanding deepens, their minds think as one.

If the electromagnetic energy force field of both minds in a relationship is attached to fear energy, both partners will find themselves creating separation, dependency, anger, fear, depression, and negative behavioral experiences. They will give the illusion of clinging, together but this will be an illusion mirrored from their experiencing fear expansion through the magnification of their fear energy. They will be sticking together as fear elements for survival not love.

The fear that separates us from the unity of self is always symbolized through the relationships that we live and the love that we experience. Fear by its very nature causes internal and external separation within our mind and within our physical relationship on some level. In turn, this fear creates stasis and devolution in our life experiences because of the internal separation and loneliness. Growth is stagnated internally and externally for both individuals if they share a fear energy in the relationship. Fear emanating from one person expands the fear emanating from the partner.

If we are not in an intimate relationship with another person, we will experience this phenomenon in the intense separation of our own body, mind, and spirit. Seeking the unity of a physical relationship is the symbol of our infinite search for the internal unity of our intellect, soul, and spirit minds.

Fear is the predominant energy when we are growing within the physical dimension of our physical evolution and within the dark side of our soul evolution. It is a normal part of our growth process. And it remains part of our physical life until we consciously make the choice to change our perception of reality from fear to love at the time of rending the veil in our second dimension of our soul evolution.

Life is a personal growth experience in soul evolution. Life is a physical tool for growth experience in spirit evolution. Life must be experienced and understood as the lessons we are learning if we are to allow our own personal growth. Love is the energy of the higher levels of soul evolution and of all the levels of spirit evolution. Once our physical life is understood, it becomes the love of our soul and spirit.

Moving through the cycle of change from fear to love becomes the peak experience of the soul as it moves from the shadow side of the soul to the light side of the soul.

Our evolution moves the fourth level of our soul growth beyond the veil of the intellect and allows the intellect to open to the wisdom and ingenuity of the soul and the love and truth of the spirit. At this moment we invite our integrated mind to search for absolute truth rather than relative truth.

The veil of our ego separates our intellect during the level of soul evolution that is focused upon knowledge. As long as the veil is intact, the intellect is attached by karmic streams of memory to the primitive, examination, and reflective levels of the shadow side of the soul. We will then make all of our intellectual judgements relative to the knowledge from our earlier physical experiences

Moving from the fear cycle of change to the love cycle of change is "rending the veil" in the peak experience of the knowledge level of our soul evolution.

The explosive feeling of release that we experience in physical orgasm is symbolic of the feeling that accompanies the rending of the veil for the soul. But the rapture and ecstasy for the soul in this experience cannot be totally duplicated emotionally by our physical senses. Since all physical emotion has elements of fear within its foundation until the rending of the veil, the true emotion of physical love cannot be enjoyed completely until the peak experience has occurred.

As a society we reflect the electromagnetic energy of the collective consciousness of multiple individuals. If the majority of individuals are living the energy of fear, our society will reflect the consciousness of fear in all aspects of our experience, including intimate relationships.

Our government, politics, education, health care, corporations, banking industry, religion, and media will be focused upon fear. Each event of our daily experience will be dramatized, sensationalized, and analyzed from our fear perception. This same pattern of fear reaction will occur within our intimate experiences in relationships creating the drama of individual wars.

Fear will support us in staying attached to dramas by allowing us to experience the physical adrenalin rush with negative events. Our ego will provide us with the negative beliefs to resist positive change as we join in the drama energy. In intimate relationships this will be acted out as fear through anger, depression, competition, and habit. It will be seen as quarreling, fighting, divorce, abuse, and murder.

All of these emotions resist physical and emotional change because there is a fear of the unknown. Our intellectual mind will belabor or struggle for an absurd amount of time over each and every aspect of the information of the physical experience and the emotional trauma that accompanies it. Yet our intellect shakes in terror at the unknown events that might accompany our change of beliefs and behaviors. The intellect will test the event against every perception it knows as it tries to comprehend why change is an inherent factor in our physical experience.

We are energy. Our physical body is energy. Our intellect and ego are energy. Our soul and spirit are energy. We are totally energy and energy by its very nature must move and change. Energy that is stagnant or inert will begin to decay.

Change is inherent within us and is at all times a driving force for movement and growth. Change is a constant within our cellular structure, our physical body, our mind, our beliefs, and our knowledge. The energy around us is in a constant state of movement and change. Disease is created within the body when the energy of our mind that is attached to our beliefs and behaviors does not move and change. Disease is the decay of stagnant energy within us. Aging is a symptom of slowing energy that is becoming stagnant. To stay young, continue to think young and be physically active and connected to nature. *To avoid stagnant energy of the mind and body, continue to be active and young within your mind and heart.*

There is no acceptable logic to our power of love for the intellect; therefore, we have been taught fear within our physical world. We are seeking an overall understanding of life and our relationship to the Universe which can only be found in our love. Knowing our value to the expansion of the Creator allows us to acknowledge our power and the value that we have in living our life. As we love ourself, we will be happier, healthier, and inspired with hope.

We are on Earth to expand the love, truth, and perfection within our Creator. As we grow and change in our love, the Creator grows and changes in His love. Our intimate love relationships are sought in our physical life as the image of the love we are truly seeking within us from our soul and spirit.

When we understand that our physical experiences of life are designed by us as lessons to help us change and grow in our soul and spirit, we will welcome change. Being attached to the physical experience only ties us to our habitual physical perception of fear. The more intense our intention of soul and spirit to grow and to learn, the more dramatic and chaotic the lessons of our physical life can become if we fail to listen and to act from our soul and spirit love.

It is now time within our human consciousness growth to move beyond the fear, to move beyond our terminal attachment to the physical details of our life drama that capture us in fear. Releasing our attachment to beliefs, behaviors, and habits is an individual choice and can only be successfully initiated when we are in complete understanding of our own power of love.

Understanding our power must become an individual commitment. No one else can walk our path of growth for us. The understanding of another can never be our understanding until we can feel, speak, and live our growth through our openness, creativity, and equality.

Competition, rage, and war are the reactive energies of fear. Each of these reactive energies has multiple levels of emotion and physical images. As the individual unites with the energy of self, the symbols of this internal cooperation will create a new and loving energy of cooperation externally.

We need only to look at the abuse and self-abuse that exists within relationships to identify the internal war that is being fought within the minds of the individuals. These internal fears that are expressed as beliefs and behaviors have a dramatic effect upon the relationships within the family. The parents fight, the children fight, and the entire family may be at war with each other. When the fears of the mind believe in war, war is acted out on all levels.

These same individuals that believe in living war within the home will believe in fighting wars within the streets. Their belief in their own powerlessness, except through the act of fighting, will create war, manipulation, greed, and crime as part of their role in society.

Any individual who believes strongly in war as a method of winning in the home and in the street will be the first to volunteer to fight in the world arena. Interference in the karmic lessons of the people of other societies is not appropriate, in the same way that interference in an individual's life lesson is not appropriate. Our lesson of non-interference is dramatic for us as it symbolizes our patience in allowing others to experience their life lessons by their own design.

Individuals in each society are within that society for their own lessons of soul growth. Change will not occur in the behavior until the beliefs change in the individual to effect change in themselves and change in their society. As a soul and spirit, we choose our parents in a society and in a nation that will support our individual lessons of our soul growth. The individuals will find their own solutions for the society as they grow, and this can fulfill their karmic lesson. When other societies interfere in the karmic lessons, the lessons will be repeated, not learned and healed. The need to fight is a karmic lesson within itself, as is the lesson of interference. *Do unto others as you would have them do unto you.*

The passion for fighting as the solution to problems will be represented in all levels of reality, as an individual member of a family, as a member of society, and as a member of the world. Fighting supports the fear energy of the shadow side of our soul and it is a dramatic indication that we as individuals, society, and the world are not evolving through the veil of beliefs and fear that makes us want to fight.

When we reach the light side of our soul, we will choose to live in our love and truth. We will choose to find peaceful and joyful solutions to any life experience whether it is as an individual, a family, a society, or a world.

Experiencing the changes within our own life through the rewards of love is the way to develop faith in the energy and power of our love.

Understand that our perception of life supports and reflects our beliefs of self, society, and the world. No one else's beliefs reflect our energy unless we accept the beliefs of others as our own. Blindly following the beliefs of history, a person, a society, or any single concept allows us to do so as a passive presence not as a dynamic participant.

The history of the world is rampant with fighting, killing, pestilence, disease, control, and religions. All wars in recorded history have had their connections to religious beliefs. All crimes have their karmic connections to religious beliefs, either as blatant denial of the beliefs or as support for them.

Crimes of greed that are considered "white collar crimes" in our society are opposite to the teachings of Jesus, although many Christian churches that are based upon the teachings of Jesus have lived from the concept of greed and abuse throughout history. When crime is committed in the name of God, it does not change the lesson of the individual. These occurrences are symbols of the lesson of love and truth for the individual and all of our religious teachings as they reflect brilliantly into society and the world as the opposite of Christian behavior, which is fear, sex, greed, and self-gratification. Having a crime of greed or abuse within the structure of religion is an indication that religion must change from the fear teachings to the teaching and the living of love and truth.

Crimes of "ethnic cleansing" within a society are symbolic of the lesson of equality that the individuals within the society are trying to learn by experiencing the opposite behavior of discrimination, fear, and judgement. When a society sees itself as separate from and superior to any other society, it will learn the lesson of equality through war, greed, crime, disease, and discrimination. This lesson is represented in the behavior of the individual as a belief in the inequality of the male and female, the races, the religions, and other ethnic groups. This is the basis of the supremacist concept of life, which has been the foundation of many wars within and between nations and religious groups. *At the core of the supremacist belief in inequality is seeing the male, the female, and God as separate, instead of one.*

The supremacist is the opposite of the equalitarian. The supremacist believes his belief is the right way and the only way, and that all people should believe as he believes. The supremacist will fight, manipulate, lie, cheat, steal, kill, and commit any other atrocity necessary to establish the supremacy of his belief. Life means nothing: it is only his belief that counts in his mind. This is a singular belief in self-supremacy and it is self-defeating in nature. Supremacy has been the role of the physical male throughout the path of our soul evolution and has always been symbolized in his discrimination of the female.

The equalitarian believes that all people are equal despite their individual beliefs. The equalitarian believes in living and allowing others to live by their own beliefs. The equality of the individual spreads out to include the society and the world. The equalitarian lives by his belief in equality, which balances us with nature and with each other.

Jesus was an equalitarian, which is ironic since religions historically believe in the supremacy of the male. Jesus and the Creator both have a consciousness of their equality as male, female, and spirit energy. *The life-giving energy of the Creator began as female energy and only extended into male energy when it created the human body as physical matter. We are equal as physical matter, female energy, and spirit consciousness in our role as humans.*

We must always value the freedom of choice that is inherently ours and we must accept the responsibility to use our freedom of choice. We must live in our love, truth, and equality at all times.

If accepting beliefs becomes our choice and we live by those beliefs, we have fully accepted our personal responsibility for our behaviors. No one else is responsible for the way we think or for what we do. Whatever we give to others in life, we will receive in return. If we give fear, we receive fear. If we give love, we receive love.

We have freedom of choice in all that we do. We all have the power of our spirit energy. That power within us is reflected into our experiences of life as love. If we attach ourself to fear, fear is what we reflect into our life experience. We get back exactly what we give.

If we are a religious believer in fear and judgement, we will find our life controlled by fear and judgement. Control is a lesson of freedom that is being learned in the opposite energy of fear and judgement. It is our choice to stay in the lesson or to learn the lesson of growth and change. Change allows us to move from our belief in fear and judgement to a belief in love, truth, and equality.

To learn how to live from the love that is within us and to attract that energy of love from others, we must understand our physical beliefs that attach us to fear. We must seek to find out who we are so truth can set us free. When we can see the cycles of fear that we experience as part of our growth, we can learn the lessons that we seek and change our pattern of beliefs.

We make our life what it is, moment by moment, day by day. It does not matter that we create our world in this manner from our subconscious and unconscious energy of the soul and spirit— because, regardless of the source of creation, we live what we create. We have the opportunity to choose to live in the energy of love, truth, and equality at any time within our soul path.

Expanding our understanding of how we create our life gives us an opportunity to create what we want, rather than the crises, chaos, dramas, and traumas of what we don't want.

Our soul and spirit designs the dramas of our life experiences and we create them within the physical experience to get our attention. If we are willing to understand ourself through our integrated mind, we will choose fewer crises to awaken us.

Understanding is a higher level of soul and spirit evolution than the level of knowledge. The shifting of our consciousness that we are now experiencing is from the Cycle of Awareness to the Cycle of Understanding within our soul level of knowledge. Our shift from awareness of self to an understanding of self shifts us from our male, physical energy to our female, soul and spirit energy.

Knowledge is based upon learned beliefs and learned facts. Many of our learned facts are firmly attached to the primitive levels of our soul growth. We have a choice to repeat these primitive beliefs on a daily basis within our life or to change our perception of self and life. We effectively live our repetitious creation as our daily behavior when we live through our fear, judgement, inequality, and greed beliefs. Each of these behaviors are the opposite of love and truth, and therefore we consistently fail to respect, honor, and value self as well as others.

We are evolving souls that are ready for the peak experience of our soul growth, and yet we hold ourself attached to the primitive beliefs of fear. Evolving souls are seeking a more peaceful and relaxed physical experience than what is being created through the fear of our ego and intellect. Our soul is ready to live from the love, truth, and equality of the light side of our soul. We want to celebrate our love and our growth.

Understanding allows us to explore our fear beliefs and our facts from a different perception of mind energy and to consciously choose to live by those beliefs which are valid for us at this time in our growth and to release those beliefs that no longer serve us.

Love, truth, and equality is the inherent energy of our soul and spirit and it lives eternally within us. Love, truth, and equality is the energy of us, and it is there to be used when we can accept the beauty, magnificence, and courage of our female power as our divine nature.

Truth

◊

"The highest truth is truth of the Spirit; a Spirit supreme above the world and yet immanent in the world and in all that exists, sustaining and leading all towards whatever is the aim and goal and the fulfilment of Nature since her obscure inconscient beginnings through the growth of consciousness is the one aspect of existence which gives a clue to the secret of our being and a meaning to the world."

Sri Aurobindo, On Himself

*T*his is the truth of our human destiny. Our spirit consciousness is the most important energy within us. If we have no awareness of our spirit self, we have no awareness of our female self and no awareness of our eternal self. Our spirit is our eternal self and our female self. Accepting the spirit within us as the truth of our being gives us a new perception of life.

Our spirit energy is our internal mother energy that nurtures us in our moment of need. Without our spirit we are only a shadow of our ego fantasy lurking within a hollow shell of physical matter. Without our spirit being acknowledged by our intellect, we are vain and shallow, breaking under the slightest pressure. It is our ego that becomes an immediate victim and succumbs to pathos.

Spirit is the eternal, internal energy of us that is forever our inspiration to love, truth, and perfection. Spirit gives us the strength and courage to live in the physical world through our compassion, freedom, equality, responsibility, and humility. As we respect and value our dignity, we live a life of mercy, learning, growing, and being in our ideas, enthusiasm, joy, choice, and open awareness. It is our spirit that acknowledges the truth of our physical life through joy and happiness.

Spirit is the good within us. It is always positive, happy, joyful, and playful. It is kind, thoughtful, peaceful, and concerned. The expansiveness of our spirit can only be imagined within our linear intellect because our spirit cannot be limited by boundaries, roles, or identities. Our spirit is magnificent, powerful, all knowing, and it is the truth of who we are.

We are the physical child of our spirit, and our spirit is symbolized in the physical world by our mother. We see our mother as our nurturer, our stability, our friend, and we recognize that our mother loves us despite our behavior or our relationship. Despite the physical relationship that we have with our mother, everyone recognizes that it is through the life-giving energy of the mother that we came into the world. We remain a physical child to our mother spirit until we rend the veil that separates us. Only the physical child can live with the image of being wounded by life and living in pain and fear. Our inner soul and higher spirit knows that fear is the illusion of the physical world.

Our female energy has been the acknowledged symbol of our liberty and freedom for many centuries. The power of our female, spirit energy was instilled upon Earth numerous times throughout history by spirit messengers such as I am. When the United States was established as a nation, it was guided by divine spirit energy to represent the three dimensions of the human condition experiencing soul evolution.

Our physical nature was represented by the red in our flag and our divine nature by the white in our flag. The blue was created to represent the peace of the soul, with each star being an enlightened state of being within that field of peace. All but nineteen of the signees of the Constitution were in direct communication with their spirit energy.

Each of them were guided to separate the state from the church that had been the foundation of religious fear in the mind of man. The unity of self and the world was fully explained, as was the inalienable right to equality of each human. Reminders of our spirit power were placed in the statues of females representing equality, freedom, and liberty in this new country. We have been left with this spirit legacy of truth, but we have continued to place our trust in the male intellect and have ignored the truth of our female power of spirit.

Our spirit mother nurtures us but she is also teaching us the love of nurturing, the freedom of truth, and the joy of equality as our perfection. Our perfection is the way to liberate us from the bondage of our beliefs into the freedom of our spirit consciousness.

Love, truth, and equality is the mother symbol of the life-giving energy of our spirit. Mothers are forever symbols of the relationship that we have with our spirit self. As we get more in touch with our spirit energy, the relationship that we have with our physical mother will change and grow. The truth of our spirit and soul connection within the relationship will become clear.

Our spirit self is symbolized in our life by living from our divine nature, or living from the good that is within us. When we love ourself, we will love and honor other people. At that moment we are actively living from the influence of our divine nature. Our divine nature is positive, loving, truthful, and compassionate, and it instills us with enthusiasm, excitement, and joy.

Life is a meditation in physical experience for our spirit self.

There is no fear within our spirit. Our spirit is consumed by the divine love of who we are, why we are here, and the joy of life as our opportunity to grow. If we find ourself captured in fear, it is apparent that we are living from the ego and intellect. The path of our soul leads us through multiple physical experiences as we seek the loving energy of our spirit. Our physical nature, which is connected with our bridge of soul, knows the truth of our divine nature but our ego has blocked the love and truth of our spirit, leaving our physical nature without a conscious awareness that it knows.

The beliefs that we become attached to within our intellect form the veil of our ego that separates the intellect from our spirit energy. This creation of fear is the natural energy of the ego as it seeks to separate our minds by threatening beliefs. The intellect feels small and insignificant when it feels separated from the expansive mind of our soul and spirit. As our intellect becomes attached to the fear found within the negative beliefs of our ego, it feels threatened by its sense of separateness, its loneliness, and its sense of insignificance and unworthiness. The ego is the originator of our physical fears.

The ego, when influenced by the spirit, becomes the true essence of humility and can positively influence our physical experiences of life.

The spirit instills a peacefulness that comes from deep within us. It is a solid force of power that gives us faith and trust in ourself. When we are humble we see all things with our spirit perception. The magnificence of our spirit is quite naturally a humbling experience for the self-directed ego and once the ego has basked in the true light of our spirit it is never the same again.

The ego does not begin its separation of the intellect with the intention of creating extreme fear for us. Understanding the ego becomes our lesson of releasing our fear beliefs before we can see the truth of the wisdom of our soul, and the love, truth, and perfection of our spirit self. The more fear we nurture in our physical nature, the more power we give to the ego as the veil of beliefs that separates us from our spirit.

Supporting our fear beliefs without searching for truth is the way our ego sets us up for abuse, victimization, and failure. We are totally responsible for the fear that we create to separate us from our love, because we have freedom of choice. It is our intellect and ego that plays the game of judging us and creating fear within us. It is our intellect and ego that is attached to beliefs of inequality and control, shutting out our truth because the ego fears change.

Humility is never self-serving, but it is exquisitely self-fulfilling to our body, mind, and spirit.

As spirit we have no concept of failure because failure is not a reality to the spirit within us. Unworthiness and inadequacy are unreal to our spirit energy. Our spirit has no need to judge what another person does because it understands that our life is designed totally for our benefit and that all experiences that we have are about us. Each life event is a soul design to help us see within our own closed mind. As spirit we also understand that each person is living the moment that is perfect for him or her in his or her personal growth. Without the lesson of the physical experience we would not grow and change. Our truth is found in accepting the truth that is being acted out within our lesson.

Our individual beliefs symbolize our level of growth, and that level of our growth is always visible within our words, emotional behavior, and the physical actions of our daily life.

The old saying "our actions speak louder than our words" has its foundation in the reality of our lesson of truth. Thoughts and words fall on infertile ground as profusely as a summer rainfall and are as quickly absorbed, but it is our actions that live on in the minds and the lives of others. Our presence upon Earth can only find truth in what we do physically, and learning is doing for our soul. Presence has only a shallow recognition without meaningful accomplishments of learning and doing for other people.

We cannot change another person as a spirit or as a human being. We can only be a good example in the way that we live and perceive our own human experience. If we attempt to control others with our negative beliefs, all that are involved are working with the multiple lessons of control and interference. If we attempt to control others with what we feel are the right and positive beliefs, we have not yet learned about freedom, unconditional love, and patience. Our lesson of patience is our lesson of noninterference.

Being a good example keeps us from accepting or reflecting our bad behavior to another before we rend the veil of our ego. It is important to maintain our integrity and moral virtue in all of our physical interactions at each stage of our life. We should at all times seek to be true to our individual path of soul evolution. *As we grow in our soul understanding and rend our veil, we no longer live from our mirror image of self.* As a soul and spirit we are committed to our personal growth, which can only be achieved through our physical experiences. The physical body is our way of learning to live the truth of our soul and spirit energy.

When we live as one united being using our physical body and intellect to be in our soul and spirit, we are living the truth of our integrated self. Spirit—as love, truth, and perfection—ingeminates us with responsibility, commitment, productivity, equality, and freedom. Boundaries, restrictions, resistances, and denials are no longer a part of our daily experience when we acknowledge and allow the power of truth to guide us.

Living in the purity of love, truth, and equality is living in our spirit self. In spirit, we speak love and truth from our heart in each moment of our human experience. Our actions of life express our love, truth, and equality in our daily behavior. We transcend all fear and know the energy and power of our love as we live our truth.

Thinking, speaking, and acting our truth from the love and perfection within us is living from our divine nature in our physical human experience.

As spirit becomes a part of our life, all of life begins to change. We no longer think we are spiritual, or needfully speak the language that we feel will associate us with spirituality. We feel connected to the physical world and we want to help the people, the societies, and the world to accept truth as growth and change.

We realize our connection to Earth, the Universe, and the Cosmos by the influence of nature, the sun, and the moon. Within the living of our life, we act through the perfection of our deeds. Our words become the simple, loving words of our heart. Our conduct is guided by our love, truth, mercy, and compassion. Our behavior reflects our generosity, respect, and dignity with an innate sense of equality.

Spirit is an energy that exists within us. It is the energy that inspires us to awaken in the morning and face our day with a smile. It is the joy that we feel when we watch a gull soaring in the breeze, a rose burst into bloom, or a tree growing majestically by the side of a brook. It is the love and compassion that we feel when we watch the small body of a child running across an open field. It is the pleasure and appreciation that tugs at our heart when we see a beautiful painting, hear a marvelous song, or feel the rhythm and harmony of a wonderful dance. It is the freedom that we feel when the wind blows across our cheek and gently lifts our hair. Spirit is the wonderment of our life, which we mindfully enjoy.

Our spirit allows us to be in harmony with nature, with our fellow man, and with ourself.

Spirit energy can be seen by our physical eyes, just as it is always seen by the spirit within us. Spirit energy can be measured and recognized by our scientific equipment, if we accept and understand spirit energy in our intellect. Spirit energy can be measured in the healing of the mind and body by an acceptance of change from disease to health. Spirit energy must be accepted upon faith and trust until the physical senses within us are capable of recognition. Our spirit energy gives us the power of faith and trust because it gives us the power of our spirit senses as our true nature.

Spirit is the most expansive and magnificent energy of us. If we deny our spirit, we deny our soul, and we deny our truth of self. A man without a soul and spirit lives without a heart. It is our soul and spirit that removes us from the animal kingdom and honors us with eternal life as a HUMAN.

Because of our soul and spirit we are the thinkers and the speakers of the Universe. We are HUMAN. We are Higher Universal Mana. We are Spirit Consciousness. We are truth as the image of God.

Because of our spirit consciousness, we have been blessed with the ability to discover and to merge with our divine nature. Merging our divine nature with our physical nature changes our physical personality and character traits into a superconsciousness that allows us to live from our true potential upon Earth.

As our internal senses change, we have the ability to use our soul and spirit senses in a way equal to and expanded from our physical senses. The senses of our soul and spirit far exceed the abilities of our physical senses, but before we learn to use our spirit and soul senses we must first learn to use our physical senses.

Our magnification of energy allows us to become consciously aware of the spirit realms within us and to consciously use this power within our life.

All changes within the spirit of self are simple, humble, truthful, and they happen with a speed greater than the speed of light. All changes within the physical self require commitment, responsibility, love, truth, integrity, equality, and freedom, as well as millions of years of repetition of our physical lessons.

Physical changes are measured by time and space. Spirit knows no time and is within all space.

Spirit changes can only be seen on Earth through the change of the physical personality and characteristics. It is when the merging of the physical nature and the divine nature occurs that spirit change can be seen as physical change. When we change, society changes, and the world changes.

Humans began as the *thoughts* of Divine Spirit. Our spirit within us is eternal. It is the physical body that is finite and used as a tool to help us through our human experience. As spirit we are a seed of the Divine Spirit, but we must grow and expand that seed into the magnificence of the Creator. As we grow and expand, the divine nature within us expands. When the love and truth within us expands, the Divine Spirit expands in its magnificence.

In our physical world spirit can only be made real by the love and truth we live in our human experience. When we as individuals and as a society live from our divine nature, the body of the Divine Spirit lives in health, beauty, love, and truth. When we live from fear, anger, denial, and false beliefs, we become an unhealthy cell in the body of the Divine Spirit. The Divine Spirit fills all space within us and around us. We are the body of the Divine Spirit.

When we live as physical beings from fear, anger, denial, and false beliefs, we symbolize the character of our beliefs into our physical body and life, and into the body and life of our society. We create disease within our body by the creation of unhealthy cells, and as unhealthy cells we create dysfunction and disharmony within society and within the world. We are united within us, with the

Earth, and with the Universe. Our unity is the truth of Universal Law. The unity of our intellect, soul, and spirit is the truth of Universal Law. Our unity with Divine Spirit is Universal Law.

What is above is below. We are a fractal pattern of the Earth. We are a fractal pattern of the Universe. We are a fractal pattern of the Divine Spirit. As we are living upon Earth with a divine nature and a physical nature, we have only to acknowledge both parts of our nature to be whole.

To merge our natures we must acknowledge that something smarter than our physical intellect created us and is at all times there within us, guiding and teaching us.

Only the intellect and ego resists the soul and spirit. This resistance symbolizes the fear and competition of our physical nature. Our soul and spirit are inseparable in the same manner that our intellect and ego are inseparable. Our soul and spirit lives in cooperation and is seeking the love and unity of self. But our intellect and ego lives in the fear of spirit competition and is seeking separateness of self, which the ego identifies with its survival.

The challenges of this internal tug-of-war between our ego and intellect and our soul and spirit are manifested within society through the same identical actions, which we create within us internally and within our physical experiences externally. Competition versus cooperation is seen throughout our society between individuals, businesses, governments, educational systems, health care systems, and religions.

Living the symbols of competition and fear externally supports the internal perceptions of competition and fear found in our intellect and ego. And living the competition and fear internally supports the external creation of the lesson. In this way we create a never-ending cycle of energy that captures us in competition, fear, and judgement. Fear, competition, and judgement deny the Universal Law of Love and Truth. *When our human experience supports fear and competition we expand the resistance and denial of our divine nature of soul and spirit by our intellect and ego.*

None of the resistances and denials that are part of our intellect and ego destroy the reality of our soul and spirit self. Resistance and denial simply strengthen the veil of beliefs that surrounds our ego and intellect and allow our beliefs to act out of a more intense neediness. This neediness will be the impetus that moves many people with a physical nature to invest in a relationship. Feelings of being "needed" in a relationship support the need within us to be needed. This is a physical relationship not a soul and spirit relationship until the need can be replaced with the love, truth, and perfection of our spirit. Need symbolizes the belief of the ego.

When we live in a temple with many mansions, shutting off one room by closing a door does not destroy the mansion.

The spirit of self has enfinite patience, compassion, and mercy for the physical nature as it travels through our human experience. It doesn't matter how intricate the physical experience is or how long it takes for our soul to travel through its path of evolution. Our soul and spirit will patiently wait for the door of the mind to open and the harmony and rhythm of the mind energy to become one in the Universal Law of Unity. Truth will always win out in time.

We are given the Mother/Father love of the Spirit toward us as children of our divine nature in the same way the mother/father love of the family supports us in our physical nature as a child.

The physical structure and organization of the family unit is the physical symbol of the spirit family unit. We are created as physical beings from the unity of the male and female sexual interaction in the same way that our spirit self was created by the interaction of the Mother/Father androgynous Divine Spirit. This Divine interaction was of an asexual nature, but it allowed us to have both male and female personalities and characteristics.

Our physical personality is the male within us and our divine personality is the female within us. We are one. Our dual nature allows us to have both male and female personality and character traits and two distinct minds—the physical, male mind of the intellect and ego, and the divine, female mind of the soul and spirit.

When we deny and resist the divine or female side of our nature, we will find ourself in the drama of fear and competition. Fear and competition set the stage for change that will happen at a moment's notice if a single belief or behavior of our male mind is challenged. This state of emotional instability sees all physical events as opposition to the ego comfort and our neediness increases in proportion to our fear. The competitive cycle feeds upon itself and continues to repeat itself into layer after layer of veil to protect our castigated ego.

In our total unawareness of our protective action, we veil our intellect and ego with our physical beliefs and separate ourself totally from our soul and spirit self. These personality and character traits allow us to live our life from dishonesty, control, greed, inequality, and multiple other emotions and actions that are the opposite of our spirit self. Our male mind perception of self sees only the physical, intellectual, and ego image of the physical. Our male mind has a supremacist attitude toward life, the female, and the world. When society or the world is structured from the male mind, the female will be discriminated against until the male understands that he is not supreme. *When the male mind is influenced by the humility of an awakened soul and spirit, equality will be established and truth will prevail upon Earth.*

Our physical self becomes the shadow reflection of the true eternal spirit of self that is living behind the veil of physical beliefs of our intellect and ego. The more fear that exists within the mind, the denser the veil is that surrounds the intellect and ego, shutting out that part of ourself that is divine in nature. The denser the veil becomes to surround our physical nature, the more intense the fear becomes from the separation the intellect and ego is experiencing.

This will establish a noticeable conflict within society as the male experiences the tug-of-war with the spirit in releasing his belief in his supremacy. The male is the physical, fighting, and fearful side of our nature, and it will not want to give up fighting with the other half of itself as spirit any faster than it will want to give up fighting wars. Fear, competition, and conflict is the symbol of our physical nature that has not yet merged with our divine nature. The delusion of separation that attaches us to the physical nature of self is our path of growth through the shadow side of our soul.

The shadow side of our soul gives us an opportunity to learn by living the human experiences that teach us what we do not want. It is only when we experience what we do not want that we begin to see with total clarity what we do want. We focus our life into physical purposes and goals, until we clearly see that we are not simply physical in nature. We will change our perception of God being external to us when we are willing to accept and acknowledge the spirit within us. When this acceptance begins, we are on our path of integrating our physical nature with our divine nature. This is the beginning of truth for us.

Every experience that has occurred upon Earth has occurred as a lesson for the soul. There is no progression for man in blaming individuals or the acts of history. All physical experiences are there to learn from in a passive or active way.

When history is viewed unemotionally to gain a clear perception of how we have created our reality, we will begin our climb out of the shadow side of our soul. What we have experienced on the shadow side of our soul was there to balance the scale of the negative and positive energy experiences in our lessons of life. This cycle of energy experience is understood as "an eye for an eye, and a tooth for a tooth."

As the soul grows through the seven primary levels of evolution, experiencing the multiple secondary levels of growth, it will in time reach the seventh level of absolute truth. In the present level of growth of the physical nature the soul has reached the fourth level of knowledge, which is relative truth.

Knowledge is seen as relative truth in the shadow of our soul as it relates to our physical perception. Absolute truth is found in the understanding, wisdom, and truth of the light side of our soul as it relates to Universal Law.

As knowledge expands into the Cycle of Understanding, we will be awakening to the light side of our soul. At this moment we will celebrate the beginning of the merging of the physical and divine nature within us. Because of the relationship of the ego to the spirit at this point of merging, an extreme tug-of-war is taking place between our male mind and our female mind. When our physical nature has fully merged with our divine nature, we will be living as divine humans in our physical experience without conflict or fear.

The spirit has chosen for us to live an equal amount of time in our divine nature to that which we have lived in our physical nature. This will be our opportunity for true growth as HUMANS.

As we have grown through the shadow side of the soul, we have perceived ourself as suffering. We have not suffered as eternal spirit. As we enter into the light side of our soul we will consciously celebrate our happiness.

Suffering is a perception of the intellectual mind which is manifested within the body and within the human experiences of life. Without the physical symbol of suffering to capture our attention, we would not see our plight as clearly and choose to seek change. Acknowledging what we do not want gives us the opportunity to change and grow. Through our human experiences we are simply growing into the true love and magnificence of our divine being. When we perceive the physical events of our life as lessons, we will be unaware of the perception of suffering.

The human experience, especially as it interrelates with family members, and intimate and close friends, is the supported path to our divine nature. The lessons of our soul experience are at all times reflected within these family relationships, friendships, and intimate relationships.

Close friends are many times old spirit friends that are there to help us with the lessons of life. They will frequently not be as involved in the drama of our human experience as they are in helping us balance ourself as we experience the physical drama. Love will always be understood between the soul and spirit energy, and therefore judgement will not be an issue within the physical experience from those that are close to us.

All of humanity must come to the understanding that within each of us is all that is. We have an inherent equality in each and every sense of our own energy and an equality with all of humanity. We move through our path of growth by focusing upon both male and female genders upon Earth. We are at all times both male and female, or physical and divine natures, regardless of the focus of our physical gender or our sexual orientation. *As a growing spirit we will choose to be in lifetimes of each gender, and each race, religion, ethnic group, and role of society.*

We are learning to be human by experiencing all that is. We will choose lives that allow us to experience all races and cultures. When we learn the lesson of a specific race or culture, we will choose a new lesson for our next lifetime. We will move through our soul growth by experiencing all orientations of sexual relationships within our physical nature. If we feel fear or anger towards different sexual orientations or races, we have not yet learned that lesson and we will choose the experience in another lifetime. Our divine nature is at all times asexual but our physical nature is sexual.

Our sexual nature is a gift to help us see love more clearly within our intimate relationships.

The transition from our androgynous asexual divine nature to our sexual physical nature is the true symbolism of Adam and Eve in the Garden of Eden. The asexual division of the twin soul of Eve was the true division of our spirit into the male and female physical consciousness. It also served to symbolize the lesson of unity through the lesson of procreation within the human experience. With our twin soul energy we can work through our lessons by forever receiving what we give in the physical world. If we are male and we discriminate against women, our female twin soul is receiving what we give. When our roles are reversed we will again be female and find ourself receiving discrimination from males.

With the diversity of perception that exists between the male mind and the female mind, the understanding of speech, emotions, thinking, touching, smelling, tasting, hearing, and seeing also became different.

This striking difference in perception created a need for our physical sexuality to help us maintain a symbol of unity. Without sexuality the diversity of perception between the male and female would have expanded the competition between them and humanity would have lost all semblance of unity. Sexuality became a necessary attraction to bring the male and female consciousnesses together for the purpose of procreation to maintain the human species. At the same time, the attraction of the male and female for each other was to symbolize the attraction of our physical nature to our divine nature.

The first five physical senses were developed as creation survival senses, and therefore became the primitive stimulus triggering the physical yearnings of sexual desire. Without our heterosexual attraction to each other, the human species would have become extinct.

The stimulation of these primitive yearnings was responded to with a total mindlessness. There was no comprehension of the purpose of sexual interaction. The body was not understood, nor was the mind expanded enough to have an awareness of the physical body or the physical senses as unique to self.

The emotions of the soul were not yet developed in this initial level of our soul evolution. The reactions of our physical nature were so far removed from the love and truth of our divine nature that the soul was created to bridge the path of learning from the physical to the spirit. The soul then became the intermediary between our two distinctly different natures. *It became the duty of the soul to determine that each lesson was learned thoroughly by our physical nature before it could be presented as truth to our spirit nature.*

Our soul sees the lessons that our physical nature must learn before it becomes the love and truth that will allow it to merge with our divine nature. Because of the soul's relationship with our physical nature, the soul is conscious of our physical dilemmas. The soul and the spirit can then work together to design a new structure of lessons each time the physical nature chooses a new beginning in a physical body, or each time we change our level of conscious awareness in this lifetime. As we grow and change within a lifetime, we may appear to be different people because of our dramatic change in our beliefs and behaviors.

We have used our path of human experience to move within the multiple levels of the soul to refine and expand our intellectual knowledge of the purpose of the body to expand the spirit. It is the intention of the spirit to unify with the intellect and the soul mind to allow spirit growth.

All facets of our human existence have their foundation within the unified mind and its conscious, subconscious, and unconscious influence upon our body and our mind.

We are one unified electromagnetic energy force that exists within the three dimensions of self. We are physical, we are soul, and we are spirit. We are the three dimensions of the microcosm. We are male, we are female, and we are God as spirit. Our family, society, and world are the three dimensions of the mesocosm. The Earth, the Universe, and the Cosmos are the three dimensions of the macrocosm. Each dimension has within itself three dimensions as the fractal pattern is repeated. Each dimension is divided into seven levels relative to seven levels into enfinity.

Each dimension of our soul and spirit energy and each dimension of our physical, external energy is interwoven with the other dimensions of energy being symbolized external to us, which provides the repetitious mirror images of our lessons externally to guide us in our internal growth.

At this time in our physical experience we have progressed into the second dimension of our personal energy force field. We are living our human experience as we grow in the fourth level of the second dimension of our soul energy. Our physical dimension and to midpoint in our soul dimension constitutes the shadow side of our soul growth. Once we begin to merge our physical nature with our spirit nature at the midpoint of our soul dimension of evolution, we begin to walk the light side of our path to spirit.

The differences that are apparent in the growth of individuals upon Earth are directly related to their karmic energy that ties them to earlier lessons of soul growth and reflects their willingness to change and grow.

The collective energy of those soul and spirit energies that are evolving beyond the veil can have the power to help other souls. Our collective consciousness can release the attachment to the primitive levels of soul evolution that are responsible for the conflict and competition upon Earth once the proper level of consciousness is reached.

Merging our physical nature with our divine nature changes our perception of life, sex, relationships, and our living. We begin to see the beauty of our design as HUMAN. We see our magnificence, expansiveness, equality, love, and truth. In this positive energy our growth begins to accelerate.

As we release our attachment to our primitive levels of growth and stop examining and reflecting our old beliefs and behaviors into the present, we will begin to understand who we are in the present moment.

The chains of emotion that have held us bound to our shadow soul of fearful beliefs and behaviors will at last be released. As we release our attachments to the shadow side of the soul, we can begin our human experience in the light side of the soul.

To discover our emotions, beliefs, and behaviors that we live by and that attach us to our shadow soul, we must not be afraid to look closely at what we are and why we are on Earth. We must have insight into our own beliefs that attach us to our comfort zone and hold us captive in our present behaviors. These beliefs and behaviors of our ego will be cast back to us as the image of perfection, encouraging us to avoid change, which the ego fears.

Perfection is not now found within our physical nature but it is inherent in our spirit self. When we accept the perfection that we see within ourself from our physical standard of judgement, we will deny our challenge to change and grow. Believing and accepting ourself "as we are" in our physical life strengthens our veil of resistance to our soul and spirit and resists our acceptance of equality and balance as our perfection. Equality and balance within the shadow side of our soul become subjective as they are judged within our mind by our perception of relative truth.

This perception of our perfection "as we are" plays into the ego need of our intellect, and it has no resemblance to the perfection of our spirit. The ego provides support through its adequate excuses to the intellect not to change and grow. Our complacency towards our sense of perfection creates a dramatic sense of inequality within us, which is reflected outward as a separateness of stagnant energy.

We use our separateness to insulate ourself from life, always relying upon the ego claim that we are perfect as we are. The stronger our insulation becomes, the denser the veil of beliefs is that we hide behind. When our perception of our perfection is at its maximum, any and all behaviors become acceptable within our mind because the trigger of spirit and soul has been dramatically insulated from our physical behavior. This insulation has the ability to produce what are considered to be pathological personalities. Losing contact with our moral and divine nature leaves the intellect and ego open to aberrant behavior. Our path of growth is perfect for us because we are living our soul design that has been uniquely designed by our soul and spirit to help us we learn our lesson.

We become perfect in our physical nature when we liberate our intellect from the bondage of our ego beliefs and behaviors and allow it to merge with the divine nature of our soul and spirit.

Releasing our repetitious attachment to our perception of physical perfection becomes our opportunity and our challenge to return Earth to its initial splendor as symbolized by the beauty of the Garden of Eden. In healing ourself, we will heal our society and Earth as expanded external dimensions of the reflection of ourself. Knowing that all healing must begin with the merging of our physical and divine natures can show us the wisdom of the soul in seeking the liberation and freedom of our spirit self. *The restoration of equality within us is the restoration of balance and unity within humanity, the world, and the Universe. It is our balance that protects us from all crisis.*

When the human began the primitive growth in the first level of soul evolution, the fear that arose in the male focus set the stage for inequality and the loss of balance in our physical nature. Each soul has been exposed to this imbalance countless times as it sought incarnation through the opposite focus of gender with its twin soul. *When we created the breach of inequality between us as males and females we symbolized the breach that we created between our physical nature and our divine nature.*

Inequality between the male and female clearly shows us the symbol of separation of our intellect and ego from our soul and spirit and the tenaciousness that exists within our physical, male self in maintaining that inequality. This symbol of separation is then repeated throughout our society and our world as mesocosmic and macrocosmic examples of inequality, just as the female has been held as unequal from the days of Adam and Eve.

When we can perceive that all of humanity has contributed to inequality during our lifetimes of the male focus, we can release our attachment to blame and judgement and we can embrace total equality for all of humanity as the true nature of our spirit.

Releasing our attachment to the examination and reflection levels of the primitive beginnings of humanity allows us to see how our physical perception of self has perpetuated control, fear, and inequality for many millions of years. When we have the courage to look and clearly see the design of life that we have created, we will be ready to liberate ourself in total freedom and joy.

For change to occur within us, we must acknowledge that we are all of equal station in our divine nature. We appear unequal because of the physical manifestation of our levels of growth that are being lived through our human experience. Our judgement of self and others allows us to attach more credence to some physical roles and identities than to others. Because of the religious foundations from which we have learned, we have also adopted the male and female inequality as our perfect lesson for learning about our soul and spirit equality.

Our primary lesson in our physical nature is to truly learn to love ourself. Once we have mastered the art of loving ourself through our unconditional love of body, mind, and spirit, we will perceive others through the love we feel for ourself.

In our physical nature we reflect the fear that we feel within us to everyone around us. When an emotion is reflected to another person, it compounds the energy of both individuals. Reflecting fear expands the fear within us and within those around us. Fear produces judgement of ourself as we begin to compare ourself to our ego standard of beliefs to which we have become attached. Because we judge our beliefs as right, we judge ourself as wrong.

In our divine nature we radiate the love that we feel within us to everyone around us. Radiating love expands the love within us and within those around us. If we radiate love to those individuals who are attached to fear, we begin to neutralize their fear. Neutralizing fear for another individual creates the illusion within them that they have no fear.

Another person's spirit energy can serve as an insulation to a fearful person and can allow him or her to react within the spirit energy of another with enthusiasm and excitement, even when he or she does not feel enthusiastic or excited. This feeling of insulation from fear through another's spirit energy can form a dependency. This emotional dependency allows an increase of ego insulation, which establishes an image of being spiritual. If another's spirit energy is used as a trigger for our soul and spirit, we will have the belief that we live from the love of our divine nature. This masquerade can only be seen by observing the behavior of the individual who is in the radiation glow of spirit energy but not living through spirit as truth. When love begins to trigger the soul and spirit energy, we will observe the life of the individual being lived through the respect, value, and love he or she has for self.

As our shift in consciousness occurs, allowing all of humanity to move from our physical nature that is controlled by fear into our divine nature that is created from love, we will experience a dramatic change in all of society. The shift in our consciousness will emphasize the power of the female that is symbolized as the love, truth, and equality of life.

Living our life within a society that is based upon the freedom and courage of love, truth, and equality will liberate us from our fear. This shift of consciousness will become our living symbol of change in all three dimensions of our energy, society's energy, and the world's energy. Our belief in fear captures our intellect and ego and hopelessly attaches us to the primitive beliefs and behaviors of the shadow side of our soul. Society and the world are reflecting back to all of humankind the desperate need for us to change our primitive beliefs and behaviors by acting out bizarre, greedy, and war-like behavior on a daily basis.

As the change takes place within our minds, allowing the merging of our divine nature with our physical nature, our behavior will begin to reflect the love and truth of our spirit self. This dramatic change of perception will be reflected in the conduct, behavior, personality, and character traits of all of humanity. When we are living our life from love, truth, and equality there will be no war, fighting, starvation, poverty, disease, or discrimination.

Our conduct will begin to reflect generosity, mercy, compassion, equality, respect, dignity, and value as the reactions of our love, truth, and equality. Our relationships and interactions will become pure and honest because the spirit within us is seeking the perfection of equality and freedom. Truth will be found in the consistency of our thoughts, words, and actions every moment of our life. Violence will increase as this shift occurs because those souls who are not willing to change will choose to die fighting.

Living the human experience through our divine nature is an occasion for timeless celebration. We will find joy in all that we do. We will seek play and laughter with the rediscovered freedom of a child. We will speak lovingly to others with the love, truth, and freedom of our hearts. We will become mindfully aware of each and every miracle of life. We will live each moment, knowing it is the only reality of life. We will accept the freedom to let our minds soar into imagination, dreams, ideas, and enthusiasm. We will perceive the value of our spirit and soul, and we will live in their harmony, rhythm, and balance. We will look at the shadow side of our soul and laugh at ourself for our superstitious beliefs that have held us captive for so long.

Life is not about miracles, life is the miracle.

Living in our divine nature will create a new world for us. We will relate differently to the power essence of our physical senses and our physical body. Each thought, word, and action will become an aware and mindful action of our one mind. We will no longer indulge in physical reaction without a conscious awareness of our intention, which will be guided in purity and love.

It will be our choice to reach others at whatever level of aware consciousness they are living, and to help them rise above their veil of beliefs to live in truth. We will have an intense consciousness of the various levels of soul growth, and it will be our purpose to invite others to grow and change. When we are consciously seeking our soul and spirit energy, we must not be afraid of emerging from the shell of our veil. The insulation of our veil of beliefs becomes our limitation in discovering the truth of our physical experience.

Those physical and technical supports that are now seen as complementary to our life will be obsolete in relationship to the power of our mind. Our space program will be seen and smiled at as the struggles of our intellectual mind. We can happily give up our telephones as obsolete. We will create only for the joy of creation. Disease will disappear as the mind is understood. When we are all merged with our divine nature, our judicial system will be unnecessary, as will prisons, crime, and conflict. Schools will exist only as repositories for gathering and communication, but not with that name or structure. *Government will be of the people, by the people, and for the people to live in their inalienable right of equality.*

We will see the female as the guardian of our divine power of intuition, and she will be honored and revered as the symbol of the Creator upon Earth. The female energy within the male will become acknowledged and revered as soul and spirit. Our female power will be cherished in the actions of our daily human experience of physical life. And our female energy will be acknowledged as our true source of healing as love, truth, and balance.

Acknowledging our female power will liberate us, whether we are male or female in our physical appearance. Separation of the male and female personalities and characteristics within our mind is symbolic of how we separate our thinking, choosing to use as little of our mind as possible to survive. As we act out our internal mind separation during our stages of growth, we set ourself up for the dramas of relationships, society, and the world. We set the stage for our world and societal dramas through the design of our own individual resistance to the truth about who we are.

The unity of each soul and spirit internally within ourself and externally to others will be understood with the wisdom and ingenuity of our soul and the love, truth, and perfection of our spirit. The unconditional love that we have for ourself and others will dissolve all judgement from within our mind. The effect of our spirit love within us will in time change all of humanity. Life will become a celebration of enthusiasm, excitement, and joy. Work will become inspired and fun, and each day will be seen as an opportunity to learn, to grow, and to change. We will not accept intellectual restrictions because we will find the balance of our internal minds and live from our external balance.

Those individuals within our world who are thought to be mentally handicapped are suppressing their intellect in this lifetime as a method of expanding their soul and spirit. Suppression of our intellectual mind is frequently chosen as the result of multiple lifetimes when the soul and spirit could not tear a rip in our veil of beliefs. When the intellect is partially suppressed, we can live lifetimes from the energy of our soul and spirit because we enter a state of timelessness where we have an awareness of only the present moment.

As our intellect rests comfortably in its beliefs, it symbolizes the seed within us of the Cosmic Christ that is waiting for its release. When the veil of beliefs that has formed our shell is torn open, the awakening to our divine nature will be the second coming of the Christ Consciousness upon Earth.

We are the seed of the body of Christ, and our physical seed must germinate and grow into its divine nature to fully experience the magnificence of the Christ Consciousness. We are the image of Christ that exists as love, truth, and perfection. As our intellect rests within the shell of our beliefs, our Christ seed is lying dormant within our physical nature upon the Earth. When the shell of our beliefs is shattered, we can emerge from the dormant state of our physical nature and join with our divine nature. At that moment we become the second coming of the Christ Consciousness upon Earth as we live in the energy of our love, truth, and perfection. As we amplify the vibrational tone of our mind energy into the purity of love and truth, we will create our "Heaven upon Earth."

We can change our mind thought with ease if we feel the responsibility to change and make the commitment to ourself to grow and change. The truth of change can only be found when our thoughts, words, and actions are consistent and it is the intention within our mind to always be open to change and growth.

In our physical nature we accept that we are perfect as we are. This is an illusion that is created by the perfection of our growth and being where we are upon our path. Our perfection is found only when our physical nature merges with our divine nature and we become the Christ Consciousness. If we are refusing to grow and change, we are living the fantasy of our perfection and we begin to live in the decay of our own beliefs and behavior.

Thoughts and words can come from our intellect or from our soul and spirit. If our thoughts involve commitment and responsibility and we are inspired and motivated to follow through with our ideas, dreams, imagination, and inspirations, our thoughts come from our soul and spirit. Our soul and spirit produces excitement within the physical world because of the joy of creativity.

The soul and spirit is inspired and motivated to create without any assurance of reward. The reward is found in the joy of doing. Many great artists have worked from their inspiration and motivation of soul and spirit energy with the soul and spirit intention of creativity. The rewards for their work frequently did not materialize within the physical world until after they chose a new beginning, but they learned their lesson of creativity with clarity. In their next life they were assured creativity with the perfection of intention.

If we find our thoughts and words becoming our physical actions only because of our sense of physical need or reward, our thoughts come from the intellect. Our intellect will focus upon task orientation, not the motivation of our soul or the inspiration of our spirit. Our perception of success will be judged and measured by our sense of reward, which may be how much money we make or the number of physical possessions that we have, and by our affluent lifestyle. Without the physical presence of the reward they have no inspiration or motivation to do the work. This is the belief within our mind that has established the labor ethic.

True success can only be felt within our heart. Our success is determined by our ability to love ourself and all other people and cannot be judged by our reward. True success is happiness.

When we judge ourself and others by an intellectual standard of success that is interested only in external gain, we are not evolving in our soul growth. Our external focus of reality upon the physical reward creates the revolutionary repetitions of life that attach us to our habits of unworthiness, fear, anger, and failure. These are the stages of life where we play out our lessons of giving and receiving by living the truth of the physical lesson.

In our physical nature we see giving as getting something in return, which belies the term giving and creates a barter system as an illusion of truth and love. In our soul and spirit nature we learn to give from the heart and we learn to receive from the heart. In soul and spirit we give with the acknowledgement of our gratitude, respect, and spirit value that we see within the receiver and we receive from a giver with the same exchange of love, truth, and perfection.

The behaviors that emerge from our physical nature are the behaviors that are acted out daily within the world. These behaviors will focus upon repetitive beliefs, greed, crime, killings, war, fear, and obsessive fanaticism that is unable to release repetitious beliefs.

When the mind resorts to criminal activity, it is hitting the shell of its mind egg with a two-by-four. This is a plea to society through a gesture of helplessness, begging for someone to understand and help the person emerge into growth and change.

Restructuring the systems of judgement and punishment into teaching growth and change would be a step forward for society, but teaching growth and change from the beginning of life would avoid the need for judgement and punishment. Those who focus upon conflict, fear, judgement, punishment, and all adversarial roles of life, are learning the lesson of freedom through the experience of control. This is a lesson of great magnitude for us and is one that symbolizes a stage of growth for the intellect that is still firmly encased in its veil of beliefs. Having a conscious awareness of the fears that are taught to our youth and changing them would alleviate fear in adults.

Habit can allow us to ignore conscious thought and our body will perform mindlessly by rote. Violent habits learned in childhood create difficult life lessons that can be avoided. If adults have a conscious awareness of the mind pattern that is being developed in the child when he or she is exposed to violent and angry behavior, they can change the child's exposure to positive behavior.

Physical need will be seen as a short-term effect. Once we have accomplished our physical goal we will lose interest in continuing with our present physical process. The intellect has a low boredom level because it recognizes that it is missing something. When the soul and spirit are merged, our mind will no longer be the same nor would we ever want it to be.

We will seek constant physical change as we seek to find happiness and satisfaction with our life. When our need to change comes from a sense of desperation, dissatisfaction, and disinterest, it is because we cannot identify what we want and our physical nature is searching. When we consciously plan change into our life, it is because we have chosen to grow and change and our physical nature is aware of the guidance of our divine nature. Changing our conscious awareness will change our life, because our perception of ourself and our reality changes as we become absorbed in truth.

If we are living from the desperation of our physical nature, we will feel no commitment or responsibility in a relationship. Our search will be pursued without a conscious awareness of what we are searching for and we will not be motivated to improve our awareness or learn from the relationship. Our intention in searching for a relationship will be to find someone to make us happy, and we will have no concern about the feelings of our partner.

When we approach any relationship looking for a happiness reward, we are setting ourself up for failure. In our personal need for attention, we will indulge in negative behavior to attract attention to ourself. We will have an expectation that the attention we get will make us happy, and we will not see how we sabotage ourself. No one can make us happy. We become happy within ourself when we understand the beauty and magnificence of our inner and higher self. When we understand ourself, we allow our intellect to unite with our soul and spirit and we become happy internally.

Our physical approach to the unity in the relationship will be reflective of ourself, unless we understand the unity within us. It will be very self-centered and we will see ourself as separate from everyone and everything else that is affected by the relationship.

The thoughts within our mind will blame and judge others in the relationship for the sequence of the events and circumstances. This perception of reality may be found in any facet of our life where vanity and greed are the goal. In our divine nature the games of our vanity and greed will amuse us as the antics of our physical child, who was selfishly seeking self-gratification through reward.

Perceiving any event or relationship from the mind of our soul and spirit instead of our intellect allows us to acknowledge immediate satisfaction with our actions. We feel satisfied and at peace. We have instant fulfillment and gratification from our spirit self, not from our physical body. We love ourself for giving and caring about us and others.

Our act of love will be patterned from our spirit mind and it becomes a welcomed part of our life. We learn from the relationship and we see the effect of the lesson in every facet of our life. Our commitment and responsibility toward our own expansion allows us to be considerate of the feelings of others as they grow and change.

In our spirit self we care and we share in our thoughts and feelings. We are open and concerned. We will perceive the reactions of others and ourself, and we will want the experience to be a growth expansion for all involved. There will be no judgement. There will only be love. We will understand that our change is motivated from within us as our freedom of choice, and we will happily assist others as they seek change.

As we grow into stages that are different from the stages of our friends, we will need to release those friends into their own stages of growth, or we will restrict our own growth. Each level of our soul and spirit evolution creates a disparity of awareness between friends, but the most significant disparity will occur when the veil is removed and we change from the Cycle of Awareness into the Cycle of Understanding. The difference of perception that exists between an awareness of life and an understanding of life is profound. Communication will become a challenge as these cycles create a dramatic difference in the function of our mind. In our Cycle of Understanding we are seeking absolute truth as it relates to self, our creation, and our purpose on Earth.

We can easily see how our intellect and ego within our physical nature and the soul and spirit within our divine nature perceive life from different levels of understanding. If we were walking up a mountain path and after going only a short way we stopped and looked down, our view would be limited to that part of the valley directly below us. If we walked to the very peak of the mountain and looked down and around us, we could see the panoramic view of the land as it stretched out from all sides of the mountain. Our understanding of the relationship of the mountain to the surrounding terrain would be completely different than our view from the side of the mountain after walking only a short way up the path.

Our intellectual view of life can be beautifully compared to the limited view we would have from only a short way up the path of the mountain. Our view is obstructed when the intellect and ego deny the presence of the soul and spirit. What the intellect cannot see does not exist in its perception. The ego supports the intellect in its sense of supremacy and our veil of beliefs obstructs the view of our soul and spirit. As we walk up the mountain, the fog thickens and shrouds the mountaintop above us. Not being able to see the top of the mountain as we begin our climb does not assure us that the mountain does not exist beyond our limited view.

Our spirit views our life from the top of the mountain. Knowledge must continue on its path until it breaks through the denial fog of our physical beliefs. Our awakening happens when we can dissolve the veil at the peak of the mountain, allowing our view to broaden and expand without the veil of fog obstructing our vision of the magnificent view.

When we awaken, all parts of the puzzle of life begin to make perfect sense. We begin to identify the connectedness of all of life and the purpose of our physical experiences begins to glimmer and sparkle as diamonds within the sands of time.

At birth we begin to walk the path from the foot of the mountain. With each moment of life we add another step up the path if we are open to learning. If we aren't open to learning, we step in place at the foot of the mountain, not climbing but busily repeating each step over and over again.

We aren't going forward and we aren't slipping backwards, but we continue to repeat over and over again the same dramas as our steps of life without an aware consciousness of what we are doing. The intellect and ego firmly and sincerely believes that each step is carrying us forward, so we innocently continue plodding along, carrying our same baggage in the same beliefs of life. In our separateness we do not have an aware consciousness that the rest of our group has continued with their progress up the mountain. Our self-consciousness has kept us focused on the physical steps as our priority of life. As we have stepped in place at the foot of our mountain, everyone else has left us. As we become aware of our separation, our fear begins to overwhelm us and we cannot see the path through our fog to move forward and change.

We prevent ourself from ever having a peak experience at the top of the mountain because we are afraid of the climb and the changing view. To reach the excitement of the peak experience at the top of the mountain, we must be willing to grow and change. If we choose to go forward with total commitment and responsibility until we reach the top, we will live with constant change. As we begin to change we will recognize that we are being challenged with multiple opportunities to grow and change as we climb. In reaching the top we will experience our most dramatic change. Each step of our growth requires change, but in reaching the peak of knowledge as the peak of our mountain in soul growth, we must change our perception of knowledge.

The level of knowledge in our soul evolution must change from a closed system of learning as memorization of historical facts as our accepted belief, to knowledge as an open system of inspiration and motivation from which we create new perceptions and understandings of our life.

Knowledge as our fourth level of soul growth is divided by our veil of beliefs separating the Cycle of Awareness and the Cycle of Understanding. Rending the veil is also our change from the shadow side of our soul, as we climb this mountain of awareness, into the sunny, light side of our soul as we descend the mountain in our search for perfect understanding. This change allows the freedom of creativity within us as the merging of our physical and divine natures takes place.

When we pass through the obstructions that our veil of beliefs forms around us, we liberate ourself into the freedom of being male, female, and spirit while having the tool of our physical body to consciously use as our way of creation.

As we awaken from our long sleep of separateness and isolation, we will open our eyes to the Garden of Eden in which we live. We will be motivated and inspired to create more beauty and magnificence through our connection with nature. Life will cease to be a struggle in which we are captured in fear, and it will become a joy of love, truth, and perfection. *The merging of our dual natures of the physical and divine changes our perception of life from the physical perception of fear to the spirit perception of love, truth, and equality.*

When we start up the path of soul evolution we experience many fears. We fear change, the journey, the unknown, our feelings of loneliness and loss, separateness, survival, and life. Life is seen as a struggle, an effort, a dramatic climb to the "top." Our soul climb is symbolized in the repetition found in each of our lifetimes as we seek our physical climb and growth to the "top" in our profession.

When we reach the peak of our soul journey and look around the mountain, we see that our path down is leisurely and beautiful. We chose the hardest part of the mountain to climb. We chose our path through the shadow side of our soul. When we climb out of the dark side of the mountain, our fear has dissolved. We look at our path with love and truth and we feel good about ourself.

We don't leave our physical body or our intellect behind in our path of soul evolution. We merge our intellect with our soul and spirit mind, and our one integrated mind becomes loving and honest as we use our physical body as the tool of our one mind.

We change our perception of ourself, others, and the world. We focus our attention on the good within our life. We feel a calmness, peacefulness, and mercifulness. We have no fear, judgement, or blame within our divine nature. As we remove these negative thoughts and words from our intellectual mind by the merging of the love within our soul and spirit mind, we will also remove all fear, judgement, and blame from our physical actions.

Our change in the perception of ourself and our life will change the way that we relate to others in all of our relationships. This will bring about a transformation of us as individuals, our society, and our world. The transition from our Cycle of Self-Awareness to our Cycle of Global Understanding will be putting our awakening into truth as the actions of our daily life.

Fear, judgement, and blame are the opposite of unconditional love. Our divine nature is unconditional love.

Our change will be evident to us by the way we feel, the thoughts that we think, the words that we speak, and the actions that we live. Our intentions of living will lose the greediness, separateness, and loneliness of our physical nature. Our perception of ourself, others, and our purpose in life will change dramatically as we view life from our spirit love and not from the reflection of our fearful beliefs.

Perception that is based upon love and truth understands that the actions of others are based upon their lessons, whether or not the lesson is known and accepted. We will continue to act out our lessons on our stage of life, whether or not we have a conscious awareness of the script that we have written. Working upon our lesson places us at the perfect place at the perfect time, regardless of the drama or trauma that occurs.

Perfection is the Universal design of our soul growth, which is based upon equality and balance. It is because of the soul and spirit's intention to equalize and balance our physical nature that we must experience all that is within life. We must be black, white, yellow, and red. We must be male, female, and spirit. We must be heterosexual, homosexual, and bisexual. We must be Jewish, Catholic, Baptist, Muslim, and so on. We must receive what we give and give what we receive. We will be a doctor, lawyer, and Indian chief. We will be a mother, father, and child. We will be rich, poor, and middle class. We will be a glutton, we will starve, and we will eat normally. Because of our equality, when we judge anyone, we judge ourself.

Our soul growth is designed to elevate us to the level of our spirit perfection. The ego will lead us to believe that we are perfect as we are rather than show us where we are in our path of growth. That is the booby trap of the ego that captures us and holds us behind the curtain in our stage of life. When we are captured in a belief, the elevator of life stops running and we find ourself stuck in one place.

Our attention should always be directed towards what we learn, not the drama or the other people who are acting in our drama. Learning our lessons in a state of aware consciousness removes our fascination with the lives of other people and allows the change to gradually occur as our life becomes our truth.

As we consciously stop reflecting our energy into the lives of other people, we lose our curiosity about their lives because we suddenly realize that our life is about us, not them. All that our aware consciousness can find in other people is the image of our own reflection.

As long as our awareness is limited to the reflection, we haven't come to the realization that we are seeing ourself. Without a realization of the reflection, we continue with the blame, fear, and judgement. Therefore, when we judge, blame, or fear the actions of another, we are judging, fearing, and blaming ourself. When we see our reflection as our moment of truth, we are open to change and growth in our life.

Our physical beliefs attach us to blame, judgement, fear, resentment, victimization, and unforgiveness. It is our physical beliefs that produce the veil around our intellect and ego. It is the density of our veil that is created by the excessiveness of our beliefs that limits our perception. Our veil creates the reflection of our own image at all times, and until we become conscious of our own reflection, we can't recognize the truth of what we see. No one else is responsible for our reflection, but our energy will attract others of like energy to symbolize the reflection of self in others.

Seeing ourself in others does not make the other person responsible for what we see. Our reflection of self is mirrored to us from our own reflection that is being imaged in our veil of beliefs that surrounds our mind. It is the veil that our soul and spirit is seeking to remove so that we can open our eyes and see who we are in perfect clarity.

An open mind will not deny the whisperings of the soul and spirit. To hear the whisperings of our soul and spirit, we must listen to the silence. Our intense focus upon physical activity, sound, and vision uses our eyes and our ears constantly at a lower level of vibrational energy. The constant stimulus of our physical senses in hearing and seeing keeps us from listening to the silence within. When our eyes and ears are overwhelmed with negative perceptions, visions, words, and actions, we are strengthening our veil of beliefs in fear, judgement, and blame.

Our attachment to television, radio, music, conversation, telephones, reading, computers, traveling, working, and partying gives us an unlimited opportunity to be lonely. Activities of the external world cannot remove the loneliness that we feel from the loss of our inner world. We seek activity as a cure for loneliness, loss, separation, grief, and fear, but once the dramas of life are quiet the emotions all rush back into our intellectual mind, perhaps even stronger than before.

Our loneliness is a trigger from our soul and spirit that is seeking to become one with our intellect. Loneliness cannot be cured with the activities of the physical world. Loneliness is felt in our heart and our stomach by our intellect because it is conscious of its separation from our soul and spirit. Loneliness, loss, and grief symbolize the search for unity of our intellect, soul, and spirit as it seeks the truth of its being. Our loneliness, loss, and grief in the physical world bring about the same emotions within us when we experience the separation or loss of someone we love.

Our physical activities reach a frantic pace in our desire not to think about who we are or why we are here. We keep ourself frantically busy with our daily pace of life, giving ourself little if any time to listen to the silence within and without. Facing the truth of reality within our internal mind becomes a terror to ignore and deny at all costs. The frantic pace of life moves faster and faster until at last the physical pace is overwhelming. This hyperactive physical state is used as a shield to reinforce the veil within our mind and protect us from seeing truth as our internal soul and spirit.

When we can no longer mentally cope with the multiple stresses of our physical life, our body and mind will collapse and we will become sick, diseased, or emotionally impoverished. In our debilitated state we cannot continue our physical merry-go-round and we force ourself to look within to find our truth and change.

We frequently design our lifestyle to initiate crisis within our life when we reach this stage of mindless vegetation. Crisis makes us change our pattern of behavior. It slaps us in the face and gets our attention with a drama of tremendous magnitude. Crisis brings us back full circle to our self-consciousness and challenges us to use our inherent strength and courage.

Our return to self-consciousness brings us back to our internal memories of pain, loss, grief, and separation that we first felt when the veil began to form around our intellect to protect us from our soul and spirit. When we are not paying attention to our soul and spirit, we create a drama to let us experience these emotions again, reminding us of how we felt when we began our mind separation.

Our body, intellect and ego, our soul mind, and our spirit consciousness cannot be separated within us without our subconscious soul mind and our unconscious spirit mind designing dramas into our life as reminders to our external self of who we are. We can resist, deny, and reject the trinity of our mind, but we can never destroy our eternal soul and spirit. We will repeatedly destroy our physical body and intellectual mind by our efforts to resist, deny, and reject our soul and spirit. When the power of the trinity of our mind is honored, respected, and valued, we will live long lives of joy, health, and happiness. When we become consciously aware of the truth of our mind power to destroy our body, we can choose to consciously live long lives of magnificent soul growth.

The physical body, the intellectual mind, and the ego are one. When one suffers, they all suffer. When one is sick, they are all sick. The physical body, the intellect, and the ego are the illusion or mirror image of the male, female, and spirit energy that we truly are. The image of self is created by the perception of self that is accepted within our physical reality. What we think we are, we are.

Listening to the silence will allow us to recognize the inner dimension of the soul and the higher dimension of the spirit. We can see, hear, smell, touch, taste, and have a total consciousness of our soul and spirit energy within. We can have conversations, receive advice, see pictures, scenes, movies, and we can touch, taste, smell, hear, and see the energy that fills the space around us.

We can experience memory of past lives, future lives, and Earth in its evolution. We can see the levels of growth in ourself and others as clearly as we can see the steps of a stairway that we climb. Spirit energy is loving energy. There is no fear, judgement, or blame to be heard or seen when we listen to our spirit self. In listening to our soul energy of past lives, we view the experience from our spirit energy, which is once again loving and truthful energy that will clarify our soul lessons if we are open to listening.

We have within us guardian angels, caretakers, and discarnate spirits that live within us, guide us, teach us, and inspire us to greater and greater accomplishments. They are all loving and are an integrated part of our energy. This is our own spirit, soul, and physical energy that is helping us to evolve.

When we speak of angels, spirits, and guides external to ourself, we are viewing them from our intellectual, external perception. We are not possessed by spirits, we are spirit. The negative spirits that have been believed in from the beginning of time are the symbols of negative thought from our fearful intellect and ego. We have the mind power to call upon our symbolic demons as well as our symbolic angels.

Each and every point of power from which we have created our parallel lives and our simultaneous lives remains eternally within our life cycle of energy to help us grow and change. We are the unity of all of our past life energy, future life energy, and present life energy. This is the unity of our eternal life which symbolizes the unity that we seek within ourself in each physical life. When we are through the veil we can consciously use this energy of our soul and spirit. When we are behind the veil our perception of our primitive lives can be thought of as demons or devils within us.

Our spirit energy is loving and protective. It comes to us as intuition, inspiration, and enthusiasm. We can sense answers before we can hear answers. Touching or feeling was the first of the physical senses to be developed at the time of our creation. It allows us to sense the presence of others, know answers, find lost objects, and know that someone is thinking about us.

We may experience deja vu, visions, voices, vibrations, smells, tastes, or touches from our spirit senses as well as our physical senses. This will become common as we rend the veil of our ego.

If our intellect and ego believe only in the physical dimension of self and do not acknowledge the soul and spirit energy of self, any experience of sensing that is not within the intellectual and ego understanding will be denied by the physical mind. When the physical nature refuses to accept the senses of the soul and spirit, it must find a way to suppress or block all senses that it refuses to acknowledge. Our intellect and ego can conjure up multiple perceptions to explain any physical occurrence that is not understood. Truth itself will not be acceptable by the intellect because it continues to see itself as separate behind its ego veil.

Multiple addictions that are now present within our society are being used to suppress the soul and spirit energy. By attaching ourself to physical addictions we strengthen the veil of our beliefs, adding strength to our denial and resistance of soul and spirit. Addictions are a stage of growth in our soul evolution that can be chosen and used as the chains that will bind us to our physical beliefs. All addictions suppress our physical senses and paralyze our soul and spirit consciousness. Addictions are behaviors of absolute fear and denial.

Each level of our soul evolution is divided into seven levels relative to seven levels. Our stages of growth are found within the secondary levels of soul growth and are an indication of severe and determined resistance by the intellect and ego to any growth and change. Many stages of growth are found in the level of knowledge as we resist the peak experience of our cycle of change from fear to love. Addictions are common in the interim stages of growth during our period of evolving through our soul level of knowledge.

At this moment we can be compared to the full-grown chick that finds itself still in the egg and unable to break the shell to free itself. We are desperately attaching ourself to physical dependencies that will hold us behind our veil of beliefs, and many times beliefs alone will become our dependency.

Our ego knows that we are flush with our veil and that one small word could be the trigger that dissolves our veil forever. If we suppress our aware consciousness with dependencies, we give ourself less opportunity to react to the trigger of our soul and spirit. Hiding behind a dependency adds another layer of strength to our veil and distracts our attention as it dulls our physical senses.

The more advanced humanity becomes, the more intense and extensive addictions become as our physical mind uses them as a means of hiding from what we cannot accept within ourself.

If our beliefs do not include a belief in the inner and higher self of soul and spirit, our natural physical response is to deny and reject that which we do not accept. Denial and resistance act as a challenge to the soul and spirit energy within us. The more we kick and scream in our physical resistance, the more insistent the soul and spirit becomes in trying to get our attention. Our soul and spirit never gives up on us. When we yell "uncle" we yell from our finite physical nature and release our physical body to death. But the game of life and learning begins again three physical days later as we re-materialize into the beginning of human development and start a new life with a new soul design to approach our old lessons from a slightly different angle.

The story of the resurrection is the symbol of our "reincarnation" into physical life, which was acted out for the benefit of humankind to support their belief in the crucifixion while symbolizing "the way" of our eternal life.

Our ego, spirit tug-of-war is symbolic of the mother and child conflict of our physical life. As physical beings we are the child and the spirit energy within us is our mother. If the mother wants us to pay attention and we in our childish rebellion refuse, our mother will become more insistent. As the pressure increases from our mother, we in our childish rebellion adopt physical beliefs and behaviors to demonstrate our resistance.

At the beginning of the conflict we may only kick and scream in our fear and anger, but as the pressure increases we may begin to hide from our mother. In the physical symbol of the child hiding, he or she may run away, go to the attic or basement, or find a closet that will offer temporary seclusion.

When we refuse to acknowledge our soul and spirit that is seeking a change in our beliefs and behaviors, we will find a diversion of alcohol, drugs, sex, or any other dependency that happens to pass by. The dependency will focus our attention on the dependency and it will drown out the inner and higher voices that are speaking to us. Our addictions take over with such cleverness in our daily pattern of life that we fail to see the symbol as a pattern that is also being acted out within our trinity of mind energy.

When the intellect and the soul and spirit interaction is perceived as the male and female interaction, we can also see the pattern of resistance of the male to accept the female within himself. To accept the female as being equal to himself within any part of his life, from the intimacy of relationships to the government and corporate board rooms, would require a change in his beliefs. As the male rejects the soul and spirit female energy within himself, he symbolizes his rejection by rejecting the value and equality of the female in his physical life.

The intellect and ego considers the spirit contribution to life unimportant, unnecessary, unreal, or inferior. The male considers the female contribution to intellectual matters unimportant, unnecessary, and inferior, but he will accept loving, nurturing, and caretaker activities within the home.

Many men are dependent upon having a woman in their bed and in their life. This dependency is an indication of the male need for the female or spirit to love, nurture, and protect him, and it is symbolic of his search for the female within himself.

When the intellect and ego faces a crisis it begins to ask God for help. This becomes the acknowledgement of the soul and spirit ability to love, nurture, and care. When we face an emotional crisis it is many times rooted in sex and religion.

Our emotional crises are symbols of the ego and spirit tug-of-war that is raging within our mind. Our physical nature has its foundation in our supreme sexual sense and in the religious foundations of our beliefs. The beliefs that constitute our religious foundations are symbolic of our physical nature not our divine nature. All religious beliefs were structured through the physical mind of the male and therefore the female, as the symbol of our soul and spirit, was shut out of all religious activities and influence. Religion was based upon the perception of our male, physical nature which focused upon fear, sin, guilt, sex, and judgement. Our divine nature of love, truth, and perfection was ignored in the early foundations of religious thought in the same way that the female was ignored. The early foundations of religion continue to be tied to our present level of soul evolution by karmic energy streams which are acted out as physical beliefs and behaviors.

Therefore, sex and religion are the two chains that bind us strongly to our physical nature and will be the strength the ego depends upon during an emotional crisis to resist the soul and spirit merging with the intellect.

This influence is seen today in individuals, societies, and the world, as sexual orientation, AIDS, religious issues, and wars are the focus of our daily experiences. The continued rejection of the female, especially by religions actively perpetuating sexual abuse and inequality, is an example of the denial of soul and spirit by those who claim to be Godlike.

The male intellect lives in fear of the spirit within, which is symbolized by our female energy. The male has accepted the female into his bed because the spirit energy of the female is loving, nurturing, caring, and giving when the physical child of the male is ready to receive. It may take a male many thousands of lifetimes to acknowledge the female within him and to acknowledge his soul and spirit.

The physical male or female does not see the spirit within us seeking to give love and truth to our mind, as it seeks to add the wisdom and ingenuity of the ages to our limited intellect. Our resistance, denial, and rejection of the truth of our internal self increases as we get closer to the veil in our soul evolution.

The loving and truthful interaction that occurs in all intimate relationships is the spirit and soul within teaching us how to relate on a physical basis so that we can eventually learn how to relate to the intimate energy of our internal minds.

When our relationships are based upon conflict, competition, jealousy, resentment, revenge, and unforgiveness, and are acted out through our irresponsible and uncommitted behaviors, we are learning the lesson of loving ourself. We set ourself up with a pattern of beliefs and behaviors that we know will attract the attention of others to us. This is the way that the ego shows us that we are unlovable. Feeling unloved strengthens the ego's position of "truth" as it reflects to our intellect the lack of respect and value we have for ourself as truth. As we feel judged by others, we are judging ourself.

Our physical mind must learn how to interact by physically experiencing the juxtaposition of multiple relationships so that we can understand the interaction of our intellect, soul, and spirit as the energy of our one mind.

Our physical relationships cannot be isolated mentally, emotionally, or physically if we expect to grow and change. We must interact with our own emotions, mind trinity, and physical body, and we must interact within multiple types of relationships. On a soul and spirit level we are constantly changing our relationships as we return to physical life. Our soul and spirit lessons are acted out through our multiple physical lives.

When we continue to see God in terms of a deity external to ourself, we are failing to accept our own power of creation, which includes each minute activity of daily living. The energy force of the Creator gave us the perfect symbol of our power of creation when He gave us the power of creation from our mind to our body.

We have accepted our ability to have children and our ability to think and to speak as our natural abilities. These abilities are natural to us as physical capabilities, but they are also a symbol to us that we are spirit. We are made in the image of God. We have the power to communicate as the spirit communicates with us. We have the power to have children, as we are children of the Creator. With our power of creation we are also given the responsibility for what we create.

God as our Spirit Creator is energy. He looked at the physical world that He had created and He longed to experience that world. But His energy was much too powerful to be contained in one small speck of physical matter. But as He *thought*, He realized that He could seed the Earth with His own *thought* energy and live through His own *thought* energy as a physical being.

God created us first as *spirit thought* energy, or as seeds of His own image of energy. As the seeds of God, we were given the power of creation. It was through our power of creation that we created our physical bodies. As God observed our adeptness at creation from the cosmic pattern of our seed energy, He knew that He could live through us as a Higher Universal Mana. God knew that He could live and expand Himself by creating His own *thought* image as HUMAN. He also knew that it would take the physical nature of His seed a long time to learn and to grow and to change, and so He gave us eternal life.

God was pleased with what we created as our physical temple, so He gave us consciousness as our gift of awareness and expression. Now, as a thinking and creating spirit consciousness, we could also communicate through thinking and speaking. We could learn to be HUMAN.

In the beginning, we were only the love, truth, and perfection of our new female spirit consciousness. We were joyous with our new energy of *thought*. We understood our power to create. In total innocence our divine nature began the journey of teaching our male, physical nature to live in our spirit consciousness with the purity of love, truth, and perfection.

Our spirit is not concerned about our paralysis of fear. It has always known that those things that were created by God can never die, and those things that were not created by God are not real. With this knowledge, our soul and spirit has total faith and trust that we want to grow and change and it loves us enough to always be there helping us.

Our spirit energy, which knows only love, truth, and perfection, continues to mother us in total patience as her sleeping physical children. Our soul and spirit accepts our physical life only as our dream of judgement and fear. Our spirit knows that our understanding of ourself as the perfection of love and truth is only a matter of awakening to our eternal life.

Yes, God loves us unconditionally, and He is patiently waiting for us to awaken to our Christ Consciousness while we are living on Earth. The Christ Consciousness is the symbol of our physical nature merging with our divine nature. Our merging as one divine spirit energy will expand the energy of God to include the male, physical nature, ingeminating all of humanity with the magnificence of our Divine Grace. Until then, God will remain in female nature upon Earth.

7

Spirit Logos

◊

"I am physical, but I am also a creation of the experiential learning of the soul within me. I have been through this Universal system for thousands and thousands of lifetimes and I have taken unto myself multiple lessons and images of lessons. I have learned through experiencing that I have all of the knowledge that is available within the Universe. I have within my soul unlimited knowledge. I am also a spirit energy that was created by God. In that spirit energy I am love, truth, and perfection. I have the power of creation that has been given to me as an inherent birthright."

H.S., from Sharing: Self Discovery in Relationships

absolute truth—knowledge that is understood on the light side of the soul and that is consistent with Universal Law.

abuse—is a soul lesson of learning to love ourself in which we inflict abuse upon ourself physically, emotionally, or sexually as part of our life design. When we learn the lesson of loving ourself, we no longer tolerate abuse.

asexual—having no physical sexual desire but capable of reproduction by thought intention of the male and female energy existing internally but independent of the physical sexual process.

channeling—originates from the internal acceptance of the multiple electromagnetic energy forces that exist within the mind and that we are capable of accessing when our ego allows us the freedom to do so. Energy waves within the mind can be compared to the energy waves within space that are accessed by radio, television, and satellites as a method of communication. Our energy waves can be accessed within any of the three primary dimensions of our own eternal life energy and will then relay messages from the dimension that is used. If communication is from the physical level of the Cycle of Development it will be from the primitive level of past memory or the present level of the physical reality. If communication is from the Cycle of Awareness it will be from the shadow side of the soul. If communication is from the Cycle of Understanding it will be from the light side of the soul. If communication is from the Cycle of Integration it will be from evolving spirit energy. If communication is from the Eighth Realm it will come from the oversoul or guardian angel energy of absolute truth. The ability to channel switches the focus of the mind energy from the intellect into a point of energy within the individual's eternal life cycle connecting the energy of past, present, or future to the physical body through any or all of the seven physical senses.

civilization—when the foundation of a culture is based upon love, truth, equality, compassion, humility, unity, and cooperation. As yet in history upon Earth, true civilization has not been reached.

closed mind—a mind firmly encased behind a solid veil of beliefs that can see nothing beyond its own mirror image of fear.

collective consciousness—mind thought that has become commonplace as connected energy streams that are focused upon a single perception of thought, giving it the strength to change beliefs within our society and our world.

competition—is an energy of the ego that is based upon fear and judgement and it is the beginning energy of all conflict which expands into crime and war.

conscious mind—is the level of awareness from which we live under the control of the intellect and ego while we are learning on the shadow side of our soul evolution.

Cosmic energy—the enfinite energy of thought from the Divine Creator or God.

creativity—the resulting action of the inspiration of the spirit, and the motivation of the soul being put into physical action by the intellect and physical body.

cults—used as a metaphor in the present society—cult denotes cultures within a society that ascribes to differing beliefs under the leadership of someone or some group of people that establishes laws, ideology, and practices for the people to live by. The more excessive the control of behavior, money, and thinking the more cultist proportions they are displaying. Many religions can be defined by their cult behavior although they don't recognize their own mirror image. Cults present control over sexual activities and religious beliefs and behaviors by fear and reward influences patterned from the judgement and wrath of God.

Cycle of Awareness—the physical mind purpose of the shadow side of our soul during the first half of our soul evolution. It is the intention of the mind to become aware of our physical nature and our need for growth during this cycle.

Cycle of Development—the thought purpose of developing the human form as physical with the exact fractal of the cosmic pattern.

Cycle of Integration—the divine mind purpose of living as the integrated energy of our physical and divine nature during the last dimension of our spirit growth.

Cycle of Understanding—the physical mind purpose of merging with the soul and spirit to search for the absolute truth of creation and the purpose of being human during the last half of the soul path of evolution.

dimensions—the human was given three dimensions of energy: the physical dimension which is our Cycle of Development when we create our physical body as human form; the soul dimension which is our Cycle of Awareness on the shadow side of our soul, until we pass through our veil of beliefs and transcend into the Cycle of Understanding on the light side of our soul; and the spirit dimension of our energy which is the Cycle of Integration and is devoted to living the merged energy of our physical nature and our divine nature in the love, truth, and perfection of our spirit consciousness. Each dimension of our energy is divided into seven primary levels relative to seven to infinity. These three dimensions of energy and their divisions of seven levels relative to seven constitute the fractal pattern of our path of growth. Each dimension is repeated as a smaller fractal of energy in each physical lifetime.

disease—the decay of physical matter due to an obstructed energy flow resulting from the excesses and deficiencies of life which create an imbalance within the mind and body. Fear as an excessive emotion is the primary originator of disease within the mind and body.

divine nature—the female soul and spirit in human form.

Divine Nature—the integrated energy of our divine nature and our physical nature that is consciously aware and in full understanding of self, creation, and our purpose of expanding the Creator energy.

dreams—messages that are sent to the intellect from the soul and spirit during sleep periods. Dreams are a method for the soul and spirit to capture the attention of the intellect by transforming the message into physical symbols that can be understood by the physical mind. Each symbol is unique to the life activities relating to the individual soul and spirit and the symbols will always be true to Universal Law not physical belief.

Earth consciousness—a fractal pattern of the Cosmic energy that was created as a school for the creation and growth of humanity. We are a fractal energy of the Earth which is our primary support energy for our physical matter of mind and body, and this responsibility is clearly understood by the Earth. Because of the Earth consciousness, Earth will continue to replenish its life for our life if we don't interfere.

ego—the interwoven fiber of our physical, fear beliefs that creates a veil as a cocoon to encase our physical, intellectual mind. The ego lives in the energy of fear and sees it's role as one of survival protection for the intellectual mind through separation. Once the veil is dissolved the ego changes into humility, and unity replaces separateness.

embodyment—a physical lifetime that has been chosen to work upon the lessons of the soul for the purpose of growth by the eternal spirit consciousness. Physical embodiment as life is used as a tool for the growth of the soul, and a meditation for the eternal spirit.

energy—we are electromagnetic energy that exists in three different force fields of physical energy, soul energy, and spirit energy. Energy by its very nature must move and change, and therefore as human energy we must move and change or decay will result.

enfinity—the immeasurable energy of eternal life.

equality—the balance that we seek in our energy of male, female, and spirit self as we begin to understand that all of humanity is equal. Our internal equality can only be learned from the experience of living in physical equality.

eternal life—an energy of spirit consciousness existing as a seed in the energy body of the Creator. Our life is eternal within the Creator and as we grow and expand we will become One with the Creator existing into enfinity as Creator energy.

fact—that which has been learned by the intellect and defined in relationship to theory, observation, or experimentation relative to physical awareness.

fractal—an exact smaller pattern of a larger energy force.

Higher Universal Mana—a thinking, speaking, spirit consciousness found in physical matter as a human being.

HUMAN—the first anagram denoting the Higher Universal Mana of Spirit Consciousness in human form.

human—the highest form of physical life upon Earth that has been given seven physical senses, with the senses of thinking and speaking setting him and her apart as a unique and expanding system of electromagnetic energy fields.

infinite—immeasurable in physical time and energy.

ignorance—an uninformed state of mind that is produced by ignoring change through physical resistance, rejection, and denial.

inspiration—the energy of the spirit as it transcends to the intellectual mind. It can be recognized as an idea or as imagination, and it will always be felt with enthusiasm and excitement as it is unconsciously accepted by the intellect. The ego acceptance then determines the inspirational progression to creativity.

instinct—is the wisdom and ingenuity of our soul mind that is given to us as a soul sense of knowing which can be directly communicated to the intellect. The intellect has the ability to receive or deny this communication, which can be physically felt in the lungs and the liver. Denial of our soul instinct frequently results in asthma or other breathing disorders, as well as liver disease.

integrated mind—the merging together of our intellectual mind, soul mind, and spirit mind into one mind that functions in an unbroken cycle of energy with total harmony and rhythm. An integrated mind is a superconscious mind using all levels of consciousness as a unified energy of one mind.

intellectual creation—the physical energy of the mind that lives and creates in fear, separateness, and greed within the external world, protected by the ego from the influence of the soul instincts and spirit intuition.

intellectual spiritualism—a sense of being spiritual that is conveyed by the ego to the intellect. Once there is an opening within the fiber of the veil that allows images beyond the veil to be discovered by the intellect, the ego convinces the intellect that it has become spirit and there is no further need to search.

intuition—is the truth of our spirit consciousness and it is consistently given to us as a spirit sense of understanding and inspiration which can be felt in the heart and intestines before the intellectual mind develops a conscious awareness of the intuitive sense. Denial of our spirit intuition will result in heart and intestinal diseases.

karmic beliefs—beliefs that have their origin within past lives but have been continued into the present life as a lesson that is not yet learned. Original sin is a karmic belief that has not yet been completed in those who view themselves as a victim, unworthy, inadequate, or as a failure.

karmic energy—relationships that exist between people that are continuing a lesson from a past lifetime. Karmic energy is never punishment but is a lesson that will be approached from different images to allow it to be seen with clarity. Karmic energy involves lessons for everyone that is involved and it is never exclusive to only one person. Disasters of all types are frequently the result of shared karmic energy for everyone involved.

karmic memory—is misunderstood in the present society as memory originating in this lifetime, rather than karmic memory from past lifetimes. As the soul is evolving our conscious, intellectual mind is being bombarded with electrical current from the soul and spirit which opens the intellect to karmic lessons of soul memory that are not yet learned. Karmic memory will be a frequent occurrence in the decades to come as we rend the veil of the ego and develop a conscious awareness of soul memory. This phenomenon will expand the judgement in many egos as it searches for someone physical to blame. Until karmic memory can be accepted, the mind will remain under the fear and judgement influence of the ego.

life design—each physical lifetime is designed by the energy of our soul and spirit to include our lessons of choice. Our life experiences symbolize images of the lessons that we are learning. Many alternatives are designed into each life regarding specific experiences but the soul and spirit has the freedom to change the life experience if the lesson is learned or the need for intensity within the lesson changes. We have total freedom of choice with each experience. There is never absolute predestination or predetermination in a life design. Our life design is an integrated mind choice that is open to change and growth.

love—is the predominant energy of our spirit consciousness and it is an energy that is searched for in the physical discovery of self. We are love as spirit consciousness and all searching within the physical world is symbolic of the internal search for the love of our eternal spirit.

Mana—spirit consciousness

mirror image—a reflection of our own energy of fear emotions, beliefs, and behaviors that are mirrored back to us by the ego veil that surrounds our intellectual mind.

motivation—the energy of our soul as it transcends into our physical consciousness, subcionsciously accepted by our intellect as an inherent knowing.

Nature consciousness—an awareness of nature that allows us to feel, taste, and smell Earth as our life-giving connection.

open mind—a mind that is open to changing habits, beliefs, and behaviors. This intellect is no longer imprisoned behind a solid veil of ego beliefs and it searches out and welcomes change and creativity.

pattern—making an impression through identical repetitions.

perception—the intellect and ego conscious mind response to reality, which defines our impression of self, life, and our physical world by patterns of thought, beliefs, behaviors, and habits.

perfection—living through a balanced, equal, and cooperative behavior of love and truth toward all of humanity, nature, and Earth.

personal civilization—when an individual lives from love, truth, and equality as "the way" of physical life and positive perception is consistently found in his or her thoughts, words, and behaviors in the physical world.

physical energy—the male, external focus of beliefs and behaviors that is based upon fear, judgement, competition, separateness, greed, inequality, and supremacy.

physical nature—our personality and character traits that reflect the beliefs and behavior of our physical energy and is directed with an external focus into the world around us.

prayers—thoughts of our mind.

primitive times—that period of time that is spent by humanity living and growing in the early levels of the shadow side of our soul. The most primitive level is the first level of soul growth, which continues to influence all levels of the shadow side of the soul.

relative truth—all fact that is determined as knowledge during the shadow side of our soul evolution. Relative knowledge as factual belief will change as life circumstances change.

religion—an external expression of an internal energy that allows all behavior to emanate from love, truth, equality, compassion, humility, unity, and cooperation in our living. When this energy can be found in the individual, society, and the world, religion will be a reality as the inspirational behavior of people living within civilization.

sensing—consciously using our physical senses as well as our soul and spirit senses to increase our soul and spirit connection to self and others.

sexual—an energy found only in our physical nature, pertaining to our sexual organs, desires, and reproductive capabilities.

sexual promiscuity—indiscriminate sexual activity that has no love, commitment, or responsibility of mind intention but is indulged in with the intention of physical pleasure and release. A dramatic soul lesson of self-abuse that becomes the external search for the internal peak experience that symbolizes loving self.

sleep—our way of giving equal time to our subconscious and unconscious mind by focusing away from the conscious mind of the intellect and into the soul and spirit. Sleep is a physical process that allows the mind to change the accepted energy channel that it normally uses. While the focus is changed to the soul and spirit channels of the mind, work is being done within those realms to evaluate the progression of the life design within the physical realm. If the soul and spirit needs to send the intellect a conscious message it must transform the message into coded physical symbols before the ego will allow the intellect to accept the message. When the mind is open to soul and spirit we remember the soul and spirit work that takes place during sleep, because the intellect will be present rather than separated by the ego. When the ego is dissolved into humility we will use power pauses rather than sleep to go deeper into our soul and spirit consciousness.

soul—our true mind energy that bridges the intellect and ego and our spirit consciousness. The soul bridges our physical and divine nature and it accumulates memory of all our physical experiences that have served as lessons in our soul growth. When all physical experiences are learned with clarity in the soul they will merge with the spirit consciousness and we will be of one mind.

soul devolution—sliding backwards into primitive physical beliefs and behavior that imprison the soul in a downward spiral.

soul evolution—consistent growth of our soul.

soul revolution—repetitious physical behavior that captures the soul and holds it in the same pattern of life experience preventing forward growth and in time creating devolution.

spirit consciousness—the seed of God that was given to us as the purity of thought at our moment of creation and that is eternally connected to our soul mind, with both our soul and spirit being symbolized as our female energy of our divine nature.

Spiritualism—is a living energy not an intellectual energy and it can only be realized by the way of life. Thoughts and words become insignificant if they are not supported by our actions in living our spirit energy. The spirit lives in love and truth as its emotional perfection and its physical perfection is found in our behavior when it is focused upon equality, compassion, humility, unity, and cooperation.

stagnant energy—our physical intellect and body in a state of stasis, obstructing the flow of our energy pattern, allowing inertia and decay to create disease in our mind and body. This can be found in people who refuse to change their habits, beliefs, and behaviors to allow growth.

static energy—our physical intellect and body that is in a state of imbalance, allowing fragmentation and confusion to interrupt and divert the flow of our soul and spirit energy. This energy creates hyperactivity, frenetic activity, anxiety, and disorientation.

subconscious mind—the soul mind that is always available and motivating to our intellect but remains separated and unacknowledged by the ego energy, allowing only a subconscious influence to occur through the intellect.

thought—our original form of creation and our subsequent beginning form of physical creation.

unconscious mind—our spirit mind that consistently inspires our intellect but is dramatically resisted by the ego, allowing only an unconscious influence to occur within the intellect.

Universal—another fractal pattern of Cosmic energy that is populated by other planets and beings.

Universal consciousness—massive streams of energy that collectively merge to strengthen the energy and create changes within the world of Earth, as well as other planets.

veil—the interwoven energy of the beliefs of our ego that acts as an unbroken shield around the intellectual mind. Our veil of beliefs mirrors the image of all thoughts, emotions, words, and behaviors back to us as our own image but allows them to appear to be external to us. When the veil is thick and heavy, acting as a true shield, God is felt to be external to the intellect and rightly so as the ego has created the illusion as the reality with its intentional separation of our minds by our veil of beliefs.

About the Author

Kathy Oddenino is a native of Salem, Illinois. After graduating from St. Vincent De Paul School of Nursing in Indianapolis, she moved to Arlington, Virginia. For the past fifteen years she has lived in Annapolis, Maryland.

Traditional nursing has provided numerous opportunities for Kathy to test the power of her philosophy, uniting holistic principles with traditional nursing practice. Her 35 years of experience as a registered nurse include work with Georgetown University Medical School, the National Institutes of Health, the Naval Medical Research Institute, the Uniformed Services University of Health Sciences, and other major medical centers. As the Director of *LIFEFORCE* Holistic Health Retreat Center, Kathy's expertise "bridges the gap" between traditional and holistic medicine. With her 12 years of medical research expertise and 25 years of health care administration and management, Kathy Oddenino sees *LIFEFORCE* Retreat Center as a natural progression of her work. *LIFEFORCE* is a resource for positive change in the quality of life, health, and human understanding for people with diverse health issues.

Since 1984, Kathy Oddenino has presented seminars and classes teaching body, mind, and spirit consciousness. She delivers lectures, conducts seminars across the United States, and frequently appears as a guest on radio and television talk shows to discuss a diverse range of topics from health to spirit philosophy. She sees all of humanity as a connected whole in the same way that she sees our body, mind, and spirit as one. A prolific writer, Kathy has published four books through Joy Publications, including *The Joy of Health: A Spiritual Concept of Integration and the Practicalities of Living, Bridges of Consciousness, Sharing: Self Discovery in Relationships,* and *Love, Truth & Perception.* Joy Publications currently distributes her four books and over 150 audiotapes of her self-actualizing seminars and presentations.

Kathy has never slowed her search for the true meaning of life and our purpose on Earth. In *Love, Truth & Perception* she has embraced the spirit philosophy that reaches to the depths of our cultures and societies to give her readers a new and beautiful perception of themselves and their humanity. As she treads upon this hallowed ground, she is looking forward to others having the strength and courage to walk with her during this magnificent time of change.

Books by Kathy Oddenino

The Joy of Health
ISBN 0-923081-00-3; QP $14.95, 300 pp.

The definitive mind/body resource from a career RN and long-time holistic counselor. A brilliant overview of our physical, mental, and spiritual lifeforces, *The Joy of Health* empowers us to change our minds about healing. Contains the *Body/Mind Cleansing Program* and *Healing Meditation*.

Bridges of Consciousness
ISBN 0-923081-01-1; QP $14.95, 312 pp.

"You hit the jackpot with *Bridges* ...." Oddenino shares the secrets of our superconscious mind energy with riveting clarity. What we think, we are. Change the perception of your male and female minds. A new perception of equality, balance, and power. It is the most explicit, detailed, accurate, useful work on spirituality and truth I have found." *V.F., College Park, MD*

Sharing: Self Discovery in Relationships
ISBN 0-923081-02-x; QP $14.95, 376 pp.

"A very important book that tells us the true, profound meanings behind relationships. A mysterium is at the core of relationships and Oddenino comes closer to it than any other writer in recent memory." *The Book Reader* Oddenino unravels the mystery of relationships with wisdom, clarity and truth, defining relationships as the foundation of our learning experiences. A must for anyone with issues about abuse, divorce, co-dependency, bi-sexuality, heterosexuality, homosexuality, communication, and intimacy.

Love, Truth & Perception
NEW! August '93 Release
ISBN 0-923081-03-8; QP $14.95, 288 pp.

Kathy Oddenino's fourth book brilliantly answers these questions in her same illuminating style: *"Where do we come from? Where are we going? What are we?"* This book will change your perceptions, your beliefs, and your life! Within these pages is a new interpretation of the traditional religious and philosophic views of life, our purpose of creation, and our path of human destiny. "The most profound information in print today.... these books will become classics in helping people improve and transform their lives...." *Susan Williams, Talk Show Host, Reno, NV*

Distributors: New Leaf, Baker & Taylor, and DeVorss & Co.
Publisher: Joy Publications, 133A Lee Dr, Annapolis, MD 21403
(410)268-3752

※ *Notes* ※

◊ *Notes* ◊

Notes

Notes

Notes